MW01629104

ZIONISM TODAY

Challenges for the Jewish Nation in the 21st Century

RABBI URI PILICHOWSKI

ZIONISM TODAY: Challenges for the Jewish Nation in the 21st Century
By Rabbi Uri Pilichowski

FOR ALL INQUIRIES:
E-mail: uri@uripilichowski.com

ISBN 978-965-598-630-3

COVER DESIGN & TYPESETTING:
Avi Levine, avi@simanimtovim.com

AUTHOR PHOTO:
Rebecca Zwiren

OTHER WORKS BY THIS AUTHOR:
Maximize Your Time - Eis La'asos L'Hashem
The Sedra
The Moadim

Advance praise for Zionisim Today...

"Zionism Today is part history, part political polemic, part religious tract, and part autobiography. In 101 informative and easy-to-read, bite-sized chapters, Uri Pilichowski provides any reader – student, first-time visitor to Israel, or veteran Zionist – with a comprehensive understanding of the need for Zionism and Israel, whether by the Jewish people or the world at large."

- Seth M. Siegel, author of the New York Times bestseller, "Let There Be Water: Israel's Solution for a Water-Starved World"

Rabbi Uri Pilichowski brings his unique perspective as a religious Jew, immigrant to Israel - Oleh, and a settler to some of the most pressing questions, concerns and misperceptions relating to Israel and Zionism. At a time when having certain identities means adopting a full package of opinions, Rabbi Pilichowski builds unusual bridges, such as supporting Palestinian statehood, even if it means he will need to leave his home, or recognizing the key contribution of secular Zionism to building the modern state of Israel despite his personal belief in divine providence.

- Dr. Einat Wilf, author, "We Should All Be Zionists" and former Member of Knesset

"Rabbi Uri Pilichowski has done a superb job in writing about Zionism in accessible terms for anyone, from experts to laypeople. He has given much needed context to a misunderstood history and concept and has done so with patience and love for his people and country."

Fleur Hassan-Nahoum, Deputy Mayor of Jerusalem, co-founder and founding member of the UAE - Israel Business Council

This book is dedicated to my parents:

RUTH & STUART PILICHOWSKI

Zionists through and through, they ignited my love for Zionism and Israel at the youngest of age and kept the flame for Israel strongly lit our entire lives.

and to my in-laws

ELAYNE & RABBI DOV GREENSTONE ז"ל

The dream of living in Israel was the cornerstone of your home; an everlasting message your children took to heart and has extended to your grand and great-grandchildren.

Thank You

To the generous sponsors who made this book possible. You've requested to remain *anonymous but I will remain eternally grateful for your support and* generosity.

May God bless you and your children.

Contents

Introduction

Although the headlines call the time period this book was written a moment of acute crisis in Israel, the truth is Israel is flourishing and a marvelous success. I moved to Israel from North America and raised my children here. I've worked as an educator, columnist and political commentator helping explain Torah and the Israeli reality for audiences, especially students, abroad. I have explained and defended Israel against the campaign of distortions that seeks to turn the Jewish state into a pariah and will proudly continue to do so. With all that concerns Israelis today, I'm still "Bullish on Israel" and proud of my nation. I've never had a greater sense of optimism and hope for the future of our country

Today, though, protecting Israel also means defending it from people that aim to undermine our society's cohesion and ethos, the foundation of the Israeli success story. Our ancestors couldn't have dreamed – in their wildest fantasies – of the Israel we take for granted today. Through analysis of Israel's values and policies, people of all ages can see a great future for Israeli society. The U.S.-Israel relationship has never been stronger and our sisters and brothers in the Diaspora have shown continuous care and concern for Israel and her people. These are reasons that make me proud of Israel.

While the Israeli people's divisions and differences today can be seen as a unique crisis, even uniquely heartbreaking because they come from within, there's still reason for pride and gratitude in the Jewish State. Israel has a healthy tradition of robust debate and protest. Whether it was Ben Gurion and Begin debating taking reparations from Germany, Rabin and

Peres debating outreach to the Palestinians, Rabin and Netanyahu debating Oslo, the times Israel has seemed alarmingly divided rival the times it seemed united.

Constructive national discussions on the issues is always necessary and healthy for Israel. Zionists have both the right and the responsibility to speak up about issues that concern them. Israeli leaders need to hear where Zionists stand. This book is a collection of columns I published in various media outlets over the past ten years. This book isn't a work of Israeli marketing, defense, advocacy or hasbara. I didn't write these columns to advocate particular positions but to inspire the reader to think about Zionism, Israel and the Jewish people. This is an educational work.

I thank God every day for living the dream of Zionism and Israel. King David wrote – and I'm paraphrasing – "When God restores the people to Zion, we see it as dreamers, our mouths will be filled with laughter, our tongues with praise and joy, the nations will say, 'God has done great things for the Jewish people!' So many of the Jewish people's dreams have been met, and so many have yet to be achieved. We are the people who are filled with laughter, praise and joy.

Gratitude

Expressing gratitude is a fundamental human character trait. There is no such thing as a "self-made" man; every person became who they are and achieved their success with the help of those who raised, taught and helped them. Humans do not live in a vacuum, we are the products of many other people's kindness and influence. I owe a debt of gratitude to many people for so much they have done for me.

Thank you to my teachers and mentors. You have taught me how to analyze, study and understand a subject. Rabbi Saul Zucker and Rabbi Benjamin and Shevi Yudin taught and raised me. Without their teaching, I could not have become a student.

It is only once you have been a parent for twenty years, watched your own children grow up, and leave your house, that you can fully appreciate the toil parenthood takes on a person. With all the trouble I was for my parents, Stuart and Ruth Pilichowski, I can't imagine the worry I gave my parents. I hope I've provided some joy and nachat to them in return. I am grateful to them for all they sacrificed for me and gave to me throughout my life..

My in-laws, Elayne Greenstone, and Rabbi Dov Greenstone ז"ל, gave me the greatest gift in the world, their daughter, Aliza. They have raised five amazing children, each impressive leaders in their communities. They have always been supportive of Aliza, myself and our children. Thank you for the support and help throughout our lives, and thank you for Aliza. It was with great sadness that we lost Aliza's father this year. Thank you to my brothers and sisters in law, as an only child I never had siblings, and I'm glad I have you.

Rabbi Steven Weil, Rabbi Efrem Goldberg and Rabbi Josh Spodek are mentors and friends. They've taught me how to speak, teach, lead, and inspire. They stuck with me when things seemed to fall apart, helped me put the pieces together and celebrated with me as I succeeded. Whether we're in the White House, Beit Medrash, or cigar lounge together I will always appreciate our relationship.

I've had many bosses in my life; the good ones teach you, the bad ones constantly criticize you, and the great ones do everything they can to support you. Todd Cohn is a great boss; he has done everything in his power to support me as Israel Advocacy Director of Southern NCSY. Everyday working for you is a pleasure and I am grateful for the many times you've made my life easier. Thank you to the Orthodox Union, NCSY and its leadership, especially Rabbi Micah Greenland, for allowing me to join your team.

Scheck Hillel Community School in North Miami Beach, Florida is more than a school, it is a community. From the board to the administration to the teachers, joining Scheck is joining a group of people dedicated to the Jewish people and Israel. I am grateful to everyone at Hillel. Teaching Israel advocacy at Hillel everyday has forced me to constantly study the topic. Much of this book is a product of my teaching at Hillel.

Alisa Abecassis introduced me to Israel activism. She sent me to my first AIPAC Policy Conference and supported every educational program I've attempted. She has taught and inspired me to be a better teacher, husband, parent and activist. I will always be grateful to you Alisa.

Life isn't livable without a friend and chavruta. Rabbi Aaron Zimmer has been both and I don't think I could live without his help, support and friendship. I know that whatever life throws at me, I can count on your friendship. Our discussions have honed my thoughts on Torah and Israel, and I'm grateful for your piercing wisdom.

Joining AIPAC isn't just joining an organization, it is joining a family. The board, staff, and fellow members of AIPAC are one big family. United by a common goal of strengthening the US-Israel relationship, we work together to make the world a better place. No one has taught me more about Israel and its issues than AIPAC, and I am a proud club member. If you're not a member yet, you should join today. Call your local office, mention my name and tell them you want the minyan level.

Thank you to Avi Mayer and David Jablinowitz of the Jerusalem Post, Alex Traiman, Jonathan Tobin, and Benjamin Kerstein of Jewish News Syndicate, Shlomo Greenwald of the Jewish Press, Laura Adkins of The Forward, and David Horowitz and Miriam Herschlag of the Times of Israel for giving me the opportunity to share my thoughts on your pages.

Thank you to my extended social media community. It's easy to be cynical and mock social media as a fake world, but I've made thousands of friends and developed meaningful friendships through social media. Social media has forced me to become a better writer and sharpen my ideas. I'm indebted to all those who follow me and comment on my posts and tweets.

Mitzpe Yericho has opened its arms to us. It has become our home and we love every minute living in it. Thank you to all of our neighbors, especially to Rav and Rebbetizn Kroyzer, Achiya and Penina Francis and the Mitzpe Anglo community within a community. I'm especially grateful to all those who voted for Aliza – and to those who didn't, well it's a closed ballot, so don't worry.

Thank you to the people who have taught me the most – my students. I've been privileged to teach tens of thousands of intelligent humans. My students have ranged in age from 2 to 93 years old, and have come from multiple states, countries and backgrounds. Thankfully not everyone becomes a teacher, but with students like the ones I've had, I don't understand why anyone wouldn't want to become an educator. They say those who can't teach are forced to do, and I'm grateful to my students for allowing me to teach every day. I'm especially thankful to Daniel Geller, a student and partner who I can always count on. Every day of my life is enhanced by your partnership.

There is nothing in my life I'm more appreciative of than my children. When things are great my children celebrate with me, and when things are challenging, they are there to cheer me up. Avigayil, you have grown up to be a hardworking and generous young woman, it's hard to believe you've begun life on your own already, thank you for making me a father and continuing to make me a better father. Temimah, watching you study Torah not only impresses me but forces me to learn more. Your midot and kindness show me how to be a better Jew. Thank you for bringing Yehoshua into our lives. His energy and smile have made our family so much more positive. Gila, your yirat shamayim and sense of humor always cheer me up; the humor because you crack me up and your yirat shamayim because I see Rav Sinai's influence in you. Noami, you are constantly full of surprises; you're unassuming nature and inherent modesty are deceptive. They cause people to underestimate you, but your talents always shine through. You're naturally gifted, and it's wonderful watching you apply them. Tova, you're more intelligent and perceptive than I'll ever be, and I love watching your wisdom shine through. The only thing better than seeing your knowledge is your smile – it brightens up any room. Moshe, the favorite part of my day is davening, studying Torah and discussing life with you. You're smart, funny, and caring, and you're a wellspring of joy.

Aliza, I know your rule is that I'm not allowed to write my feelings to you publicly, so I'm employing a loophole by writing to the kids about you. Kids, we are the most blessed family in the world. Mommy is the most loving mother and wife; she is constantly putting our needs before hers. She never takes time for herself, is always buying us presents, making time for us, and supporting us. Hashem gave us a gift and an unfair advantage with Mommy. Her chesed knows no bounds, as if being our mother and wife wasn't enough, she became a chaplain and then mayor! Most people will never know how great mommy is – they just get a glimpse, but we've been given an inside look, and a role model of love and chesed to emulate. Don't squander the gift!

CHAPTER

ONE

What is Zionism?

Delegates at the first Zionist Congress in 1897 might've left the conference enthused, inspired, but also confused. Many people appreciate "defining their terms," creating an action plan based on the terms, and then putting the plan into action. At the first Zionist Congress the delegates adopted the "Basel Program," but never defined Zionism.

The Basel Program aimed to establish a "publicly and legally assured home in Palestine" for Jews. It promoted moving Jewish agriculturists, artisans, and tradesmen to Palestine, create federations of Jews around the world, strengthen the Jewish sense and consciousness, and taking preparatory steps to attain government grants necessary for the Zionist purpose. These were ambitious goals for a people who hadn't enjoyed autonomy in their homeland in almost 2,000 years. Yet, with all their plans, they neglected to define what they stood for and how they defined their movement. Delegates might've been somewhat confused at the lack of a clear definition of their movement, Zionism.

While no "official" definition of Zionism has ever been declared for the movement, a consensus definition, made up of four parts, has spread throughout the world of Zionism. "Zionism is the right of the Jewish people to self-determination in their historic homeland." This definition includes (a) Jewish rights (b) The Jewish people (c) Jewish self-determination (d) Historic homeland. These four components are not givens, and over the past 150 years many have opposed one, two or all of them. To fully appreciate the novelty of Zionism, one must appreciate the four components that went into its composition.

The idea of Jewish rights to self-determination in the land of Israel is confusing for a 21st Century world focused more on progressive values than national rights. The entire notion of an ancient people rejuvenating itself and gathering its people from all four corners of the world to establish a state after a 2,000 year absence seems archaic and otherworldly to this generation. The people of today's times see little value in one's ancestry or place of origin. To be taken seriously, Zionism needs to demonstrate its relevance in a modern era.

Zionism is premised on the principle that just as individual human beings have innate rights, so do the groups that individuals form to unite themselves as a nation. Nations, just as much as individuals, have innate rights. These rights aren't earned but come automatically when the group of individuals unite together. These rights are inalienable and any nation that aims to deny another nation its rights is violating that nation's sovereignty and breaking the expected norms of relations between nations.

The Jewish people were a nation long before they were considered a religion. Many people aim to limit Judaism by calling it "just" a religion and refusing to see Jews as a separate and unique people. A Jew is a Jew irrespective of their adherence to Judaism's principles, laws and philosophical axioms. The lack of necessity to conform to religious practice while still retaining one's Jewish "citizenship" demonstrates Judaism isn't just a religion, but a full nation. Like any other nation of the world, the Jewish people enjoy the inalienable rights afforded to all nations.

One of the rights all nations of the world can expect to exercise is the right of self-determination. Each nation has the right to develop its own aims and objectives without care or concern for how other nations will think of their objections. Most importantly, each nation should have the freedom and independence to exercise their national interests without the hindrance of other nations. Even the United Nations, often used as an impediment to freedoms, recognized this right, stating its purpose was to, "Develop friendly relations among nations based on respect for the principle of equal rights and self-determination of peoples."

If Jews are truly a people, they must've come together at some point, or at least originated in one geographical location. Otherwise, without a central location, what organized them into a nation? That place is the land of Israel. In fact, the Jewish nation was originally called "Israelites," because they originally came from the land of Israel. To the Jewish nation, Israel isn't a mere place to move to, it is a place they came from. A sound argument alleges that the Jews are the indigenous people of the land of Israel.

Zionism isn't a "new" movement that strove to establish a revolutionary idea in the world. Zionism was an ancient movement, buried deep in the heart and ambitions of every Jew for millennia. While the world either forgot or worked hard at erasing the Jewish people's nationhood, rights and history in its land, the Jewish people never forgot. Modern political Zionism, a movement started by Theodore Herzl in the late 1800's, aimed to restore the nationhood and rights of Jewish people and to gather them back to their historic homeland. It achieved its success in 1948 with the establishment of the State of Israel.

CHAPTER
TWO

Are Jews indigenous to the Land of Israel?

Many assume Jews are not indigenous to Eretz Yisrael, the land of Israel. They define indigenous as being the first people on the land. Since ancient Canaanites were the first people on the land of Israel, they assume Jews aren't indigenous. Obviously, Palestinians weren't indigenous to the land of Israel either, and therefore, they argue, being indigenous isn't an applicable factor in the Israeli-Palestinians conflict. Their argument is incorrect.

In well researched analysis Ryan Bellerose and Rabbi Elli Fischer explained that indigenous to a land doesn't mean being native or the first people on the land. Bellerose and Fischer explained the term "indigenous." According to their analysis, the Jews are the indigenous people of the land of Israel. Considering the diversity of indigenous peoples, an official definition of "indigenous" has not been adopted by any UN-system body. Instead, the system has developed a modern understanding of this term based on a few factors.

First, the people have self- identification as indigenous peoples at the individual level and accepted by the community as members. There is historical continuity of the current people with pre-colonial and/or pre-settler societies. There is also a strong link between them to territories and surrounding natural resources, along with distinct social, economic or political systems. Second, the current people must also have distinct language, culture and beliefs. Third, they must've formed non-dominant groups of society and resolved to maintain and reproduce their ancestral environments and systems as distinctive peoples and communities.

Jews are indigenous to Eretz Yisrael by any reasonable definition of the term, but the criteria for an indigenous person set by the United Nations in the factors above clearly establish the Jewish people as indigenous to the land of Israel. The Jewish people refer to themselves primarily by two names, "Jew" and "Israel". Israel is the name of a people, and that people referred to its (often distant) homeland as "the land of Israel" or "Eretz Yisrael". In Hebrew liturgy, you will not find the word "Jew." At the same time, Jews have been known as "Jews" (Yehudim, Iudaeoi, Yahud, Yidn, Zhid) for a very long time - since 500 BCE. The term first appears in the Biblical books of Zechariah, Esther, and Ezra. It is a geographic term, referring to the tribal lands of Judea and its exiles.

Mordechai of the book of Esther was called an "Ish Yehudi" (a Jewish man) even though he lived in Persia and was from the tribe of Benjamin. Jesus was a "Judean" even though he

lived in the Galilee. Nowadays the term "Jew" is used differently, but there is clearly "historical continuity with pre-settler societies." If a person calls themselves a Jew and is accepted by the Jewish people, they are identifying themselves as indigenous, even if they and others protest Jews are not indigenous.

It is easy to go down the list of factors that establish a people as indigenous to a land and demonstrate the Jews are indigenous to the land of Israel. Do Jews have strong links to the territory? Yes. Praying facing it three times a day, yearning for a return to the land, millennia of sending money to support communities in the land, all show strong Jewish links to the land. For three weeks every summer, Jewish communities commemorate weeks of mourning the two Temples of Jerusalem's destruction over 1950 years ago.

Do Jews have distinct social, economic, or political systems? Yes. Wherever Jews lived, they had a high degree of cultural and judicial autonomy - until Emancipation. Did they have a distinct language? Yes, several, all of which used an alphabet unique to the Jewish people. Hebrew was not a vernacular, but Jews wrote and studied in Hebrew. Almost every Jew could read Hebrew, even if they couldn't understand it. It was a means of communication for different Jewish communities - and only Jewish communities.

Did Jews have distinct beliefs? Of course.Jewish beliefs are so well established and so unique it allowed the myth that Judaism is "only a religion" to propagate. Did Jews form non-dominant groups of society? Yes. Did Jews resolve to remain distinct? Yes, of course. Jewish resolve to remain unique manifested itself in language, culture, practice and even dress.

It is clear that by every single United Nations criterion, Jews are indigenous in Eretz Yisrael. Today, the Jewish people are privileged to be in a situation where they no longer need to demand indigenous rights. Jews, unlike so many other indigenous people, have largely attained their rights. When people and other nations have tried taking the Jewish people's rights away from them, the Jews have fought wars to keep them.

Misguided views that Jews are not indigenous to Eretz Yisrael, in addition to being wrong, only furthers the Jews and their neighbors from the type of mutual understanding that can be a foundation for peace. As the indigenous people of the land of Israel, and after a 2,000 year long wait, finally the governing power of the land, the Jewish people have shown themselves to be generous rulers over the other minority nations under their authority. Contrary to the slanderous accusations of Israel's enemies and opponents, Israel has afforded all human rights to Palestinians and equal civil rights to Arab Israelis. These rights far surpass the treatment Palestinians receive in Arab lands.

When the denials of Israel's indigeneity to the land of Israel end, and Israel's enemies and opponents agree to the Jewish people's rights to ancestral homeland, room will be created to discuss a healthy and productive way forward. Until that time, it is unlikely that a true and lasting peace can be established when there isn't consensus on the Jewish right to be in the land.

CHAPTER
THREE

Are Jews a religion or a people?

In a night of majestic surprises, The President's announcement in the State Dining Room of the White House took the cake. As a few hundred Jews stood around celebrating Hanukkah with the special feeling of privilege a White House invitation brings to an American. The President entered, welcomed his guests and announced he was signing an executive order making antisemitism punishable under the Civil Rights Act. His executive order was meant to protect college students facing antisemitism. The Civil Rights Act doesn't protect religions, only nations, races, and ethnicities. As someone who was in the room at the time, I can say that we didn't recognize the significance of President Trump's order at the moment. It was only later we'd realize the President of the United States had signed an Executive Order defining Jews as something more than "just a religion."

Zionism's ideology isn't simple. Zionism is a compound of multiple elements, all joined together to create an ideology focused on improving the condition of the Jewish people. One of the most fundamental elements of Zionism is the Jewish people. Zionism is an ideology started by Jews for Jews working hard to create a Jewish State for the Jewish people. Having a Jewish state for the Jewish people opened the question of who is a Jew? While the debate raged over who qualifies as a Jew; the larger and more important question of "What is a Jew?" wasn't given enough attention.

Answering the question, "What is a Jew?" would seem to be pretty straightforward. A Jew is an adherent of Judaism. While that seems like an easy answer, it's completely incorrect. A Jew doesn't have to adhere to Judaism at all to be a Jew. Even if they refuse to follow Judaism, they are still considered a Jew. "What is a Jew?" is anything but a simple question. What are the qualifications that make Jews a Jew?

Traditionally, the qualifications to be a Jew were twofold; If one was born to a Jewish mother or if they converted according to halacha, they were Jewish. While a person was considered Jewish by those two standards, if they maintained certain heretical beliefs, they were expelled from the Jewish community and not considered part of the nation. Conservative, Reform and Reconstructionist Jewry changed many of these guidelines, lowering the high standards of Orthodox Jewry.

The world defines religion as a social construct. The world sees religion as a group of people agreeing to believe the same axioms, maintain the same values, and follow the same laws. They see Judaism, Christianity and Islam as fitting these social constructs. Judaism isn't just a social construct; Jews believe it to be a system that follows the truth - God's word.

A nation or a people is a group of people that share certain qualities, chief among them a geographical location. A nation is more than just a social construct, it goes to the very identity of the people. The designation of a "people" or a "nation" entitles the people to unique national rights, like self-determination on their own land.

From the very founding of Judaism, the Jews were meant to be a people, and not "just" a religion. When the Jews were slaves in Egypt, when they gathered at Mount Sinai, when they traveled through the desert and entered the land of Israel, they were called "The Nation of Israel," and the "Israelites." They had a King, a legislative body, a unique set of laws and culture. Whether an individual Jew decided to accept the axioms of the Jewish religion or not, whether they believed in God or were an atheist, if they were born into or converted into Judaism, they were considered a member of the Jewish people.

Why are so many motivated to limit Judaism to a religion and refuse to recognize the national element of the Jewish people? As a people and a unique nation, the Jewish people are entitled to self-determination on their historic homeland, the land of Israel. Antisemites, whether they are or aren't aware of their bias against Jews, aim to restrict the rights of Jews. In characterizing Jews as just a religion it becomes easy to justify denying Jews the rights to self-determination and their homeland.

Modern political Zionism, Theodore Herzl's movement to establish a

Jewish state in the land of Israel, was built on the principle that Judaism wasn't just a religion, but the Jews were a nation as well. As a nation, in fact one of the oldest nations on Earth, the Jews deserved to establish their own state in their historic homeland. Anti-Zionists stood against Jewish rights and tried to stop the establishment of Israel. Even today, Israel's enemies still deny the Jewish people's rights. Zionism was a movement to free the Jewish people and gain them the rights they deserve. The modern state of Israel and its advocates still stand for those same rights today.

CHAPTER
FOUR

When did Zionism begin?

Take a survey of proponents and opponents of Zionism and ask both groups when Zionism started, and you'll receive vastly different answers spanning thousands of years. Most movements have an easily defined start date; A movement is usually founded in response to a specific event, an injustice, or a rebellion against ruling powers. While there might have been an evolution that led to the movement's formation, there's commonly a seminal date that people can point to as the day when the movement began. Zionism is an exception to this general phenomenon, there is no consensus to Zionism's start date.

Zionism's opponents claim the movement is modern in nature. They accuse it of being a modern European colonialist project. In an article titled, "A Century of Settler Colonialism in Palestine," Tariq Dana and Ali Jarbawi argue, "Throughout the past century, the Zionist movement constructed the most sophisticated settler-colonial project of our age: the State of Israel. The violent birth of Israel in 1948 and the subsequent colonization of the entirety of the land of Palestine after the 1967 war are indeed reflections of Zionism's successes in fulfilling its settler-colonial ambitions in Palestine." It is clear that Dana and Jarbawi view Zionism as a modern settler-colonial project.

In 1897 Theodore Herzl, a lawyer by training and journalist by profession hosted the first Zionist Congress in Basel, Switzerland. It was at the Congress that he founded the World Zionist Organization and published a resolution called the "Basel Program" that declared Zionism aimed to establish a legally assured home for the Jewish people. It outlined steps the WZO would need to take to achieve its goals. Herzl's movement was called "Zionism" and is more accurately called "Modern Political Zionism." Zionism's opponents use Herzl and 1897 as the start of Zionism. In using a relatively contemporary start date, the opponents of Zionism can disparage Zionism as a young movement without historical patronage.

As a movement, Herzl's modern political Zionism had a slow start, but eventually took off. Herzl passed away prematurely as the movement gained popularity and others took up his struggle. While the stated goal was to establish a Jewish State in what was then called Palestine, their underlying objective was to save Jews around the world from rising antisemitism. Early Zionists aimed to establish a refuge for Jews to escape threats that would eventually become a Holocaust. They aimed to create the Jewish State in the Land of Israel because it was the Jewish people's historic homeland and the Zionists felt they had the rights to establish a Jewish State there.

Herzl's modern political Zionism movement started in the late 1800's, but Zionism, the movement that seeks to establish a Jewish state on the land of Israel has a record that stretches much further back in history. The Jewish people count Abraham, Isaac and Jacob as their first ancestors. They sought to establish the land of Israel as the place for their children. Moses and Joshua were the leaders of the Jewish people more than 3,000 years ago. They led the Jewish people from Egypt to Eretz Yisrael and charged the Jewish people with conquering the land from the now long deceased Canaanite people and settling it. The Jewish people governed the land for over 1,000 years, were briefly exiled by the Babylonians and returned to rule the land in a second commonwealth for over 400 years.

After the Roman Empire conquered and exiled the Jews almost 2,000 years ago, the Jews strove to return to their land. Three times a day Jews prayed to return to the land of Israel, they ended their two most sacred nights of the year with cries of "Next year in Jerusalem," and spent three weeks a year mourning their state of exile in the hopes of returning to their land. During their 2,000-year exile there was always a Jewish presence in the land of Israel, and those Jewish residents pined for their fellow Jewish brothers and sisters to return home. Zionism, the connection of the Jewish people to the land of Israel, is integral to Judaism and the Jewish people.

Counting Zionism as a modern movement, let alone a colonialist settler movement, is not only inaccurate, but it also impugns millions of Jews who strove to make the Zionist dream of returning the Jewish people to their homeland as some sort of nefarious characters. Early political Zionists weren't starting a new movement in the late 1800's. Herzl, Nordau, Jabotinsky, Weizmann, and Ben Gurion strove to fulfill 2,000 years of unfulfilled Jewish dreams. Their idea and movement weren't novel. What made them stand out was thinking that dreams don't have to be the stuff of legend; with enough will there is a way to make all dreams come true. Abraham, Isaac, Jacob, Moses and Joshua's efforts were resurrected by Herzl and his colleagues.

CHAPTER
FIVE

Zionism answers the Jewish question

"When did Zionism begin?" is a question students and audiences attending lectures on Zionism appreciate discussing. Many people answer with Theodore Herzl's Zionist Congress in Basil, Switzerland in 1897, others start decades earlier with scholars writing of the need to leave Europe and move to Israel. There are more expansive thinkers who go back to the 1700's when the students of the Gaon from Vilna moved to Israel. In almost every crowd there is one student or participant who sheepishly raises their hands and answers, "Abraham."

A legitimate argument can be made that Abraham, commanded by God to move to what was then known as Canaan, to set foot in the land that was destined for his descendants, was the first Zionist. In walking the length of the land and purchasing a plot of land in Hebron, Abraham took a foothold in the land of Israel, and his children and descendants would inherit the land from him. Abraham was the first Zionist and set an example for the millions of Zionists that would follow him.

When did Zionism begin begets a more crucial question for the Zionist; what motivated Theodore Herzl and other early Zionists to begin a movement of political Zionism that included a campaign to inspire Jews to begin moving to Palestine?

In 1844 Karl Marx penned a lightning rod of an essay in response to German philosopher Bruno Bauer's contention that the only way Jews would achieve equality with their Gentile neighbors was if they gave up their religion. Ostensibly an essay about Jews, Marx used his essay to focus on the true meaning of emancipation and the state's role as a healthy replacement for religion. The underpinnings of both Bauer and Marx's essay was the "Jewish Question."

"The Jewish Question" had been asked for 2,000 years, but was beginning to get louder in the late 1700's and early 1800's. The Jew had never been accepted as equal citizens in their host countries. Jews had always been seen as their own group, never really one with everyone else. Many times, this lack of acceptance was based in antisemitism as Gentiles refused to see their Jewish neighbors as equals.

This question wasn't only being asked by Gentiles, Jews too were asking the question – albeit in slightly different ways. Justice Louis Brandeis posed the question this way, "For us the Jewish Problem means this: How can we secure for Jews, wherever they may live, the same rights and opportunities enjoyed by non-Jews? How can we secure for the world the full contribution which Jews can make, if unhampered by artificial limitations?" Brandeis continued by explaining, "The problem has two aspects: That of the individual Jew, and that of Jews collectively."

In contrast to many who advocated assimilation or conversion to answer the Jewish Question, Brandeis said, "Since death is not a solution of the problem of life, the solution of the Jewish Problem necessarily involves the continued existence of the Jews as Jews." Brandeis's solution to the Jewish Question was a return to the land of Israel, "Only in Palestine can Jewish life be fully protected from the forces of disintegration; that there alone can the Jewish spirit reach its full and natural development; and that by securing for those Jews who wish to settle there the opportunity to do so, not only those Jews, but all other Jews will be benefited, and that the long perplexing Jewish Problem will, at last, find solution."

Herzl had echoed Brandeis's answer of returning to Eretz Yisrael as the answer to the Jewish Question. In his book, "The Jewish State" Herzl wrote, "The whole plan is in its essence perfectly simple... Let the sovereignty be granted us over a portion of the globe large enough to satisfy the rightful requirements of a nation; the rest we shall manage for ourselves." He continued later in his book writing, "I think the Jews will always have sufficient enemies, such as every nation has. But once fixed in their own land, it will no longer be possible for them to scatter all over the world."

It can be argued that Zionism is a 4,000-year-old movement that required a jumpstart in the late 1800's as antisemitism and hostile Gentile attention begin to focus more and more on the Jewish question. As Jews felt hate against them rise, and pogroms began with more frequency, the requirement for a Jewish answer to the Jewish problem became necessary. Herzl's political Zionism answered that call in a practical way, calling on the Jewish people to relocate permanently to Palestine – Aliyah to Eretz Yisrael.

Unfortunately, Herzl's call wasn't answered quickly enough to save European Jewry from the Holocaust. In his work "The Scientification of the Jewish Question in Nazi Germany" author Horst Junginger described German scholars work to counter the vanishing influence of religious prejudices against the Jews with a new antisemitic rationale – a scientific "explanation" for how Jews are lesser forms of human beings. This "scientific explanation" claimed to answer the "Jewish Question" with a final solution, the extermination of the Jewish people.

It is easy to look back and say, "If only," and imagine a brighter past, but had early Zionists' calls been heard and had the British allowed Jews to immigrate to Palestine and Zionists achieved their goals, the Holocaust might've been less devastating or might not have even been allowed to happen. We will never know. Unfortunately, the "Jewish Question" was answered by antisemites before Jews were able to solve the problem.

The Jewish Question hasn't been answered; it is an ongoing challenge. As long as anti-Zionists question Jewish rights to the land of Israel and antisemites question Jews living in other countries, the Jewish question will always be asked. Zionism, the movement to establish Jewish self-determination on Israel's homeland, the land of Israel, is a healthy eternal answer to the Jewish question.

CHAPTER

SIX

The Seventy Faces of Zionism

Zionism was never given an official definition by Zionism's founders. The lack of a definition allowed Zionists to stretch the meaning of Zionism to almost absurd dimensions. Looking at the word Zionism one would've thought that the foundation of the movement would've been a move to Zion – the city of Jerusalem and the land of Israel. Yet, Zionism's founder and many of his followers accepted Theodore Herzl's "Jewish State" where he contemplated creating an autonomous Jewish State in Argentina and listened years later when Herzl suggested accepting England's offer of Uganda as a Jewish state. Creating a Jewish state in Argentina and Uganda directly contradicted the name Zionism, but because Zionists never set forth a definition of Zionism, even Zion wasn't sacrosanct to Zionists.

As Zionist plans were put into action and the Zionist dream of establishing a Jewish state came to fruition, a definition of Zionism became unofficially adopted by Zionists and the rest of the world. Zionism became known as the political movement to support the Jewish right to self-determination in its own homeland, the land of Israel. This definition was predicated on understanding that Jews were Israelites, not solely a people with a joint religion, but an independent nation. Like all nations the Jewish people had inalienable rights. Zionists defined these rights as truths that guaranteed the Jewish people their historic land. Just as every other nation has a right to their historic homeland, the Jewish nation also enjoys the right to its homeland. Just as every nation deserves to determine its own destiny, so too, does the Jewish nation deserve to determine its own destiny through an autonomous state.

The consensus of the definition of Zionism was more recently reached by the Jewish people. While the definition isn't binding, the principles - Jewish rights to self-determination and its own state on its homeland, are binding. Just because Zionists never agreed to one definition doesn't mean the Jewish people aren't entitled to their rights. Zionism became the movement that assured the Jewish people they'd be able to enjoy their rights. Even Jews who didn't support or opposed Zionism agreed the Jewish people had rights; the dispute within the Jewish people over Zionism was timing. The disagreements stemmed over whether it made sense to begin a political effort to achieve those rights at this time.

Over seventy years after the achievement of the first Zionist dream – the establishment of the Jewish State in the land of Israel – Zionists have a range of issues that concern them. External and internal enemies, economic challenges, domestic social issues, foreign policy and so many other issues test Zionists to create a better society for the Jewish people in Israel.

The Sages taught that there are seventy paths to explaining the Torah – they called them the "Seventy faces of the Torah." While Zionism's wisdom doesn't compare to the wisdom of the Torah, its lack of authoritative definition has allowed it to be defined with at least seventy different definitions. There's little benefit in fixating on the definition of Zionism. With the creation of the State of Israel, Zionism's achievements have become an undeniable reality. Whether you agreed with its original goals and methods, Zionism is now a part of contemporary Jewish life.

Today's discussions shouldn't focus on defining Zionism but should focus on the burning questions of nationhood. The Jewish people need to begin asking who they want to become? What are Zionism's values and how do the Jewish people manifest them in their own State? How do they achieve and measure their own success? What are their goals over the next 25 years? These are the questions Jewish scholars should be contemplating, educators should be teaching, adults should be discussing, and politicians should be debating.

CHAPTER
SEVEN

The Evolution of Zionism

In the late 1800's antisemitic events were rising dangerously in Europe. For almost two thousand years the Jews had been wanderers without a home. Exiled from their land by the ancient Romans and Arabs, the Jews had spread to the four corners of the world. Although finding temporary refuge in numerous places, the Jews would inevitably be persecuted by their hosts. The results of antisemitic persecution the Jews suffered under exile ranged from pogroms to a Holocaust.

In the two hundred years leading up to World War Two, the Jews and the Gentiles asked earnestly, "What should be the fate of the Jews?" Gentiles no longer wanted to host the Jews, they saw them as permanent foreigners, not a group they wanted to incorporate into their nations. The Jews sensed the world's rejection of them as neighbors and asked where they could go and find a place to call home. This led Theodore Herzl and other Jewish thinkers to answer the Jewish question in a unique way – creating a Jewish state where Jews could determine their own future. Zionism, as the movement became known, began as an answer to the Jewish question.

As the Zionist movement grew and became more than just Herzl's speeches and his best-selling book, it gained popularity, and the movement became more practical in its thinking. Aiming to save European Jewry from a coming disaster, the movement turned political and tried to garner support for the creation of a Jewish State. Herzl and his supporters put more emphasis on saving the Jews than the location of their salvation. Herzl and the early Zionists spent a few years researching Uganda, Africa as a possible location of a future Jewish State. Uganda would serve the purpose of providing a safe refuge for the Jewish people.

When the decision to accept the British offer of Uganda for a Jewish State was brought to a vote at a World Jewish Congress, it was narrowly rejected. The delegates at the Congress voted the new Jewish State would be in Eretz Yisrael and nowhere else. Zionism had evolved from a movement mostly concerned with saving European Jewry from persecution to a movement demanding the creation of a Jewish state in the Jewish people's historic homeland, the land of Israel. Jewish national rights demanded that Jews enjoy self-determination in their own homeland.

In 1948, the Zionists' dreams were fulfilled. A Jewish State, fully autonomous, Democratic, and in Eretz Yisrael was established. At this point Zionism required another evolution. The movement no longer had to worry about establishing a Jewish State, it now had to be concerned with sustaining the State of Israel and gathering the exiles from the four corners of the Earth. Almost immediately following its founding, the State of Israel faced an existential threat when five Arab armies attacked it and tried to annihilate the fledgling Jewish State. Shortly after the war, the Arab countries expelled its Jews and over 800,000 Jews from Arab lands flooded the State of Israel. The almost immediate doubling of Israel's population was almost too much for the State to handle, and Israel struggled to absorb its new citizens. Zionism had become a movement focused on the survival of the State of Israel.

Seventy-years later Zionism has become a continuously evolving movement. It has shifted from defense to offense. Zionism no longer worries about survival and focuses more on development. With one of the strongest economies in the world, the State of Israel spends its energy deciding where to invest its resources, mostly cerebral, and not how to protect them from attack. Israel is thriving, and while it still faces consistent threats, it no longer faces existential threats. Zionism is the metaphysical fuel to the physical State of Israel. The Jewish State has become the fulfillment of the early Zionist dreams.

Looking forward, Zionism will continue to be the fuel of an even more vibrant Israel, but will also evolve into a global influencer that addresses international problems like climate change, water shortages and more efficient transportation. As it has in the past decade, the world's technological advances will largely include Israeli ingenuity. Zionism can't evolve into a fully global movement; there are plenty of challenges it must face at home as well. Growing divisions within Israeli society and between Israel and the

Diaspora threaten to fracture a united Israel. Israel will have to simultaneously address internal challenges while thriving externally to ensure Zionism's next evolution is successful.

CHAPTER
EIGHT

Is Israel solely for the Jews?

Theodore Herzl began the modern Zionist movement with a practical goal of creating a Jewish State through political means. Early Zionists aimed to return the Jewish people to their homeland, the land of Israel. Herzl traveled from country to country, speaking to world leaders, influential Jews, and the Jewish community. Herzl spoke about the imperative for a Jewish State and tried to convince everyone he spoke to that they should support his vision. When Herzl died, Chaim Weizmann took over and traveled the world trying to drum up support for a Jewish state. Weizmann, along with others, succeeded in their goals.

With the dual goals of providing the Jewish people with a place of refuge to flee persecution and exercising the Jewish people's right to self-determination on their historic homeland, the Jewish State was declared by Zionist leaders in Tel Aviv in May 1948. The founders of the Jewish State declared, "The State of Israel will be open for Jewish immigration and for the ingathering of the Exiles." The Jewish people are a nation, not just a religion. The State was now the open home of all members of the Jewish people.

In 1950 Israel passed the "Law of Return" which stated, "Every Jew has the right to come to this country as an immigrant. An immigrant's visa shall be granted to every Jew who has expressed his desire to settle in Israel." The right of Jews to return to Israel extends to relatives as well, "The rights of a Jew under this Law and the rights of an immigrant...as well as the rights of an immigrant under any other enactment, are also vested in a child and a grandchild of a Jew, the spouse of a Jew, the spouse of a child of a Jew and the spouse of a grandchild of a Jew." Members of the Jewish nation, wherever they live, have the right to immigrate to Israel because the State of Israel was founded to provide all members of the Jewish people access to their historic homeland, the land of Israel.

In Israel's Declaration of Independence, the founding Zionists avowed, "The State of Israel will foster the development of the country for the benefit of all its inhabitants; it will be based on freedom, justice and peace as envisaged by the prophets of Israel; it will ensure complete equality of social and political rights to all its inhabitants irrespective of religion, race or sex; it will guarantee freedom of religion, conscience, language, education and culture; it will safeguard the Sacred Places of all religions." Immediately after the founding of the State in 1948 all Arabs were granted Israeli citizenship but were still ruled by martial law. In 1966 martial law was completely lifted and Arab citizens of Israel began enjoying the exact same civil rights as their Jewish neighbors.

Granting Israeli citizenship to Arabs is troubling to some Zionists. Today, Arab Israelis are fully integrated into the Jewish State. They are Knesset members, judges, police officers, doctors, and lawyers. There is no position denied to Arab citizens and Arab parties feature prominently in the Israeli Knesset. No longer regulated to the opposition, Arab Knesset parties have sat in the government. Why would a Jewish State, built by Zionists to be a place of refuge and home to the Jewish people, allow Arabs, members of a different nation, become citizens of its State? If Israel is a State for Jews, what role do Arabs play in it?

A legitimate argument can be made that Israel should be a State solely for the Jewish people. Jews should be accepted into the country almost immediately according to their rights under the "Law of Return." Anyone else who wants to live in Israel can be accepted as residents but not citizens. Countries around the world, from the United State to the United Arab Emirates have similar laws.

Zionists and Israelis don't see the Jewish State as a state like all other states. The Jewish people aren't a people like all other people, and the Jewish State isn't a state like all other states. Israel is meant to be a light unto the nations where a moral baseline is modeled for the rest of the world. Israel's acceptance of over two million members of other nations as its own citizens (in a country of barely ten million) demonstrates Israel's commitment to human rights, equality, and democracy. Israel's acceptance of others should be a guiding light for other nations as they develop policies towards prospective immigrants.

Zionism was a movement that worked primarily to establish a home and refuge for the Jewish people. It also aimed to establish a nation among the international community that would make the world a better place through various means, including technological innovation and medical research. Morality, kindness, and charity start at home, and before Israel could reach out and help foreign nations, it had a responsibility to help those within its own borders. In offering citizenship to a Jewish State to non-Jews, the Zionist leaders of Israel demonstrated the moral policies it hopes other nations will adapt to make the world a better place for all its inhabitants.

CHAPTER
NINE

Is Zionism a movement or an ideology?

Zionists will forever debate when their movement began. There are Zionists who fervently argue their first member was Abraham. When God told Abraham, "Go forth from your land to the land I will tell you…" and Abraham arrived in a land to be named "Eretz Yisrael," he became the first Zionist. More contemporary thinking Zionists will claim Theodore Herzl, the founder of modern Zionism, was the first Zionist and started the drive of the Jewish people to return to their homeland. There's no end to the debate, but there's also no question the Zionist movement is built upon millennia of history, personalities, and ideas.

Zionism is often called a modern movement. When describing Theodore Herzl's efforts to establish a Jewish state in the land then called Palestine, it's accurate to call his efforts the start of a modern political movement others coined, "Zionism." Many argue that Zionism isn't just a 150-year-old movement, but rather an ideology. The idea of the Jewish people establishing their own authority in the land of Israel is much older than a century and a half. Arguably Moses and Joshua who led the Jewish people back to Israel after their enslavement in Egypt could be seen as the first Jewish leaders to inspire the Jewish people to return to Eretz Yisrael to govern their own nation.

Theodore Herzl's modern Zionist political movement was founded based on an ideology that was thousands of years old and multifaceted. The ideology started with the belief that God had promised the Jewish people the land of Canaan to become their land of Israel. It evolved to believe the Jewish people had a national right to self-determination as their own nation. That self-determination was considered a necessity to ensure the security of

Jews around the world facing Gentile and Arab antisemitism. Zionism also maintained that the Jewish people deserve to enjoy self-determination on their historic homeland – the land of Israel.

Zionism didn't only discuss the Jewish people on their own land. Dovetailing with traditional Jewish values, Zionism understood that the Jewish people were to be a light on to the nations, modeling exemplary behavior for the global community. Zionism aimed to create a State for the Jewish people whose values, scientific, technological and medical advancement would help the world. The values of the Zionist ideology are what fueled the Zionist movement.

If Zionism was "just" a movement, the opposition to Zionism from within the Jewish community would be more understandable. A movement without an ideology is a dangerous headless monster. It can distract and pull Jews away from traditional Judaism – however you define it. Without an ideology Zionism could be seen as a movement that comes to replace Judaism's age-old values with nothing more than political machinations. Politics for political sake is not a Jewish value. To gain acceptance, Zionism needed to be based on an ideology.

While many Jews – from all walks and sects of Judaism - play ostrich and refuse to look into Zionism's ideology, preferring to assume its values instead of learning them, others take a critical look at Zionism and see its consistency with traditional Jewish ideology. It's easy to point to individual Zionists and policies of Israel and demonstrate their inconsistency with Judaism's tenets; those discrepancies aren't representative of Zionism's ideology. The ideology of Zionism that stands for a return of the Jewish people to Eretz Yisrael, ensuring the security of the Jewish people and modeling behavior for the rest of the world, is the exact ideology of traditional Zionism.

Many argue that after the creation of the Jewish state in 1948, Zionism has outlived its purpose. This viewpoint sees Zionism solely as a movement that aimed to create a Jewish State and once the goal was achieved what purpose could the movement have going forward? As an ideology, Zionism extends past a movement and lives eternally. The State of Israel is the vehicle to manifest Zionist values into the coming decades and centuries. As the State of Israel grows in so many ways, it is able to display its values for the benefit of the world and humankind.

CHAPTER
TEN

Is Zionism an aspect of Judaism?

When Theodore Herzl began his Zionism movement over 125 years ago, Jews didn't know what to make of it. The movement was clearly intended to attract Jews and change the course of Jewish history, but it didn't fit into the neatly drawn boxes of establishment Judaism. The question of whether Zionism was a part of traditional and established Judaism or just another modern political movement is still being debated today. There isn't a week that goes by where the question of whether Zionism is an aspect of Judaism isn't taught, discussed, or written about in columns the world over.

Whether or not a modern movement can find a place in traditional Judaism is an engaging question. The debate of Zionism's role in Judaism is made even more fascinating by the players in the debate. The question doesn't fit classical religious vs. secular or left vs. right quadrants of the Jewish issues box. The debate puts the usual opponents together on the same side of the debate, and pits usual allies on the opposite side of each other.

Normally secular anti-religious Jews would never be found aligned with Ultra-Orthodox religious Jews. It's hard to find many areas where the ultra-progressive and the ultra-conservative communities meet. Zionism is the issue that unites them. Both camps find Zionism abhorrent. Progressives can't imagine a movement they see as displacing native Palestinians (sic) from their lands as part of a tikkun olam Judaism and the Ultra-Orthodox refuse to admit a secular movement into the traditional Judaism they hold dear. In today's partisan world, left-wing Democrats see right wing Republicans as their natural political enemies, the Israeli analogous parties are the same; Meretz finds Likud repulsive and led by corrupt leadership and Likud views

Meretz as a weak party set out to destroy the very structures causing Israel's success – yet all four of these groups are staunch Zionists and gladly join forces to protect the Zionism they adore.

Many of the above parties would argue that Zionism is a secular movement, and while it is aimed at Jews, it doesn't have anything to do with Judaism. They explain Judaism as a religion, and traditionally religions focus on a belief system, and in most cases the relationship between the person and God. That is a partial description of Judaism. As a religion, Judaism does have a philosophy with a set of axioms. It does instruct Jews on their relationship with God, and it informs them of how to act in interpersonal relationships from the boardroom to the bedroom. In the above description of Judaism, Zionism wouldn't seem to have a place.

Judaism isn't a religion like other religions the world has become familiar with over the past two thousand years. Judaism isn't just about God, beliefs, and action, it is about peoplehood. Judaism began with a mass revelation to a people recently emancipated from the slavery of Egypt. These people were chosen by God to convey ethical monotheism to the world. It wasn't each individual standing at Mount Sinai that was chosen, it was the new nation – the Israelites – that were chosen and formed as a nation that was chosen by God. A central tenet of Judaism is that it isn't just a religion, it is the system of the Jewish nation.

A nation isn't complete without its own homeland. This might seem like a foreign idea to many, but it is an axiom of Judaism. Throughout the Torah God charges the people to enter the land of Israel, conquer it and settle it. "You shall take possession of the land and settle in it, for I have assigned the land to you to possess," is just one of the many commands God tells Moses and the Jewish people. The land of Israel isn't ancillary to Judaism. The land of Israel is a central aspect of Judaism.

The land of Israel isn't just the homeland of the Jewish people. The land of Israel plays many roles within Judaism. The land of Israel is a focus point of Divine reward and punishment. Throughout the Torah we read God promising the land will prosper with Divine blessings of peace and produce if the Jews observe God's commands and will be plagued with war, famine, and pestilence if the people defy God's commands. An entire category of the 613 commands is only applicable in the land of Israel. These mitzvot cannot be observed outside the land – and to do so would be sinful. The land itself was divided among the Jewish tribes and then individual families, with many laws designed to ensure families and tribes didn't give up their portion of the land.

Theodore Herzl was not a Torah observant Jew. He began Zionism as a modern political movement primarily focused on saving Jews from concerning rising levels of antisemitism in Europe. Herzl's motivations were consequential in how the Zionist movement was shaped at its inception, but as the movement took on a life of its own many recognized the practical objectives of the movement – to inspire Jews from around the entire world to gather and return to the Jewish homeland - was perfectly consistent with the tenet of Judaism that charged the Jews to live together in the land of Israel.

Judaism has seen many different communities and leaders create campaigns that focus on one aspect of Judaism and encourage the Jewish people to renew its commitment to that part of Judaism. The Chafetz Chaim, a Torah scholar in the early 1900's, created a movement to inspire Jews be careful with their speech and guard themselves from speaking loshon hara – gossip. The Lubavitch Hassidim encourage Jewish men to wrap tefilin every day. Of the same importance as loshon hara and tefilin is having a united Jewish nation living in Eretz Yisrael. Although clearly not its intention, Zionism is the movement to return the people to Judaism's tenet of living in Israel. A legitimate argument can be made that Herzl's modern political movement of Zionism wasn't an aspect of Judaism, but it's undeniable that gathering the Jews to live as one nation in the land of Israel is just as much a part of Judaism as any other aspect of the religion.

CHAPTER

ELEVEN

Israel and the Holocaust aren't connected

When former Iranian President Mahmoud Ahmadinejad called the deaths of millions of Jews during the Holocaust a "lie and a mythical claim," and said, "Why should everyone be forced to accept the opinion of just a few on a historic event?" people were astounded. How could a world leader, even an Iranian leader, deny a recent historic event that so obviously occurred? Simple hate and antisemitism wouldn't lead someone to make absurd claims. There must've been a method to Ahmadinejad's madness. Read between the lines and try to decipher Ahmadinejad's actual objective in denying the Holocaust.

As Israeli Memorial and Independence Day are commemorated and celebrated in Israel, the usual splicing of pictures of the Holocaust with the founding of the State and IDF soldiers were broadcast around the world.

The land of Israel was Jewish land thousands of years before the Holocaust. The Jewish people's right to the state of Israel is far stronger than a land granted in return for suffering. The Jewish people have had a continuous presence in the land of Israel since the time of Joshua, around 1171 B.C.E. The Jews never stopped considering Israel their homeland. Jews have mentioned their yearning to return to their capital, Jerusalem, three times a day for close to two thousand years.

The Jewish people are entitled to the land of Israel because it is their historic homeland. Arabs and those who stand against Israel spread a false narrative that the Jews were given this land as an empathetic gesture by the international community because of their failure to stop Hitler and the Germans. Claiming the Jewish connection to Israel is based on international empathy undermines the Jewish claim to the land, substituting Jewish rights with a gesture. When that narrative is established, delegitimizing Israel as a Jewish State is an easy next step.

On June 4, 2009, President Obama spoke to the Muslim world in Cairo, Egypt and did a great disservice to Israel and the Jewish people. President Obama linked the establishment of the State of Israel with the Holocaust. Although he presumably meant well, the well-publicized speech carried the wrong message. President Obama said, "America's strong bonds with Israel are well known. This bond is unbreakable. It is based upon cultural and historical ties, and the recognition that the aspiration for a Jewish homeland is rooted in a tragic history that cannot be denied. Around the world, the Jewish people were persecuted for centuries, and anti-Semitism in Europe culminated in an unprecedented Holocaust. Six million Jews were killed – more than the entire Jewish population of Israel today. Denying that fact is baseless, ignorant, and hateful. Threatening Israel with destruction – or repeating vile stereotypes about Jews – is deeply wrong, and only serves to evoke in the minds of Israelis this most painful of memories while preventing the peace that the people of this region deserve."

Former Israeli Prime Minister Benjamin Netanyahu made the same mistake when he responded to President Obama's speech. Instead of correcting the new American President and explaining the Jewish people's right to their historic land, Netanyahu said, "There are those who say that if the Holocaust had not occurred, the State of Israel would never have been established. But I say that if the State of Israel would have been established earlier, the Holocaust would not have occurred." Netanyahu missed an opportunity to validate the Jewish people's historic right to the land of Israel.

President Obama corrected his mistake on a 2013 visit to Israel when he said, "I believe that Israel is rooted not just in history and tradition but also in a simple and profound idea: the -- the idea that people deserve to be free in a land of their own." For his part, Netanyahu has spoken many times about the Jewish right to the land of Israel. This is the message that all American Presidents, Israeli Prime Ministers and world leaders need to reinforce.

The Holocaust was an eye opening catalyst that spurred the world into action, giving Israel to the people who already deserved it. Iranian President Ahmadinejad and Arab leaders - including current Palestinian

President Mahmoud Abbas - deny and minimize the Holocaust as a means of undermining Israel's legitimacy. Step one is tying the Jewish people's rights to Israel to the Holocaust, step two is denying the Holocaust. It is then easy to deny the legitimacy of a Jewish state of Israel. The world must stop connecting the State of Israel and the Holocaust.

When celebrating Israel as a Jewish State, renderings of Abraham, Joshua, King David, the two spectacular Temples and archeological sites around Israel that show the Jewish people's historic connection to the land should be spliced with modern pictures of the State of Israel and her people. In focusing on the Jewish people's rights to the land of Israel the world will support the Jewish people's right to its own Jewish state.

CHAPTER
TWELVE

The contradiction in Israel's Declaration of Independence

Each Spring, Israelis and Zionists celebrate Yom Ha'atzmaut, Israel's Independence Day. The original Yom Ha'atzmaut in 1948, was initiated with the signing of the Israeli Declaration of Independence in Israel's Tel Aviv Museum, today called Independence Hall. The nature of the new Jewish state was defined by the words Ben Gurion read on that first Independence Day.

It is interesting to note that there seems to be an inherent contradiction in Israel's Declaration of Independence. The first section declares the Jewish people's right to the land of Israel. "The Land of Israel was the birthplace of the Jewish people. Here their spiritual, religious and political identity was shaped. Here they first attained to statehood, created cultural values of national and universal significance...Impelled by this historic and traditional attachment, Jews strove in every successive generation to re-establish themselves in their ancient homeland... recognition by the United Nations of the right of the Jewish people to establish their State is irrevocable. This right is the natural right of the Jewish people to be masters of their own fate, like all other nations, in their own sovereign State." This first section established the Jewish people's historic right to the land of Israel. This right is inalienable and not dependent on any outside factor.

Later in the same document, the authors seem to offer a different reason for the establishment of the state. "The catastrophe which recently befell the Jewish people - the massacre of millions of Jews in Europe - was another clear demonstration of the urgency of solving the problem of its homelessness by re-establishing in Eretz Yisrael the Jewish State, which would open the gates of the homeland wide to every Jew and confer upon the Jewish people the status of a fully privileged member of the community of nations." This latter clause seems to posit that the Holocaust and the need for a place of refuge for Jews was the reason the State of Israel was established.

The two clauses, the first that said Israel was created because the people have a right to the land and the second section that said the need of a place of refuge was the reason for the establishment of the state, seem to contradict to each other. The contradiction muddies the waters of determining the purpose of the State of Israel. Was the state established so that the Jewish people could exercise their natural right to be masters of their own fate, like all other nations in their own sovereign state or was it established because of the urgency of solving the problem of Jewish homelessness, and all the persecution that came with it?

The two views do not complement each other. The difference between the two is whether Israel has a right to settle parts of its ancient homeland not needed to provide a refuge for Jews facing homelessness and persecution. An argument can be made that the State of Israel can be a haven for the Jewish people even without Jerusalem or Tel Aviv. If the purpose of the State of Israel is only to be a safe haven for persecuted Jews, as the second part of the Declaration of Independence suggests, then each piece of the land of Israel is not that significant.

The state of Israel wasn't established solely because the Jews needed a safe haven from future persecution. The State of Israel was established because like any other people, the Jewish people have an eternal right to govern and live in the land of Israel. The homelessness of the Jewish people, the persecution of the Holocaust, created the immediate necessity for a Jewish State, but did not create the right for the creation of the State. The State of Israel was created to reestablish the Jewish people's homeland. It was and continues to be their right.

The right of the Jewish people to their land doesn't expire. The right to their land doesn't terminate when others claim they replaced the Jewish people. The right of the Jewish people doesn't even end when the international community orchestrates a grand compromise that strips them of rights to half of their land. The Jewish people's right to their ancient lands is just as strong today as it ever was. Critics of Jewish control of the land of Israel use the argument that Israel was established as a haven to demonstrate that there is no compelling reason for Israel to maintain control of its land - they are incorrect.

Those that conflate the Jewish people's need for refuge with their right to the land commit an even graver mistake. They inadvertently weaken Israel's legitimacy among the nations of the world. They claim that while every other nation deserves self-determination on its own land, the Jewish people only deserve refuge. This is a grievous error with unknown ramifications to Israel's international standing. Like any other nation, Israel has a right to all of its land.

CHAPTER

THIRTEEN

Were early Zionists terrorists?

What's the difference between Palestinians, who Zionists regularly accuse of being terrorists and terrorist supporters, and early Zionists who used violence to fight the British and the Arabs before the founding of the State of Israel? This is an important question to answer, not because Zionists must defend themselves, but because Zionists need to understand if their movement is a violent and immoral one by nature. If early Zionists, the founders of our State, and an Israeli Prime Minister, were all violent and immoral terrorists, it should cause Zionists pause about their movement and cause.

Menachem Begin was the leader of the Irgun, a para-military force that existed before the founding of the State. It carried out attacks against the British and Arabs of Palestine. The Irgun, especially after its attacks on The King David Hotel and Deir Yassin, were accused of terrorism. This charge followed Begin throughout his life, especially after he was elected Prime Minister of Israel in 1977. The following excerpt from the book, "Right-Hand Man" by Menachem Michelson, discussed how Menachem Begin addressed the charges that Israeli Irgun fighters were terrorists.

"Several times, the question arose of whether Begin saw any comparison between the struggle of the Palestinians and the Jews' War of Independence. Once, Mike Wallace, the well-known American interviewer asked him directly, "Mr. Prime Minister, you were the commander of a terrorist organization. Do you see any comparison between this and the PLO?"

Begin replied, "There's nothing at all to compare. We fought to liberate our land from a foreign regime, from the British. They want to wipe us off the face of the Earth and take our land from us, because this land is ours. We threw out the British because the land is ours. What do the Arabs want? To throw us out of our land! There's no comparison between the PLO, or any group of murderers of theirs. Another issue is the method of battle. They kill every man, woman, and child, whereas we did everything to avoid harming civilians. True, sometimes disasters happened, and civilians were hurt, but this was not part of our battle tactics."

Prime Minister Begin's answer won't satisfy everyone. His first answer is predicated on the position that the entire land of Israel is the Jewish homeland and doesn't belong to the Palestinians. Therefore, Jews fighting for the land are fighting for their land. Palestinians have no right to the land, and their efforts to fight the Jews isn't a fight for their land, but rather to throw the Jews out of the land. If a person takes a different position and maintains Palestinians have a right to the land of Israel just as Jews do, Begin's answer won't come close to explaining how early Zionists were justified in their attacks against the British and the Arabs.

It's important to note Zionists don't have to accept the premise of their enemies that the land of Israel isn't theirs and Palestinians too have a right to the land. Zionists don't have to answer the charges of their enemies, and Begin's first answer is perfectly acceptable. Other people disagreeing with the Zionist position that the entire land belongs exclusively to the Jews doesn't obligate Zionists to change their position, entertain an opposite opinion, simply to answer an accusation. Begin's first answer is perfectly acceptable to a Zionist.

Begin's second answer was addressed to Zionist opponents who would scoff at Begin's position that Jews fought for their land and Arabs fought to throw Zionists out of their land. Begin's focus on Arab tactics of taking no prisoners and murdering everyone, irrespective of whether they are a woman, or a child was directed at those who maintained both Jews and Palestinian fighters were justified in their cause. The Irgun's code of only attacking those culpable of being a threat to the Jews in contradistinction to the Arab ethos of killing any and all Jews, pointed to the difference between the Zionist and Palestinian fighters.

In his book, "A Durable Peace," then former Israeli Prime Minister Benjamin Netanyahu addressed the topic of early Zionists and terrorism.

Netanyahu wrote, "The Jewish actions in Mandatory Palestine against British military targets were quickly branded by Britain as "terrorism." The Arabs have been only too happy in more recent times to try to taint the Jewish resistance with this same term, to justify by means of a supposed symmetry their own ruthless violence against Israel and others.

This effort at symmetry readily reduces the Jewish resistance to the false cliché that "One man's terrorist is another man's freedom fighter." But terrorism can be reasonably defined. It is the deliberate and systematic assault on civilians, on innocent noncombatants outside the sphere of legitimate warfare. One could argue that in the case of the Jewish underground organizations a few isolated incidents could possibly qualify under the definition of terrorism, but there can be no question that the many hundreds of operations carried out by these organizations were indeed concentrated on military rather than civilian targets (including the British military headquarters, then housed in the King David Hotel).

This is a far cry from the flood of unprovoked peacetime attacks on civilians that has characterized Arab terrorism over the past decades. In thousands of remorseless attacks, Arab terror organizations have deliberately and systematically sought out civilians as targets, attacking them in markets, airports, schools, universities, bus stops even at the Olympic games, which had been declared off-limits to violence since ancient times."

The Irgun and other Zionist fighters were just in their struggle to win freedom for the Jewish state. The land of Israel is the ancient Jewish homeland. The Jewish people spent thousands of years pining to return to their homeland and never gave up claim to the land. British and Arab forces who violently denied the Jews the opportunity to return to their land had no right to prevent the Jewish people's return and opened themselves to the same violence they were perpetrating against the early Zionists. The Irgun's struggle was a righteous fight for their people's freedom. Early Zionists owe them a debt of gratitude.

CHAPTER
FOURTEEN

Who was Theodore Herzl?

Zionists will be shocked when they read this quote and learn who said it; "The Jews have nothing to do anymore with the historic homeland... if the Jews were ever really to 'return, they would discover the very next morning that they had long ago ceased to be one people. For centuries they have been rooted in diverse nationalities, different from one another, their similarities maintained only as a result of outside pressure." The author of this quote was none other than the founder of Zionism, Theodore Herzl. Before becoming a staunch Zionist, Herzl ridiculed the idea of a mass return to the Jewish homeland.

Reading Pre-Zionist Herzl's objection to the Jewish people's connection to the land of Israel, the mystery of who Theodore Herzl was and what he stood for becomes more pronounced. People born between the ages of pictures and video mystify us. We can see their image but can't see them move or hear their voice. Forever muted, their voices and dynamism are figures of our own imagination.

Herzl was simultaneously vilified and praised by the Jewish people. There were those who felt he was undermining Jewish tradition and others who felt he was a Biblical prophet, almost Messiah-like. In his new work on Herzl's writings, "Theodore Herzl and the Jews Leap of Hope," Dr. Gil Troy wrote about the first Zionist Congress, "One delegate from Odessa, Mordechai Ben-Ami, wrote: 'Before us rose a noble, almost angelic figure whose deep and piercing stare mixed quiet majesty with unutterable sorrow. This was not the elegant Dr. Herzl of Vienna, but a royal scion of the House of David, risen suddenly from the grave in all his legendary glory.'"

Dr. Herzl was frequently compared to Moses. There were many similarities between the two men. Both Jewish leaders brought their people back to Israel but didn't actually move with them. Both set the foundations for a Jewish commonwealth but weren't able to witness its achievement. Yet, as many similarities as can be counted between Herzl and Moshe, there are differences. The clearest difference between the two men was that Dr. Herzl wasn't Torah Herzl and Moses were at first reluctant to take on their mission. Herzl's reluctance was evident in the quote we opened this essay with, and when Moses heard God say, "I will send you to Pharaoh, and you shall free My people, the Israelites, from Egypt." Moses responded and said to God, "Who am I that I should go to Pharaoh and free the Israelites from Egypt?" (*Shemot 3:10-11*) While they were both reluctant, Moses doubted himself while Herzl doubted the connection between the Jewish people and the land of Israel. This difference demonstrates while Moses and Herzl had some items in common, there isn't a real comparison to make between the two men.

Many are critical of Herzl for his being known as the founder of modern Zionism. They claim that Herzl wasn't the first thinker during his lifetime to come up with the notion of Zionism. He wasn't even the one that coined the name, "Zionism." Other critics charge Herzl didn't truly galvanize the people, and that during his lifetime, most Jews rejected the idea of returning to Israel. Many religious Jews criticize Herzl's secular approach to Israel and saw him as drawing Jews away from the Torah.

If there is so much criticism directed at Herzl, why is he so admired and considered the founding father of the modern Zionist state? Herzl made three significant contributions to the Jewish people that earned him the admiration of the Jewish people. For two thousand years the Jewish people were disconnected from each other, spread out through many lands from the Far East to the California coast. While some Jewish communities were in touch with each other, many weren't even aware of the others' existence. Herzl transformed diverse Jewish communities to think of themselves as a nation, not disparate people.

Having the Jewish people view themselves as one nation wasn't Herzl's only laudable achievement. For thousands of years Jews viewed the land of Israel as a messianic fairy tale land and not a realistic place to move and make home. With his practical approach to Zionism, Jews began to see Eretz Yisrael as a place to make home today and not only when the Messiah arrives.

Lastly, Herzl created Zionism not just to the benefit of the Jewish people, but for the entire world. The State of Israel's daily contributions to the world testify to the efficacy of Herzl's efforts.

In his book, "A Durable Peace," Benjamin Netanyahu praised Theodore Herzl, "What Herzl was able to do was to translate a native, emotional Zionism that beat in millions of Jewish hearts into a political movement that took account of the modern world. He understood the forces of politics and power, of personality and persuasion; above all, Herzl was animated by a profound understanding of history and by a vision of the impending tragedy of European Jewry and of the triumphant possibility of revived Jewish statehood. He therefore pressed the Zionist claim with all the urgency he could muster."

Herzl wasn't the perfect person, leader or Jew, but that doesn't mean he doesn't deserve the Jewish people's admiration. While many would balk at comparing him to Moses or King David, it is understandable that the founder of a movement that led to the first Jewish State in two thousand years can draw such comparisons. Whichever side of the Herzl admiration debate one falls on, all Zionists owe a debt of gratitude to Herzl.

CHAPTER
FIFTEEN

Zionism isn't a reactionary movement

It's hard to admit, but Zionism has largely become a reactionary movement. Zionism was never designed to be reactionary; it was meant to inspire the millennia-old dreams of the Jewish people. When Zionists proudly declared a State of Israel, they didn't respond to the charges laid against them as a colonizing and racist entity; they proudly declared, "The Land of Israel was the birthplace of the Jewish people. Here their spiritual, religious, and political identity was shaped. Here they first attained statehood, created cultural values of national and universal significance, and gave the world the eternal Book of Books."

The most prolific Zionist advocates have become obsessed about our opponents' slanderous accusations against Israel and the Jewish people. They feel required to constantly post and tweet answers to our enemy's claims. Jews can be a neurotic people, but the amount of worry put towards Israel's opponents isn't justified.

The most vicious non-violent opposition towards Israel has been from the BDS (Boycott, Divest and Sanction) movement. It encourages a complete embargo on anything and everything Israeli, but other than a few cultural events, and the utter failure of the Soda Stream and AirBnb boycott attempt, BDS hasn't succeeded. International sanctions, stemming either from the United Nations or the European Union, have never been levied against Israel. The many one-sided United Nation resolutions against Israel have had little effect on Israel. As Israel's opponents' voices have gotten louder, American support for Israel has only risen. The Arab boycott of the 1970's and 1980's has turned into the 2020's Abraham Accords. Israel's opponents have not been able to stem Israel's growth.

Zionism stands for much more than answering its enemy's accusations. Zionism isn't about reacting, it is about dreaming of the Jewish future. Zionism is a romantic prophetic vision of the Jewish people put into action daily in the Jewish people's historic homeland – the land of Israel. It envisions the Jewish people as their reborn Israelite nation come to life, even better, healthier and stronger than they ever were in their long history.

Zionism stands for the values and rights of the Israelite nation – the Jewish people. These are ideals Jews should be proud of and boast loudly to all who will listen. First and foremost, Zionism stands for the Jewish people's right to self-determination. This right means more than giving a Jew the same rights as a Gentile in another land. The right to self-determination grants the Jewish people as a nation the right to determine their future together. Like any other nation, the Jewish people deserve to be able to chart their future by themselves without foreign interference. Zionism is the movement that fought for that right.

The Jewish people have an historic and unbroken connection to the land of Israel. Unlike many other nations throughout history that conquered, colonized, or immigrated to Israel, the Jewish people are the native people of Eretz Yisrael. Although most of the Jewish nation were exiled and kept out of Israel for over 2,000 years, Zionism encouraged the return of the Jewish people to its land based on the right of the Jewish people to its historic homeland. Zionists need to loudly proclaim that they have every right to live, settle and govern the land of Israel as a Jewish state.

Zionism incorporates all other Jewish values within it. Being a light unto the nations is a responsibility the Jewish people have always taken seriously. From charitable giving to warfare, the Jewish people have always held themselves to a higher moral standard. Zionism stands for a world where the Jewish people can contribute to the welfare of the world as an independent nation. The world has seen Israel's contributions in science and technological innovations, medical breakthroughs and aid missions Haiti, Nepal and Florida, among so many other places. There are thousands of Africans with access to clean water and healthy food because Israelis have made Africans' welfare their priority. The generosity of Zionism must be the talking point of all Zionists.

Zionists do themselves a disservice by focusing on repudiating their opponents instead of re-emphasizing Zionism's core values. After 73 years three things have become clear; answering the accusations of Zionists' enemies and opponents will not change their minds, rebutting slander against Israel doesn't advance Zionist goals, and Zionism spreads further and is more appealing when it's talked about in a robust positive message. It's time Zionists focused their attention on the good it has done and the dreams of an even brighter future.

CHAPTER
SIXTEEN

Zionism without Israel

At the sixth Zionist Congress in Basel, Switzerland, a year before his death, Theodor Herzl offered a suggestion that will live in infamy in the world of Zionism – The Uganda Scheme. Herzl came to the Congress with an offer from then British Colonial Secretary Joseph Chamberlain. Chamberlain was willing to fulfill Herzl and the Zionists' request of securing land for a Jewish state. Unable to give the Zionists Palestine – at the time it was still in the hands of the Ottoman Empire – Chamberlain offered Herzl 5,000 miles of African territory of what was known as Uganda and is in today's Kenya.

The delegates at the conference were split, with some seeing the benefits of the offer, and others vehemently opposing establishing a Jewish State outside of Eretz Yisrael, the land of Israel. When the Congress ultimately rejected the offer, the British withdrew it. Uganda wasn't the only alternative to Eretz Yisrael considered by Herzl and other Zionists. The list of alternative lands is long, and in Herzl's book, *Der Judenstaat* (the Jewish State) he even considered Argentina. 120 years after the Uganda Scheme was proposed, with an established Jewish State in the land of Israel, it's difficult to understand how any land other than Eretz Yisrael was even considered. What motivated Herzl and his colleagues to consider a land other than Eretz Yisrael for the Jewish State?

Zion is one of many Hebrew names of Jerusalem; Herzl's Zionism was named after the Jewish people's eternal Capital. Did the leaders of Zionism not consider Eretz Yisrael to be essential to their movement? Can there be a Zionism without Zion?

The questions surrounding Zionism without Eretz Yisrael center on the assumption that the land of Israel is essential to Herzl's Zionist movement – which is a baseless assumption. Many assume Herzl's main motivation in founding his Zionist movement was to return the Jewish people to their ancient homeland, the land of Israel. Although eventually Herzl centered his efforts on founding a Jewish State in Eretz Yisrael, his main motivation was solving the Jewish question. Known for the insidious direction the Germans took the Jewish question, the question of what the world should do with its Jews was asked by the Jews just as much as the Gentiles who surrounded them – albeit differently. Recognizing the rising levels of antisemitism in Europe, the Jews knew they needed to find a place of refuge. After 2,000 years of placing their security in the hands of others – and being attacked instead of shielded – Herzl and his colleagues knew the only path to securing the Jewish people was their own state where they could protect themselves. The location of the state was a secondary consideration to the priority of finding safety for the Jewish people.

Israel's Declaration of Independence reflects the idea of the Jewish State being a place of refuge for Jews fleeing persecution. It stated, "The catastrophe which recently befell the Jewish people - the massacre of millions of Jews in Europe - was another clear demonstration of the urgency of solving the problem of its homelessness by re-establishing in Eretz-Israel the Jewish State." Israel's Declaration of Independence also listed Eretz Yisrael as the Jewish people's rightful homeland, "The Land of Israel was the birthplace of the Jewish people. Here their spiritual, religious and political identity was shaped. Here they first attained to statehood, created cultural values of national and universal significance...Impelled by this historic and traditional attachment, Jews strove in every successive generation to re-establish themselves in their ancient homeland."

The Jewish people's connection to the land of Israel is undeniable – even though many continuously try to deny it. The Jewish people's Patriarch, Abraham, passed this land down to his children, and they took up the charge when Joshua led them through the land more than three thousand years ago. There has been a continuous Jewish presence in the land, including more than fifteen hundred years of autonomous rule, ever since. Even Jews who were exiled from the land continued to look at Eretz Yisrael as their homeland. There is no such thing as the Jewish people without a connection to the land of Israel.

In the late 1800's Theodore Herzl started a political movement he coined Zionism. This movement was built on an ideology that was more than four thousand years old. The ideology of Zionism stated that the Jewish people have a right to self-determination on their homeland, the land of Israel. This wasn't Herzl's notion; this was Judaism at its core. While the movement of Zionism briefly considered other lands in an effort to save Jewish lives, it remained loyal to the connection between the Jewish people and the land of Israel.

As a successful country in its historic homeland the clock can never be turned back and the question of the Jewish State in the land of Israel isn't open for discussion. The Jews belong to the land of Israel and the land of Israel belongs to the Jews. These two institutions are inseparable and will never be divided. Zionism demands the land of Israel, and no other place can come close.

CHAPTER
SEVENTEEN

My grandfather was a slave

As an elementary school student at a Jewish day school in the New York area, I was brought, along with the rest of the students in my grade, to a "Jerry-Springer" like television show where the producers had brought together children from all different types of American life to compare and contrast their American experiences. Our Jewish school was placed next to an African American school. The students began talking and soon we were comparing which group had the worst past. We began comparing American slavery of African Americans and the Holocaust. We were too young to recognize there could be no greater apple and orange comparison than two tragedies and injustices as great as the Holocaust and slavery. I can't speak to the experience of the African American students, but the discussion gave my friends and I our first look at the African American experience.

American progressive society tells me that as a male with white skin, having grown up in the United States, I had privilege not enjoyed by females or men with black or brown skin. As an Ashkenazi male with white skin that grew up in the United States and immigrated to Israel, Israeli progressives tell me that I am privileged.

I am told my privilege was unfairly given to me and I should feel somewhat guilty over my privilege. Society's message is that I need to work hard to erase the privilege I enjoy - but did not merit - by giving advantages to the "underprivileged," even if it's unearned by merit. I have power they don't enjoy, and I must even the power imbalance by giving up some of my privilege.

Looking at a picture of me, I look like the classic American WASP. I have light brown hair and fair white skin. I speak with an American accent and grew up as a middle-class American in a classic suburban small town. Yet, I'm not white in the sense that progressives on the "power imbalance trail" qualify people as white. I'm not the classic WASP that came to America from Europe, enslaved blacks from Africa and enjoyed advantages other Americans could only dream of for themselves.

My grandfather grew up in a small Polish town. He was a poor young man, one of eight siblings. He had married relatively young, had two children and worked as a tailor. Life wasn't great but it was fine. Then came September 1939 and the German invasion of Poland. As the Germans took over Poland and swept through the cities and towns, they gathered the Jews. All skilled laborers were forced to work for the German war machine. As a tailor my grandfather had a skill the Germans needed.

My grandfather became a slave for the Germans in the 1940's. After watching his parents, siblings wife and two children gassed to death and their bodies incinerated, he suffered through Auschwitz. His life ripped apart, he was liberated and found refuge as an immigrant with nothing to his name in America in the late 1940's. He got remarried, raised a stepson, and had my father. They slowly brought themselves up from poverty to middle class. My father was the first in his family to attend college, managed a factory for a stable livelihood and brought me up in a healthy environment that allowed me to succeed. My grandfather, my father and I, weren't given any advantages anyone else in America didn't enjoy.

After a healthy upbringing in America, I came to Israel to attend a gap year yeshiva. I fell in love with Israel and realized my parents' and grandparents' dream of returning to our ancestral home and living in Israel. For two thousand years our people pined, prayed and begged to return to Israel but were always denied the opportunity. Finally, after two millennia, the Jewish people established a Jewish State in the land of Israel, how could I not return home? Although I came to Israel with much more than many immigrants from Arab lands in the 1950's, the Soviet Union in the 1990's or Ethiopian Jews at the end of the Century, I still struggled with Israel's different culture, language and high taxes combined with lower salaries. I was far from privileged. As happy as I am to live in Israel, living here hasn't been without significant challenges.

The story of our people coming to Israel and establishing a State after the hardships of Arab persecution and a German Holocaust is reminiscent of the Jewish people coming to Israel after the Egyptian slavery of Biblical times. In the Egyptian story, much like our own, a generation of children and grandchildren of slaves, fought off enemies, built infrastructure in a desolate land, and established a state. Today's Zionists are much the same; They are children and grandchildren of slaves; survivors of national trauma who rehabilitated themselves to be stronger and rebuild their own national homeland. Zionist Jews are anything but privileged.

Confusing the Jewish story with one of "white privilege" is absurd and patently false. For a theory on a people to be so incorrect requires willful ignorance or blatant bias. Mistakes this colossal are never accidental. Accusations of Jews as privileged simply because they've applied their talents to put themselves in a better position doesn't mean there's something nefarious about their power or any imbalance with other people. Demonizing Jews for having power is antisemitic and the Jewish nation will pay it no heed.

CHAPTER
EIGHTEEN

We don't have to ask, "Will you hide me?" anymore

Johannes Kleiman, Victor Kugler, Johan Voskuijl, Bep Voskuijl, Jan Gies, and Miep Gies should be well known names among the Jewish people, but very few Jews know who these people were. These were Otto Frank's friends who had prepared a secret apartment at 263 Prinsengracht Street in Amsterdam. They smuggled food and clothing to the Franks, including their daughter Anne, during the family's two years of hiding from the Germans during the Holocaust. Miep Gies had the sense of mind to keep Anne Frank's diary and presented it to her father after he survived the Holocaust. These men and women were righteous Gentiles who risked their lives to save their Jewish neighbors and friends.

The Canadian Race Relations Foundation is Canada's leading agency dedicated to the elimination of racism and all forms of racial discrimination in Canadian society. It's executive director, Mohammed Hashim, recently tweeted about a meeting of community leaders he organized and a comment by a very wealthy Jewish leader – who had no worries in the world – made that changed his perspective. Mohammed tweeted, "She roughly said, 'For me to truly have trust, I would need to believe that you would hide me.' This community leader whose name I won't share was quite wealthy and for a second I thought, hold on, you could literally buy an entire island and fortify it and you worry about who would hide you here in Toronto??? 'Who would hide me?' Has never been a thought I have had. But it is one that many of my Jewish friends have had." Hashim went on to connect this exchange to International Holocaust Remembrance Day and how differently the Jewish people feel about the Holocaust than non-Jews.

Hashim's tweet made the rounds in J-twitter and many Jews responded by saying the "Who will hide me question?" is also at the forefront of their concerns. With rising antisemitic incidents in the United States in recent years, Holocaust era questions are becoming more mainstream among many American Jews. It is almost second nature for Jews to look at their Gentile neighbors with a different perspective. Instead of judging them by the way they maintain their house and yard, they have begun asking if they would hide them from antisemitic persecution.

Many Zionist scholars and educators attribute Theodore Herzl's founding of modern political Zionism to the French Alfred Dreyfus treason trial. Dreyfus, a Jewish French army officer, was falsely accused of treason. Herzl was a journalist assigned to cover the trial and based on the ramrodding of Herzl in the trial and the crowds chanting, "Death to the Jews" outside the courthouse, concluded it was antisemitism that guided Dreyfus's conviction. The way the narrative flows, Herzl was so upset at the antisemitism openly on display at the trial that he developed a plan to gather and return the Jewish people to the land of Israel. Although it makes a good story, it probably wasn't the Dreyfus trial alone that inspired Herzl to start the Zionist movement.

By the late 1800's Europe was suffering from a wave of harsh antisemitism. Pogroms were a frequent feature of Eastern European life. Herzl wrote extensively about rising antisemitism and it motivated him to act. His solutions to "The Jewish Question" was not Zionism at first. His ideas ranged from having all Jews convert to Christianity to moving everyone to the lush farms of Argentina. Herzl even wrote that he didn't think a Jewish State would solve the problem of antisemitism! It was only as his thoughts evolved that he began to think about motivating the Jewish people to return to the land of Israel. Even after concluding Palestine was the place to move, he entertained the British offer of founding an independent Jewish State in Uganda.

Zionism is usually defined as a movement that advocated for the right of the Jewish people to determine their own future in the land of Israel. The definition rarely mentions antisemitism and the need for a place of refuge. A study of Herzl's writings clearly demonstrates that although he believed in the Jewish right to the land of Israel, he was primarily concerned with antisemitism. The State of Israel was the answer to the antisemitism of Europe.

It's easy to argue that Herzl's assumption that a Jewish State would help solve the problem of antisemitism was wrong. As the Zionist movement began Arab antisemitism kicked into high gear. Jews living in Israel would face terrorism for the next hundred years. Wars began with the declaration of Israel's independence and continue until today. Zionism and Israel didn't end antisemitism as was hoped. The counter argument is just as easy to make. The State of Israel wasn't founded to stop antisemitism, but to give the Jewish people the ability to find refuge from persecution and defend themselves against violent attack. Israel has been a great success in these goals.

One of Zionism's primary goals and one of its greatest achievements can be said to ensure that Jews no longer have to ask, "Will my neighbor hide me?" The very question that plagued Mohammed Hashim when he heard it from a Jew that seemed to have nothing to worry about, was the motivator for the Jewish people to start their own nation where their security wouldn't be dependent on other people. I'm an American immigrant to Israel and I'm gratified to be living Herzl's dream of a Jewish State that can protect its Jewish citizens.

CHAPTER
NINETEEN

Reclaiming Zionism for the Jewish People

On a trip to South Florida, I was shocked by how much Hebrew I heard. At every Kosher restaurant I enjoyed my server spoke to me in Hebrew (that rarely happens in Israel!). Walking the aisles of Target and Costco I heard Hebrew spoken at every turn. Even my students were children of Israelis, fluent in Hebrew and many with modern Israeli names. While hearing the "*Moma lashon*" was comforting, it also worried me. Just how many Israelis have moved to America?

In order for Israelis to visit America today they must apply for an interview at the American Embassy or its branch in Tel Aviv. The next available interview might only be a year from now. After receiving your interview appointment, there is generally a wait on line for hours, sometimes for an entire day, to be interviewed. If the applicant is approved, America takes the Israeli's passport for a few weeks. The Israeli can then visit America.

Applying for a visa to America is an onerous process that drives many vacationing Israelis to more accessible places like South Asia or Europe. Why does America make it so hard for Israelis to get a visa to visit? America's chief concern is that Israelis applying for a visa to visit will overstay their visa and relocate to America.

The fear that Israelis will overstay their visa is not unfounded. Shop at most major malls in America and you'll find Israelis who have overstayed their visas selling Dead Sea salt products. The draw of America, the land of dreams, with its cheaper housing, more space, and the "easy" ability to earn riches is too good for many Israelis to forego. I fear the only thing stopping hundreds of thousands, if not millions of Israelis from leaving Israel to America is the difficulty in attaining a visa. If Israel joins the US visa waiver program, I fear a brain drain as Israelis exit our homeland to America.

It worries me that some Israelis don't share my fears. There are officials working with American government leaders to allow Israel to become the 40th country America grants a visa waiver to- and they want it to be granted this year.

What worries me even more is that some Israelis don't want to stay in Israel. Even with the wonderful benefits of America - it isn't the Jewish homeland. If Israelis aren't teaching and inspiring Israelis to love Israel, stay in Israel and be a part of Israel's growth, who will teach patriotic Zionism? Parents, teachers and even television shows have the power to influence. Far from a critique, I'm calling for action – We can be spending time talking to our children about the uniqueness of Eretz Yisrael and the privilege of being the first Israeli citizens in 2,000 years!

Inspiring Israelis to love Israel so much they're willing to stay even at personal discomfort, must be a priority of all Zionists - from mail people to parents. This isn't a joking matter; entire nations have failed when their best and brightest have left for greener pastures. We can't let that happen in Israel.

President Abraham Lincoln worried about internal corrosion more than external enemies, "At what point then is the approach of danger to be expected? I answer, if it ever reach us, it must spring up amongst us. It cannot come from abroad. If destruction be our lot, we must ourselves be its author and finisher. As a nation of freemen, we must live through all time, or die by suicide." This quote is often misquoted in shorthand, "America will never be destroyed from the outside. If we lose our freedoms it will be because we have destroyed ourselves from within." President Lincoln was referring to America, but he saw America as a nation of values, and it was the erosion of pride in those values that put America at risk. Israel is also a nation of values, and it too must be concerned that a lack of pride in Zionist values poses an existential threat to Israel.

How do we inspire our youth to love Israel? Our enemies and opponents have turned Zionism into a dirty word. First, they claimed it was racist, then oppressive, and today they claim Zionism is colonialist. Survey social media posts about Israel by Pro-Israel activists and you'll rarely find the word Zionism or discussions about Zionism. We've allowed our enemies to take the word and all it stands for from us. It's time we reclaimed Zionism for its rightful owners – the Jewish people.

The answer to inspiring love of Israel among our youth lies in education (not indoctrination). At home, school, on line, and even on television, a core message must be to teach our children, in Israel and outside of Israel, about the importance of the land of Israel, the nation of Israel, and the movement of Israel - Zionism. Most importantly, we must instill a sense of pride in who we are as Israelis. The combination of love and pride will keep our people in the land.

CHAPTER
TWENTY

Zionism and Power

In a recent conversation about Zionist values, the following argument was made to me, "The Jewish people were never meant to rule over another people and doing so contradicts all Zionist values." This is a critique I receive frequently from Zionists upset with the current situation in Israel. Skipping the political side of the discussion, I'd like to focus on the use of power and whether Zionist values require limiting its power, especially over other peoples.

For 2,000 years Jews lived the existence of the victim. Powerless, the Jewish people faced persecution through Crusades, pogroms, and a Holocaust. Discussions of power were the topics of fantasy more than realistic possibilities. Jews were at the whim of the ruling government of the land they lived in and no hope of wielding power. Even the few Jews of Eretz Yisrael were subject to the ruling power's laws.

Political Zionism aimed to give the Jews power over their own destiny. Instead of being oppressed and persecuted, early Zionists sought to establish a nation where Jews could flee and find refuge, as Israel's Declaration of Independence stated, "The catastrophe which recently befell the Jewish people - the massacre of millions of Jews in Europe - was another clear demonstration of the urgency of solving the problem of its homelessness by re-establishing in Eretz-Israel the Jewish State, which would open the gates of the homeland wide to every Jew and confer upon the Jewish people the status of a fully privileged member of the comity of nations." With the establishment of Israel, Jews would forever have the ability to defend themselves.

Zionists aimed to establish peace with its Arab neighbors, including

Arab neighboring countries and Arabs who resided within Israel. Israel's Declaration of Independence is instructive about Israel's founders' true intentions, "[Israel] will ensure complete equality of social and political rights to all its inhabitants irrespective of religion, race or sex; it will guarantee freedom of religion, conscience, language, education and culture; We appeal in the very midst of the onslaught launched against us now for months - to the Arab inhabitants of the State of Israel to preserve peace and participate in the upbuilding of the State on the basis of full and equal citizenship and due representation in all its provisional and permanent institutions."

Early Zionist leaders debated how to handle the Arab inhabitants of Palestine. The debate extended from the extreme suggestion of population transfers, where Arab inhabitants of Israel would be transferred to an Arab state and Jewish inhabitants of Arab states would be transferred to Israel, to an inclusive suggestion of offering citizenship with full rights to all Arabs irrespective of their view on Israel. In the end, Arabs who lived within Israel's borders as established in 1948, were given Israeli citizenship with full and equal rights to Israel's Jewish citizens. Arabs who lived outside of those borders, but in lands that Israel controlled but never annexed, for example, Judea and Samaria (The West Bank) were given human rights but not offered citizenship.

Unfortunately for all, Israel's offers of peace weren't reciprocated. Arabs from a multitude of countries outside and inside of Israel fought against Israel instead of accepting its call for peace. Israel was forced to rule over enemy Arabs found inside Israel's borders when the armistice lines were drawn to end the Independence War in 1948. In 1967, Arab armies attacked again and, in their defeat, lost the Sinai Desert, the Gaza Strip, Judea and Samaria (The West Bank) and the Golan Heights to Israel. Millions of enemy Arabs found themselves within the borders of Israel's rule and Israel found itself ruling over millions of Arabs who did not want to be governed by Israel. Israel's immediate offers of land for peace as an end to the conflict and a dysfunctional situation were rebuffed.

Many Zionists and Jews were upset with the power Israel was exercising over non-Jews under their rule. A debate opened in Israeli society and Diaspora Zionists about whether exercising power over non-Jews was consistent with Jewish and Zionist values. As former Deputy Prime Minister and Israeli Ambassador to America Dr. Michael Oren wrote, "Today, as an

Israeli, I must confront questions that derive from having power. I had to decide, for instance, whether to support the construction of a fence which may provide greater security against terrorist attacks, but which evokes the very ghetto walls that Zionism aspired to topple." Ruth Wisse echoed these sentiments writing, "In trying to withstand the Arab assault, Israelis, Jews, and concerned third parties tripped again and again over the same issue of power that had impeded the development of Jewish political history to begin with."

Jewish tradition is clear about ruling over others, as Maimonides wrote, "If the enemy accepts the offer of peace ... they should be subjugated. If they agree to tribute, but do not accept subjugation or if they accept subjugation, but do not agree to tribute, their offer should not be heeded." In his well-known essay, "The Iron Wall," Ze'ev Jabotinsky wrote, "The inhabiting of the land can, therefore, continue and develop only under the protection of a force independent of the local population--an iron wall which the native population cannot break through...This does not mean that any kind of agreement is impossible, only a voluntary agreement is impossible...But the only path to such an agreement is the iron wall, that is to say the strengthening in Palestine of a government without any kind of Arab influence, that is to say one against which the Arabs will fight. In other words, for us the only path to an agreement in the future is an absolute refusal of any attempts at an agreement now."

Former Israeli Ambassador to America Ron Dermer addressed Jewish power in the context of the Holocaust, "What is the lesson of the Holocaust to the Jews? Is the lesson that we have to teach tolerance? Did we need six million to die to teach tolerance?... We didn't need the Holocaust to teach tolerance. The lesson of the Holocaust is that the Jewish people need power. That's the lesson of the Holocaust." Jews are uniquely uncomfortable with the idea of power because there's a price of power. You know what that price is? It's imperfection. When you are sovereign, you are imperfect. When you are a victim, you can be morally perfect. I would rather be sovereign and imperfect."

Today the debate continues in a healthy way. Zionists disagree whether they should be ruling over others. Zionists on the left side of the political spectrum strongly oppose ruling over non-Jews and are willing to sacrifice land to exit a situation they feel erodes the moral fabric of Israeli society. Zionists on the right see ruling over others a part of Jewish tradition and have no issue with it. There's a third school of thought that prefers not to rule over others, but doesn't see a viable alternative to ruling over those not willing to make peace with Israel. While the Knesset ultimately decides policy for the State of Israel, each Zionist must draw their own conclusions about Zionism and power.

CHAPTER
TWENTY-ONE

Israelis are good people

In the middle of the night on June 24th, the Champlain Tower came crashing down in Surfside, Florida. While chaos ruled for days, eventually 98 people would be found dead and four people would be rescued from the rubble. Two days after the collapse, the Israeli Defense Forces sent a search and rescue team to aid the Florida team on the ground. This wasn't the first time the IDF had been sent at its own expense to aid non-Israelis around the world. In countless situations the IDF has been sent to aid countries suffering from disasters. No other country Israel's size helps others as Israel does. Israel's value of helping others reflects the Israeli people's character and their role as a moral light onto the nations.

The Israeli people are a good people, deserving of accolades and praise for their "Hadar," their refined dignity. It is the Israeli values of helping others, acting with humility and including the needy in larger society. These values are thousands of years old and began with the Jewish people's forefather Abraham in the land of Israel. Abraham had four openings to his tent, one opening facing each direction. Through his multiple entrances, Abraham was able to see if travelers were passing by and he could reach out and invite them into his tent to refresh and have something to eat. Helping others was the moral value system Abraham passed to Isaac, who passed it to Jacob and it has carried on until today.

Israel's system of helping the needy isn't limited to Jews, it extends to its non-Jewish citizens as well. Israeli Arabs are given equal rights to Israeli Jews. Arabs in Israel have reached the highest offices of Israeli society. Arab Israelis are Ministers in the government, Supreme Court justices, mayors, doctors and lawyers. An Israeli Arab party sat in the government for the first time in Israel's history. Arab placement in the government after 70 years speaks to Israeli determination to repair societal ills and become increasingly more inclusive.

Israel doesn't only aim to include and help Israeli Arab citizens but has helped Palestinian Arabs more than all other Arab countries combined. After 19 years of neglect by Jordan, Palestinian Arabs came under Israeli rule in 1967. At the time few Palestinians had electricity in their homes and only four cities had running water. Palestinians were using cisterns from Roman times. Palestinian quality of life was horrific but in line with the rest of the Arab world. No world body attempted to help them.

Israel doesn't measure its policies by the neighboring countries around them. While Israel's neighboring Arab countries have treated its Palestinian residents as less than human, restricting their access to jobs, rights and at times even executing them in mass numbers – as King Hussein of Jordan did during the "Black September," Israel treats Palestinians with full human rights and has remarkably improved their lives.

Since 1967 and Israeli control of Judea and Samaria, Palestinian Arabs have seen their lives drastically improve in three areas. Palestinian quality of life has improved, life expectancy has improved, and Palestinian population numbers have risen. Palestinian cities and villages have seen development beyond their wildest dreams, and they enjoy every modern convenience. While it might seem obvious that every town should have electricity and running water, Palestinians living in other Arab countries do not enjoy the same quality of life.

Israel is constantly holding itself to higher standards. Israel's justice system is independent and holds criminals responsible for their nefarious actions. Unlike its stronger and older ally America, Israel has convicted and imprisoned a Prime Minister, President and Chief Rabbi. It has a penal system that holds criminals, irrespective of place in society, guilty for their crimes. Israel's commitment to justice ensures that its society is run by the rule of law, not the elite in society getting away with crime while the poorer of society languish in jails.

Israel's military has long been known as the most moral army in the world. The Israel Defense Forces sticks to a code of ethics that far surpasses its responsibilities under the international laws of war. Israel will take all steps to ensure it does not harm civilians in a battlefield situation, often calling off missions immediately before they are conducted because a civilian has entered the battlefield arena and could be harmed in the operation. Israel also drops dud bombs on building tops before blowing them up, drops leaflets in neighborhoods about to be targeted and calls the cell phones of residents of the area – all to warn innocent civilians of impending harm.

Israel is a good country full of good people. This doesn't mean Israel is a perfect society. While the overwhelming number of Israelis are kind, law abiding citizens who look to help those around them, Israel also has jails full of inmates who have not led their lives by traditional Jewish values. Israel is also plagued by extremists who paint Israel dark and sully Israel's name around the world. These people feature front and center of the world's headlines making it seem at times as if Israel is a basketful of bad apples.

Israel's bad apples are a small, even tiny, percentage of its overall population. Any honest look at the Israeli people will show them to be the best of the best of the world. Every Zionist should be proud to call the Israeli people their people and should spread the message of Israel's kindness, inclusiveness and desire to help the needy in Israel and around the world.

CHAPTER

TWENTY-TWO

Days that should never, shouldn't, and didn't have to be on the calendar

Jewish history is made of fulfilled dreams and nightmares come to life. As a people, Jews weren't intended to be a people of such great degrees of loss. The Jewish people were meant to be a light onto the nations, modeling moral policies and behavior with their successes a testimony to the fulfillment of their national mission. Unfortunately, as a people, the Israelites rarely met the challenge of their destiny and suffered the consequences. As nations didn't perceive a positive uniqueness to the Jewish people, they began to persecute them. The Jewish people were left to suffer at the mercy of foreign nation.

During the two weeks following Passover Israel marks three national days, Yom Hashoah (Holocaust Remembrance Day), Yom Hazikaron (Israeli Memorial Day for war and terror victims) and Yom Ha'atzmaut (Israeli Independence Day). The proximity of these three dates send Israelis on a roller coaster of emotions from the lowest of lows to the highest of highs. While there is an imperative to commemorate these three days, an argument can be made, Yom Hashoah and Yom Hazikaron, memorialize events that should never have happened and Yom Ha'atzmaut celebrates an event that didn't have to happen.

The Holocaust was a singular moment of tragedy that both included and surpassed all other tragic days of Jewish history. The Jewish people hope it was a culmination of their national catastrophes. Like all antisemitism it should never have happened. Elie Wiesel wrote about the global indifference that allowed the Holocaust, "Sometimes we must interfere. When human lives are endangered, when human dignity is in jeopardy, national borders and sensitivities become irrelevant. Wherever men or women are persecuted because of their race, religion, or political views, that place must—at that moment—become the center of the universe."

Not only should the pervasive hate of Germany and Europe have never occurred, but the indifference that permitted it shouldn't have happened either. Yom Hashoah commemorates two tragedies, the tragedy of the dead of the Holocaust and the tragedy of the Holocaust itself. The Holocaust should never have happened, and Yom Hashoah should never have been instituted.

This year's Yom Hazikaron, Israeli Memorial Day for war and terror victims, will commemorate almost 24,000 victims. None of these victims should've been killed. The world has accepted the reality that nations must go to war and lose their citizens to violence – but this isn't true. In the Israeli Declaration of Independence, Israel's founders wrote, "We extend our hand to all neighboring states and their peoples in an offer of peace and good neighborliness, and appeal to them to establish bonds of cooperation and mutual help with the sovereign Jewish people settled in its own land. The State of Israel is prepared to do its share in a common effort for the advancement of the entire Middle East." Had the Arabs accepted our hands extended in peace, there would've been no wars and no one to remember.

Benjamin Netanyahu famously paraphrased former Prime Minister Golda Meir, "If the Arabs put down their weapons today, there would be no more violence. If the Jews put down their weapons today, there would be no more Israel." Wars against Israel should never have been fought and Yom Hazikaron should never have been put on the Israeli calendar.

Israel's national law states, "The right to exercise national self-determination in the State of Israel is unique to the Jewish people." Zionism was a movement that advocated for the right of the Jewish people to enjoy self-determination in their own historic homeland. Miriam Berger explained the Israeli national law, "Supporters of this declaration say that Jews have the right to a place of their own just like other people have, and that enshrining this principle in the law is necessary to ensure that Israel remains under Jewish control."

The founding of the State of Israel was nothing short of astonishing and deserves to be celebrated daily. Within the celebration is a reminder of the wrong the Jewish people suffered before Israel was founded. Israel had to be founded because 2,000 years ago the Romans defeated the Jewish nation and exiled its people. In a continuous act of injustice, the global community refused to grant the Jews a right to return to their land for 2,000 years. If the world hadn't mistreated the Jews by robbing them of their homeland, there wouldn't have been a need to establish a Jewish state or create an Israeli Independence Day.

A danger presented by the juxtaposition of the three national calendar days is the mistake of conflating the days and assuming a cause and effect relationship between them. In an address to the Arab world in Cairo in June of 2009, American President Barack Obama said, "America's strong bonds with Israel are well known. This bond is unbreakable. It is based upon cultural and historical ties, and the recognition that the aspiration for a Jewish homeland is rooted in a tragic history that cannot be denied. Around the world, the Jewish people were persecuted for centuries, and anti-Semitism in Europe culminated in an unprecedented Holocaust. President Obama was criticized for connecting Israel's existence to the Holocaust, implying that it was the Jewish people's tragic history and not their rights to their homeland, that created the State of Israel.

Four years later, on a visit to Israel, President Obama corrected his mistake by declaring the Jewish people's eternal right to the land of Israel, "More than 3,000 years ago, the Jewish people lived here, tended the land here, prayed to God here. And after centuries of exile and persecution, unparalleled in the history of man, the founding of the Jewish State of Israel was a rebirth, a redemption unlike any in history. Today, the sons of Abraham and the daughters of Sarah are fulfilling the dream of the ages -- to be "masters of their own fate" in "their own sovereign state." And just as we have for these past 65 years, the United States is proud to stand with you as your strongest ally and your greatest friend."

As Israel marks its most meaningful national days it is important that along with the wave of emotion, recognition of the cause of the events that brought these days is crucial to properly commemorating them. Ironically, it's only by acknowledging the reason these days shouldn't exist can we properly respect the people and events these days are meant to honor.

CHAPTER
TWENTY-THREE

Zionist Particularism vs. Universalism

The modern political movement known as Zionism began in the mid to late 1800's. Theodore Herzl, largely credited with starting Zionism, was concerned with the safety of the Jewish people. During his lifetime antisemitic violence was rising in Europe and Herzl was convinced only a Jewish State that provided protection to the Jewish people could guarantee the security of the Jewish people. A secondary goal, and one that only came later in Herzl's plans, was the actualization of the Jewish right to determine their own future in their historic homeland, the land of Israel. It was Herzl and other Zionists' focus on Jewish security and return to their homeland that caused people to characterize Zionism as a purely particularistic movement.

Zionism was once slandered by the international community as a racist movement in an infamous United Nation resolution. Only one of two United Nation resolutions to be rescinded by the international community, it has been revealed as the misrepresentation of Zionism's true values. The resolution ironically accused Zionism of being a supremacist movement that aimed to deny people self-determination. How was such a distortion of Zionism allowed to be perpetuated in an international forum as significant as the United Nations?

Zionism was a revolutionary nationalist movement unparalleled in its time. It aimed to gather millions of Jews from around the world, unite them as a single people, and bring them back to their historic homeland they had been exiled from almost two thousand years before the movement began. Zionism claimed the Jewish people had sole rights to the land of Israel. While Zionist leaders eventually acquiesced to the United Nations' partition plan which severely limited greater Israel to a small sliver of land, they never thought anyone but the Jewish people shared the same rights and historical connection to the land of Israel as the Jewish people. It's easy to characterize a movement whose primary concern is one people as a purely particularistic movement. It would also be a great misunderstanding of Zionism.

Jewish tradition maintains the Jewish people have a unique role in the community of nations. The Jewish people have been Divinely chosen to act as a model of exemplary behavior for the nations of the world. There are hundreds of commands just for them, and they have a unique relationship with God. The Jewish people have specific directives of how they are to treat their fellow Jews, lending money to them without interest, supporting the Jewish poor and building robust Jewish communities. These traditions point to Jewish particularism. Zionism took many of the Jewish values and positions as its own and Zionism became known as a particularistic movement.

There are universalistic aspects to Judaism as well. The directive for Jews to be a light unto the nations isn't just about Jewish behavior but also relates to the imperative for the Jewish people to help improve the world around them. The Jewish people can't look away when faced with the world's problems, they must come to help the world. Universalism is inherent to Jewish values and practice. Just as particularistic Jewish traditions and values extended to Zionism, so too, the universalistic aspects of Judaism extended to Zionism as well.

Zionism was never meant to be a movement that focused purely on the Jewish people and Jewish State. Early Zionist leaders always saw the Jewish State they aimed to create as one that would lead the world in technological innovation, medical discovery, and scientific research. They couldn't perceive the hi-tech world Israel has flourished in, but more modern Zionists have taken up their charge ensuring the State of Israel has become a world leader in hi-tech and business.

All too often modern thought and concepts are projected onto old systems. The old systems and movements are expected to align to values the world adopted decades after they existed. This kind of retroactive judgment is unrealistic and can never meet the verdicts of future generations. This is true of Zionism as well. The modern political movement of Zionism was founded in a specific time in the history of the world when the values of the world sharply contrasted with today's values. To expect Zionism to have foreseen the progressive values of today, especially when none of the world's movements matched it isn't reasonable. Considering it was a movement bent on saving Jewish lives through a nationalist movement and still focused on the rest of the world, Zionism itself was a progressive movement whose values matched today's values well.

Zionism was a movement constructed to mirror the dual Jewish values of particularism and universalism. To succeed and remain relevant it must always give primacy to ensuring the Jewish people's security and guarantee the Jewish people's rights to self-determination on the land of Israel. But to meet its original mission it must also look past the Jewish people and aim to improve the world by solving its most vexing problems. To peg Zionism as purely particularistic or purely universalistic is inaccurate. Zionism is an expansive enough movement to encapsulate both particularistic and universalistic goals.

CHAPTER

TWENTY-FOUR

Left and Right-Wing Zionism
Two Sides of the Same Coin

"Zionism seeks to secure for the Jewish people a publicly recognized, legally assured homeland in Palestine. For the attainment of this purpose, the Congress considers the following means serviceable: (1) The promotion of the settlement of Jewish agriculturists, artisans, and tradesmen in Palestine. (2) The federation of all Jews into local or general groups, according to the laws of the various countries. (3) The strengthening of the Jewish feeling and consciousness. (4) Preparatory steps for the attainment of those governmental grants which are necessary to the achievement of the Zionist purpose." These points form the Basel Program, developed by a committee at the first Zionist Congress in 1897. It's interesting to note that the program covers the aims and methods of Zionism, but never defines Zionism. In fact, Zionism was never actually defined.

As Herzl's Zionist movement grew, it began to split into different sub-groups, each with their own approaches to Zionism. Political Zionism, Practical Zionism, Religious Zionism, and Revisionist Zionism are just some examples of different forms of Zionism, and many were not only different from each other, but opposed each other's positions. As each group jockeyed to prove it was most aligned with Zionism, the lack of a consensus definition of Zionism prevented any one group from claiming to represent Zionism more than any other group. While Zionism has never been officially defined, there is a widely used description of Zionism that almost all Zionists ascribe to when discussing Zionism. "The Jewish people deserve self-determination in their historic homeland, the land of Israel," is widely used by Zionists to describe their movement.

A perceived notion exists that right-wing Zionists are "More Zionist" than left-wing Zionists. This notion is given fuel by a numbers game: loud and prolific Zionist on-line voices tend to be right-wing Zionists. While many right-wing Zionists argue it's no coincidence that right-wing Zionists are louder and more prolific, raised voices and proliferation aren't metrics of greater Zionism. The only data point to be taken from the online right-wing voices is that they're louder and more prolific. Great Zionism is measured in many ways, on-line advocacy is only one way of many different metrics.

The left-wing Zionist is accused of not being sufficiently Zionist because of the policies they advocate for Israel. It is easier to sound "more" Zionist when you're advocating for more right-wing and conservative policies. Issues like land expansion, taking a strong stand against enemies and opponents, and refusing to compromise, come off as proud Zionist stands. Opposing building and development in favor of peace, advocating for reconciliation with opponents and enemies and preaching compromise can make one's Zionism seem weak or even secondary.

While none of the above stereotypes are true, and an argument can be made for opposing building as a method of bringing peace is more Zionist than stubbornly building and offending Israel's enemies, the left-wing Zionist opens themselves to the accusation of not being a staunch enough Zionist with their more liberal positions. Rarely is the accusation made against the right-wing Zionist that their ideology can damage Israel's long-term future and is therefore anti-Zionist. In truth, right and left-wing Zionism agree on so much, their differences can be ascribed more to tone and emphasis rather than significant partisan divisions.

Left wing Zionism is more liberal in its approach. It stands for pluralism, equality in all social areas, and normalized relations with Arab and Palestinian neighbors through granting Palestinian freedoms and independence. Left wing Zionists are more willing to compromise and more open to a Jewish State whose diversity is shown by both Jewish and Arab citizens. Right wing Zionism is more conservative in its approach. It stands for land expansion; it puts more emphasis on Israel as a Jewish State than a state for all its people and is less willing to compromise.

No one side of the political spectrum has a monopoly on Zionism.

Israel's longest serving Prime Minister, Benjamin Netanyahu, was a right-wing Prime Minister and its second longest serving Prime Minister, David Ben Gurion, was a left-wing Prime Minister. Zionist leaders, soldiers, artists, and scholars have come from both the left- and right-wing camps. While a little bit of each of us wants to live in an echo chamber of our own positions constantly echoing back to us, Zionism is richer when it has more members, and its ideas are more diverse. Instead of each side trying to best its opponent by arguing it has the more authentic Zionist approach, each side should celebrate Zionism's inclusivity and diversity.

CHAPTER TWENTY-FIVE

"It is more important to be smart than correct."

There is an Israeli phrase, "It is more important to be smart than correct." I had an Israeli boss who would drill this mantra into me and my coworkers. At every point of conflict between staff and clients, when we knew we were right, our boss would say, "You're right, but 'It is more important to be smart than correct.'"

Jews, Zionists, Israelis, are correct in their claim to a historical connection with the land of Israel. When comparing claims to the land, the Jewish people have the longest claim to the land of Israel. Relative to the history of the land, Arabs are newcomers. It is a credit to Israel and their people, that Israelis treat Palestinians under their administration far better than their Arab brethren do in neighboring countries. It has become the consensus position that there's little chance of ending the Israeli-Palestinian conflict in the coming years. Unlike harsh treatment of Jews in Arab lands, Israel has accepted two million Arab citizens into its Jewish state and granted them equal rights.

Jewish people have been targeted and killed in Israel for over 75 years. Zionists abhor their unnecessary losses to violence and never want to pay another shiva call to a terrorist victim's family. Zionists want their army to decrease in size and not have to defend against terrorism. As stated over and over in Israel's Declaration of Independence, Zionists thirst for peace.

This has led many Zionists to the position that would seem counterintuitive to the Zionist goal of returning the Jewish people to their land. They advocate giving portions of the Jewish homeland to other nations in exchange for peace. If peace means losing some of the land, then it is a loss for a greater good. If it meant recognition of Israel's legitimacy and of the Jewish people's indigenousness in this land, they would be willing to give up parts of the Jewish homeland to other people. It is here that I hear my former boss's voice echoing in their position, "It is more important to be smart than correct."

These people are fully aware that Zionism sought a return of the Jewish people to the land of Israel and by giving up land, they'll be moving away from that goal. Zionists could lose their homes and the communities they've built and developed for years. These Zionists know many of their brethren will accuse them of betraying the Zionist dream and the Torah command to settle the land, much as Israeli Prime Ministers Menachem Begin, Yitzchak Rabin, Ehud Barak and Ariel Sharon were accused when they gave up Israeli controlled land. But they reason, "It is more important to be smart than correct."

Most importantly they know there is no chance of a solution anytime soon. They are fully aware that Palestinians and Israelis are as divided as they've ever been. There is little trust between the two peoples, and in many cases, there is no mutual recognition of each other's positions. As long as enemy leaders teach hatred, worship terrorists as heroes, and refuse to negotiate, there is no chance of a peaceful resolution to the conflict.

Whatever a Zionist's positions on land for peace, all Zionists continue to pray for peace, even if they're not optimistic of seeing it in their lifetime. While Zionists certainly don't advocate for a process that will fail in an attempt to bring peace, the basis of Zionism is the search for peace. Zionists are practical and rational, and irrespective of any particular policy, their success will come from heeding the advice that, "It is more important to be smart than correct."

CHAPTER
TWENTY-SIX

MLK, Justice & Zionism

Zionism isn't a movement solely dedicated to the return of the Jewish people to their homeland. Zionism is a movement of justice. For thousands of years injustices were perpetrated against the Jewish people. Jews suffered from Crusades, pogroms, and the Holocaust, among a host of economic injustices. Vile among the other injustices was the forceable exile of the Jewish people off their homeland – the land of Israel. As long as Jews were prohibited from reclaiming and returning to their land an injustice was being committed in the world.

When Dr. Martin Luther King Jr. received the Nobel Peace Prize he spoke passionately about oppression and justice. "Oppressed people cannot remain oppressed forever. The yearning for freedom eventually manifests itself. The Bible tells the thrilling story of how Moses stood in Pharaoh's court centuries ago and cried, 'Let my people go.' This is a kind of opening chapter in a continuing story. The deep rumbling of discontent that we hear today is the thunder of disinherited masses, rising from dungeons of oppression to the bright hills of freedom, in one majestic chorus the rising masses singing, in the words of our freedom song, 'Ain't gonna let nobody turn us around.'

We know through painful experience that freedom is never voluntarily given by the oppressor; it must be demanded by the oppressed. Frankly, I have yet to engage in a direct-action campaign that was 'well timed' in the view of those who have not suffered unduly from the disease of segregation. For years now I have heard the word 'Wait!' It rings in the ear of every Negro with piercing familiarity. This 'Wait' has almost always meant 'Never.' We must come to see, with one of our distinguished jurists, that 'justice too long delayed is justice denied.'

The Zionist struggle to return to their homeland and the African American struggle for equal rights in America are similar pursuits of justice. The late Congressman John Lewis, contemporary of Dr. King and hero of the American civil rights movement wrote, "[King] knew that both peoples were uprooted involuntarily from their homelands. He knew that both peoples were shaped by the tragic experience of slavery. He knew that both peoples were forced to live in ghettos, victims of segregation.

He knew that both peoples were subject to laws passed with the particular intent of oppressing them simply because they were Jewish or black. He knew that both peoples have been subjected to oppression and genocide on a level unprecedented in history. King understood how important it is not to stand by in the face of injustice. He understood the cry, "Let my people go."

Congressman Lewis wrote about Dr. King's appreciation of Zionism, "On March 25, 1968, less than two weeks before his tragic death, he spoke out with clarity and directness stating, 'Peace for Israel means security, and we must stand with all our might to protect its right to exist, its territorial integrity. I see Israel as one of the great outposts of democracy in the world, and a marvelous example of what can be done, how desert land can be transformed into an oasis of brotherhood and democracy. Peace for Israel means security and that security must be a reality." During an appearance at Harvard University shortly before his death, a student stood up and asked King to address himself to the issue of Zionism. The question was clearly hostile. King responded, "When people criticize Zionists they mean Jews, you are talking anti-Semitism."

At the opening of the Madrid Peace Conference between the Israelis and Palestinians in 1991, Israeli Prime Minister Yitzchak Shamir echoed Dr. King's sentiments on Zionism and justice, "The Zionist movement gave political expression to our claim to the Land of Israel. And in 1922 the League of Nations recognized the justice of this claim. It understood the compelling historic imperative of establishing a Jewish homeland in the Land of Israel. The United Nations Organization reaffirmed this recognition after the Second World War."

As a movement promoting justice, Zionism is a righteous movement. The continual affirmation of Zionism and rights of the Jewish people to self-determination in their own historic homeland is the continuous struggle for justice. Fighters for justice anywhere must fight for Zionism, as Dr. King said, "Injustice anywhere is a threat to justice everywhere." Unfortunately, Zionism must continuously defend itself, but I pray for a day when Zionism doesn't need to defend itself. I pray for the day when justice reigns and the world recognizes the justice of the Zionist ideal.

CHAPTER
TWENTY-SEVEN

The Only Existential Threat Facing Israel

Golda Meir's bodyguard, Adam Snir, told reporters that Israel's Prime Minister during the Yom Kippur rejected her Defense Minister's suggestion that Israel use a nuclear weapon to defend itself against attacking Arab armies. "That's the last thing I need," Meir told Moshe Dayan according to Snir. Supposedly, Israel had committed to America not to use its nuclear arsenal unless its very existence was under threat. In the first few days of the Yom Kippur War, it seemed to Dayan that Israel could be looking at its end.

The Yom Kippur War wouldn't have been Israel's first time facing an existential threat, but it would be its last. From its very inception, and arguably before, Israel faced multiple Arab armies who outnumbered them and potentially would have defeated Israel. In 1948, 1956 and 1967 Israel faced looming threats, went to war, and successfully defended itself. After its successful defensive victory in 1973, Israel never again faced an existential threat.

In 1981, Israeli Prime Minister Menachem Begin was told that Iraq's nuclear program was designed to be a weapons program and could be used against Israel. In 2007 Israeli Prime Minister Ehud Olmert was told the same news about a Syrian nuclear reactor. Both Prime Ministers understood that if either country attained nuclear weapons they would be used to end Israel. Instead of waiting until the nuclear threat was realized, both Prime Ministers preemptively bombed their enemy's nuclear reactors and ended the threat before it began.

Israel has faced years of Fedayeen attacks from Egypt, two intifadas, tens of thousands of rockets, thousands of terror attacks, and boycotts, all aimed to scare Israelis out of Israel and end Israel as a Jewish State. Palestinians began campaigns of delegitimization to ostracize Israel in the international community, accusing it of occupation, apartheid, war crimes and even grotesque slander of harvesting Palestinian organs. They recruited the United Nations to their efforts, all to shame Israel and have it face pressure from the international community to turn their Jewish state into a Palestinian State. All these attacks and efforts failed. Today, Iran is trying to develop a nuclear weapon with the explicit aim of annihilating Israel. To date, Israel and its allies have kept Iran from developing a nuclear weapon, but Iran is still trying. Currently, there are no enemies that pose an existential threat to Israel.

The lack of an existential threat should give Israelis a sense of security, but it's becoming clear that Israel is facing an existential threat of a different nature. Only by studying Jewish history can we understand the existential threat Israel currently faces. The end of Israel's second commonwealth, when the Roman Empire destroyed the second Temple and exiled the Israelites from the land of Israel, was brought about by baseless hatred between groups. Baseless hatred is difficult to identify, anyone accused of baseless hatred is bound to justify their hate by claiming their hate is warranted.

Rosh Chodesh often a horrific scene played out at the Ezrat Yisrael section of the Western Wall. Conservative Jews held a prayer service which included a bar mitzvah. Some Haredi Jews, opposing an egalitarian service with mixed seating, attacked the worshippers. I won't recount exactly what the Haredi attackers did, but antisemitism expert Deborah Lipstadt wrote, "Had these acts been anywhere else in the world, they'd be considered antisemitism." Around the world people couldn't help but be shocked at the hate filled scene at the Western Wall that day.

The existential threat Israel faces today doesn't come from an external enemy but from internal division. Nothing is more corrosive for a functional and healthy Jewish nation than internal division. Healthy debate over important issues is encouraged and always produces a better society – usually through compromise. When healthy debate turns into hateful division, society begins to fall apart and violent scenes, like the one at the Ezrat Yisrael section of the Western Wall, begin to occur.

Creating unity between different groups of our people doesn't require uniformity in thought or policy. It requires respect and a healthy dose of nuance. Listening to other groups of people doesn't validate their positions or declare your agreement with them. Hearing other viewpoints demonstrates a willingness to come together and stop unhealthy divisions and the threat it brings.

The mission of Zionists must be to build internal bridges among our people. Zionists must improve the infrastructure of our society just as much as they improve the physical infrastructure of the land. The focus of the Jewish people, from Haredim to the secular, from Reform to Orthodox and anywhere in between, must be to move past division and focus on the issues that unite. To ensure this third commonwealth succeeds and develops into something even greater, Zionists must work hard at uniting the Jewish people. The first step is listening to each other.

CHAPTER
TWENTY-EIGHT

Welcoming New Friends

It was a day like any other day in the yeshiva in Mevasseret Zion, Israel. Rabbi Sinai Adler zt"l, a Holocaust survivor, sat in the front of the study hall studying Torah in his well-known sing-song tune. A student approached him to let him know that German supporters of Israel were visiting the Yeshiva. Enraged, Rabbi Adler had them removed not just from the Yeshiva, but from the Yeshiva campus. Rabbi Adler quoted a teaching from the Talmud to explain why he insisted on ejecting the Germans from the Yeshiva, "*Eisav Sonei Es Yaakov*," (The descendants of Eisav will always hate the descendants of Yaakov) he explained. "The Germans are not our friends." Rav Sinai ejecting the Germans from the Yeshiva stuck with all who saw the episode that day. The lesson Rabbi Adler taught about Jews never being able to trust non-Jews made an impression on everyone who heard his explanation.

A great deal of Israeli history and destiny changed in 1977 when Israel's most formidable enemy, the Egyptians, reached out to Israel to make peace. The President of Egypt, Anwar Sadat and Israeli Prime Minister signed the Camp David Accords that made peace between two of the world's most severe enemies. Many Israelis were skeptical about the Egyptians true intentions and whether they should be trusted to make peace with Israel.

The world was surprised again when Palestinian Yasser Arafat and Israeli Prime Minister Yitzchak Rabin agreed to the Oslo Accords that created a process to bring the Israeli-Palestinian conflict to a close. The Palestinian Liberation Organization was responsible for hundreds of terror attacks against Israel that were responsible for thousands of dead Israelis. Once again

Israelis were skeptical about whether the Palestinians were genuine about peace. Protests broke out all over Israel and unfortunately, skeptics became violent and Prime Minister Yitzchak Rabin was assassinated.

The next peace accords Israel signed were met with less skepticism by Israelis. In 1994 Israel signed a peace deal with Jordan's King Hussein. It was widely known that Israel had been dealing clandestinely with the Jordanian royal family and its government for decades and peace with Jordan was seen more as a formality than a breakthrough. Israelis didn't see peace with Jordan as a former enemy changing its ways like Egypt and the Palestinians claimed to be when signing agreements with Israel, but rather as a concretization of an already existing reality.

In much the same way The Abraham Accords wasn't seen as the end of Israeli-Arab conflicts, but more as normalization with countries Israel didn't have previous relations with – at least not publicly. The people of the UAE, Bahrain, Sudan, and Morocco weren't former enemies on the battlefield but rather political and diplomatic opponents. Israelis weren't as skeptical about the genuineness of the Arabs of these countries because there were no battles or wars ended with the Abraham Accords. Unlike with the Egyptian and Palestinian accords, Israelis didn't have to extend themselves and trust previously untrustworthy enemies to sign these accords and treaties.

Rabbi Adler was once asked if all non-Jews could never be trusted, and if "*Eisav Sonei Es Yaakov*," (The descendants of Eisav will always hate the descendants of Yaakov) is an evergreen principle with no exceptions or a general principle that can have exceptions built in. Rabbi Adler answered that although we assume that non-Jews will eventually turn against the Jews, if the non-Jews support the Jewish people or Israel because it is in their interest to do so, the non-Jews can be trusted.

The various peace accords brought skepticism among many Israelis. For years Israelis were always waiting for the "trick" that the Arab countries would pull on the Israelis and demonstrate that the peace was fake. Many Israelis point to the failure of the Oslo Accords with the Palestinians to support the skepticism and distrust of the Arab countries. The success of the Abraham Accords has drawn Israelis in the other direction, showing the great potential of turning former opponents into supporters.

Rabbi Adler's principle that "*Eisav Sonei Es Yaakov*," and its exception, that non-Jews who support the Jewish people and Israel because it is in their interest to do so can be trusted, act as a guiding light to Israelis on how to understand non-Jews and their enemies, especially when there's a potential for peace.

CHAPTER
TWENTY-NINE

The aspersions cast on left-wing Zionism

There are Zionists who regularly denigrate left-wingers as anti-Israel and even antisemitic. Some left-wing perspectives are often seen by more conservative Israelis and their advocates as inconsistent or even conflicting with Pro-Israel positions. Progressive Democrats like Alexandria Ocasio-Cortez, Bernie Sanders, Ilhan Omar and Rashida Tlaib and their anti-Israel positions make it seem as if all Democrats, left-wingers and progressives, share their hostile positions.

Many left-wingers, in Israel and outside of it, are Zionists and care deeply about Israel. If Zionist feelings could be measured, there are many left-wingers who would rate highest on the "love Israel" scale. Calling left-wingers anti-Israel or antisemitic is inaccurate. Lumping all left-wingers together as followers of progressive elected officials and their anti-Israel positions is also a mistake.

Progressive and left-wing political thought leaders both lean left, but they are not the same in their values or ideals. They ascribe to two different political philosophies and grouping them together is just as ignorant as grouping libertarian and conservatives together. Progressives work hard to change the current systems, mostly to right the imbalances of power – as they understand them. Progressives perceive Zionists as immoral and oppressive because they have power.

Left-wingers don't subscribe to that same equation. left-wingers want everyone to be treated equally, and the poor given additional help to overcome the societal challenges they face. Left-wingers want to help the weak because they need help, not because they are victims of oppression. Left-wing

Democrats want the best for Israel and they should not be conflated with anti-Israel progressives. Left-wing Democrats in Congress are Pro-Israel and while they might not show as much support as other politicians, they should be included as friends of Zion. Many left-wing Democrats consider themselves Zionists. After landing in Ben-Gurion airport for the first time as President of America, Joe Biden said, "I had the great honor of living part of the great history of this great — and I did say and I say again, you need not be a Jew to be a Zionist."

Zionism is the political movement to secure the Jewish people's right to self-determination in their historic homeland. For 2,000 years the Jews were wandering exiles, moving from country to country, at times settling – but always only temporarily. The Jews deserved to return to their homeland, and left-wingers, starting with President Harry Truman, recognized their rights to the land of Israel. There is nothing about left-wing doctrine and Zionism that is mutually exclusive of each other. In fact, many left-wingers argue that left-wing doctrine and Zionism are consistent with each other.

Many Zionists differentiate their approach to Zionism from other streams of Zionism with social issues like welfare, women's rights and healthcare; but these are issues that aren't exclusive to Zionism. When pressed for Zionist issues that separate left-wingers from other Zionists topics like support for the two-state solution to end the Israeli-Palestinian conflict, the need for an Iran nuclear deal, and a pluralistic approach to religion in Israel are the most frequently mentioned.

There are Zionists who disagree with the left-wing approach to these three positions and think supporting any of them is dangerous and unhealthy to Israel. Yet, they can't know with certainty their position is correct - maybe their ideas will be better for Israel in the long run. Without prophecy, neither side can state with certainty they're correct. It is also absurd to state that left-wing positions are anti-Israel. Judaism has a rich culture of "Elu-v'elu" where multiple opinions are considered without canceling any of them.

On the left-wing side of the aisle in the American Congress, many of Israel's greatest friends can be found. These are elected representatives who have written, sponsored and pushed through the most important Israel supporting legislation ever passed. To demonize the Democratic party as anti-Israel without the nuanced approach of recognizing friends in the party is insincere.

To look at left-wing Zionism through the lens of only the three areas of disagreement, is a shallow approach to the topic. The most left-wing left-wing Zionist and the most right-wing conservative Zionist agree on far more areas than they disagree. Each side of the political spectrum must advocate for the positions they feel are best for Israel's future, but the Pro-Israel community needs to focus on the issues that unite them more than the issues that divide them.

CHAPTER
THIRTY

A Zionist Victory – the Visa Waiver Program

Early Zionists never imagined that their goals would solely focus on Israel and the Jewish people. They saw the Zionist movement at first achieving a State for the Jewish people, and then being a light on to the nations that would help global advancement. World leaders understood the benefits of Zionism extending past the borders of Israel, as former English Prime Minister Winston Churchill said, "The cause of Zionism is one which carries with it much that is good for the whole world, and not only for the Jewish people; it will bring prosperity and advancement for the Arab population."

Most attention focused on Israel's application to the American Visa Waiver Program will focus on the inner politics of the Knesset and American Ambassador to Israel Tom Nides's pressure on Israel to pass legislation necessary for Israel to enter the program. There is also a strong Zionist lesson about values and accomplishments to be taken from America's willingness and eagerness to have Israel participate in the program. Let's look past the politics of the issue and see the larger lessons of Israel and the American Visa Waiver Program.

The American Visa Waiver Program permits citizens of participating countries to travel to the United States for business or tourism for stays of up to 90 days without a visa. Currently, Israelis wishing to visit America must apply for a Visa. The process is expensive, requires waiting on line for hours in the hot Tel Aviv sun, sitting for an interview, multiple call backs, bureaucratic headaches – and at the end of the application process a high percentage chance of rejection. Israel's participation in the program will allow Israelis to skip all of this and simply purchase a ticket to America and enjoy themselves. Recently, American Ambassador to Israel Tom Nides tweeted, "I've been working around the clock since I arrived to help Israel meet all the requirements to join the Visa Waiver Program. Don't lose momentum now. This will help Israeli citizens travel to the U.S. – put them first!" While Ambassador Nides is concerned with helping Israelis, there's another perspective to the program as well.

It's not only Israelis that will benefit from the visa waiver program, but America will also benefit as well. While writing in his new book, "Let My People Know," about the challenge China poses to America, Aryeh Lightstone, former American Special Envoy for Economic Normalization in the Middle East, connected Israel and the Visa Waiver Program to the China-America rivalry. Lightstone wrote, "In various technologies of the future, breakthroughs will come from China and Russia, or from the United States and Israel. China will overpay to invest in technology; it will not open its market in a fair way. What's more, China's immigration policy currently gives it a big advantage in attracting talent from Israel, because it is far easier for Israelis to get a visa to China than to the United States. This is especially true for recent graduates of the Israel Defense Forces."

Lightstone continued, "The default position of the U.S. consular service is that people who enter the United States will choose to remain unless there is a strong indication that they would feel compelled to return to their home country. This is a reasonable assumption regarding people from most other countries. Many young Israelis like to travel for six months after completing their mandatory service in the IDF, to decompress and regain some of their youth before going on to university or a vocation. The U.S. consular service views most of the people in this group as not having strong enough ties to Israel that they will likely return there rather than stay in the United States. Consequently, they are subject to a higher-than-average rejection rate for visas. The Chinese government default is that recent graduates of the IDF are likely to be startup entrepreneurs in the next few years, so every single applicant from this group receives a visa."

Lightstone saw past the benefits of easier travel for Israelis through the Visa Waiver Program. He understood the benefit to America by having young Israelis travel to the United States, become familiar with the country and their familiarity leading to greater partnerships between American and Israeli companies in the future. Israeli partnerships will only add to American intellectual and corporate prowess and its ability to shut down competition from China.

Early Zionists envisioned creating a Jewish State that benefited the world through creative ingenuity and technological advancement. With great pride their vision has been achieved. Israel exports technology that helps the global community in areas like water availability, COVID research, farming and so many other areas that change lives for the better. It is challenging to recognize Israel's value to the global community when so many of Israel's opponents slander Israel in forums like the United Nations. With all the help Israel provides so many countries around the world, Israel should be winning accolades in many global forums. It is frustrating and disappointing to see Israel denigrated instead of praised. America's eagerness to have Israel participate in the Visa Waiver Program shows America's desire for Israeli ingenuity and the fulfillment of the Zionist dream has come to fruition.

Zionism stands for Jewish self-determination on its ancient homeland, but it isn't limited to that goal. Zionism is about the Jewish State contributing to the world in all areas. Most nationalist movements are focused on its constituents, not the global community. Zionism differentiates itself by looking to see how it can help the world at large. Zionism is a movement that is built on a foundation of Jewish values; a value of Judaism is to be a light on to the nations and to be a force that makes the world a better and more moral place. Zionists never imagined building a state that would divorce itself from key Jewish values. To count itself truly successful, a Zionist state measures itself not by its own achievements, but by the benefit it has provided to the world.

CHAPTER

THIRTY-ONE

It's not just Yom Yerushalayim

The Jewish people are proud of their return to their historic homeland, the land of Israel. Jews around the world take great pride every year on Yom Ha'atzmaut (Israeli Independence Day), boasting of their 2,000 year wait and success in reestablishing sovereignty on their own land. The truth is the Jews had returned to their land, but not all of it. In its 1947 Partition Plan and vote, the United Nations voted to only give the Jewish people only half their historic land. The Land of Israel that was promised to the Jews by God, that the Jews had prayed to return to, that Jews pined for through Crusades, pogroms and in Concentration Camps, is double the size of the land granted by the United Nations. The land Jews had waited 2,000 years to return and establish their own state on stretches from the Jordan River to the Mediterranean Sea, and includes the Capital City of the Jewish people, Jerusalem. Even though it was half of what the Jews desired, they accepted the United Nation's plan, for the Jews weren't willing to give up the opportunity of a return to their land.

Jewish historical records from the time record that there were mixed emotions in Jewish and Zionist communities when the United Nations' partition plan was announced. On the one hand, after two thousand years the Jews were going to return to their land, yet they weren't given what they desired. These Jews were probably apprehensive about defending half the land; Israel wasn't designed to be so thin. The borders seemed indefensible to many of them.

It wasn't until nineteen years later that the Jewish people's prayers to return to the land of Israel from the Jordan River to the Mediterranean Sea came true. In June of 1967, Israel won The Six Day War and took control over the land they had been praying for all those years. The Jews were finally back in control of Biblical and historically Jewish cities such as Jerusalem's Old City. For the first time in two millennia, Jews could travel to the cities of their past, the cities which existed as prayers for the future, and call them the cities of the Jewish present.

Yom Yerushalyim, Jerusalem Day, is celebrated on the 28th of Iyar on the Jewish Calendar each year. It celebrates the victory of The Six Day War and the reunification of Jerusalem. For nineteen years, an unnatural split between the Eastern and Western parts of the city existed but the victory of the war recaptured the entire Capital City for the Jewish people. It is a day of great festivity in Jerusalem.

There were many great things that happened in June 1967 and the Jewish people recognized that they couldn't celebrate them all. They picked the biggest event, the reunification of Jerusalem and said they'll just celebrate that event each year. They decided to name the day after that great achievement, have parades that celebrate it, and be satisfied with the pride and gratitude of that day. Israel celebrates the reunification of Jerusalem, and calls it Yom Yerushalayim, Jerusalem Day.

The other achievements of that war besides the reunification of Jerusalem are no less significant and less worthy of mention. In the days leading up to the war, the Israeli population thought they'd certainly lose the way and might even face another Holocaust. Mass graves were dug in major cities like Tel Aviv, and over 25,000 coffins were prepared. The stunning and overwhelming victory was incredible. The return to the Biblical sites of the land of Israel and its heartland back in Jewish hands for the first time in close to 2,000 years. For the first time Jews were able to freely visit the Jordan River and see where Joshua crossed with the Jewish people after the forty years in the desert, pray at the Cave of the Patriarchs and Matriarchs, and travel the land of Israel from the River to the Sea with no inhibitions.

Many around the world still deny the Jewish historical connection to the land of Israel. In response we need to celebrate the victory of June 1967. Jews need to proudly declare that we have a historical connection to all of Eretz Yisrael. Jews and Israelis need to educate and explain that political calculations and narratives aside, history cannot be denied out of political correctness.

Yom Yerushalayim's celebration should be extended past the reunification of Jerusalem to all of the miracles that occurred during and resulted from the Six Day War. Jews need to take pride in their land and their accomplishments. Jews should let the world know that they aren't going to leave their historic homeland simply because anti-Zionists demand we leave. It is time the world knows that Israel is here to stay.

CHAPTER

THIRTY-TWO

There's no dual loyalty when it comes to Israel

Some American Presidents and members of Congress have been recorded speaking to Jewish Americans and calling Israel "Your country." Referring to Israel as American Jews' country - as their country as opposed to America raises concerns that American Jews have dual loyalty to Israel and America. The accusation is a classic antisemitic dual-loyalty trope that accuses American Jews of being more loyal to Israel than America. It is rare that American politicians use the "Your country" statement as an accusation of dual-loyalty, it's mostly just pandering to an electorate and politicians selling themselves as Pro-Israel to American Jews.

America and Israel aren't competing nations. Dual loyalty isn't a real concern for Americans because it can never have practical applications within American Jewry. America and Israel aren't just allies because of shared interests, business partnerships or common enemies. America and Israel share values. Americans who hold American values dear should love Israel and Israelis who hold Zionist values dear should love America. If you love America for what it stands for, you should love Israel. Anyone who doesn't understand this point hasn't understood what America and Israel are actually all about - their values. American Jews can't be accused of dual loyalty because of their dedication to Israel; it is American values that drive a love for Israel.

There's a larger point to address than issues of dual loyalty and antisemitism, larger than any President's careless remarks. Is Israel the home of American Jews? American Jews must define home and country for themselves. It is important to note that most American Synagogues that display an American flag, display an Israeli flag as well. The Israeli flag isn't an ancient Jewish flag, Judaism has no flag, it is an Israeli flag, and Synagogues display it to show an affinity to the land and state of Israel.

Eretz Yisrael is the homeland of the Jewish people - and each and every Jew. Jews don't yearn to be in Washington, New York, or Los Angeles next year, and they don't pray three times a day to return to Berlin, Baghdad or Morocco. A core value of Judaism is that Eretz Yisrael is the Jewish homeland. The Rabbis of the Talmud instructed that "A Jew should always live in the land of Israel." Unfortunately, this lesson has been taught harshly to so many Jewish communities decimated by antisemitism and recognized their attempts to make someone else's homeland their own had failed.

American Jews are Americans just as much as any other American. The values that the founding fathers were guided by make America a natural place for Jews to thrive. American Jews should feel grateful for the home and refuge that America has offered to the Jewish people. As a grandchild of Holocaust survivors who found a welcoming home in America, I will always have tremendous gratitude to America and a loyalty to its ideals. The homeland of the Jewish people is Eretz Yisrael. American Jews don't need a President of the United States to remind them.

CHAPTER
THIRTY-THREE

The Israeli Flag

Flying high above the sky on dark nights, the Israeli flag inspires Zionists with pride over their country, land and people. When staring at the flag during an induction ceremony at the Kotel, in the bright sunlight over Masada or at the front of our Synagogue during the prayer for the welfare of the State of Israel, one can't help but get choked up over the turnaround of our nation during this past century. What's the meaning of the Israeli flag?

Judaism is a religion of the abstract. While it's true that there are many mitzvot that require use of physical objects and actions, like wearing tefillin, lighting Shabbat candles, and reciting kiddush on a cup of wine, the priority of the Torah is to know and form a relationship with God. Forming a connection with God is an abstract endeavor; it is achieved through prayer and study. Objects, places and actions all seem to distract from the goal of living in the world of thought.

There are exceptions besides the objects of mitzvot to the emphasis on prayer and study. There are a few occasions when the Torah emphasizes the use of an object. One spot where the emphasis is placed on an object are the flags in the desert. God instructed the Jewish people, "The Israelites shall camp each with his people, under the banners of their ancestral house; they shall camp around the Tabernacle, but at a distance." The scholar Rashi wrote, "Each banner shall have a different sign — a piece of colored cloth hanging on it, the color of one flag not being the same as the color of another, but the color of each tribe's flag shall be the same color of that tribe's stone that is fixed in the breastplate of the Cohen Gadol in the Tabernacle. It is with these unique colors that everybody will be able to recognize his banner." The flags were held high above the people to draw a connection between each tribe's camp and the service being conducted on behalf of the people by the Cohen Gadol who would wear each tribe's color on his chest.

Today's Israeli flag features two long blue stripes and the "Star of David." The two blue stripes look and symbolize the tallit, the shawl worn during certain prayers, and the blue color is reminiscent of the Biblical blue techelet color used in the tallit and the Tabernacle. The flag is widely accepted among all streams of Jews, although it isn't without controversy. Many great modern Rabbinical scholars including Rabbi Moshe Feinstein, the Chazon Ish, and Rav Ovadia Yosef were critical of the Israeli flag.

The Star of David is a frequent source of controversy. Although named after King David, the Jewish people's great king never saw it, and especially never adopted it as his own royal crest. The hexagram shape didn't start off as a Jewish symbol at all. It is definitively not Biblical or even Talmudic. It doesn't contain any Jewish symbolism and didn't appear on any of the tribe's flags in the desert. It was only a few hundred years ago that Jewish communities in Europe began using it as an identifying symbol. The Zionist movement used the Star of David as its symbol, and it gradually morphed into Israel's symbol on its official flag five months after Israel's founders declared their independence.

In his three-book series on Theodore Herzl, Dr. Gil Troy wrote about Herzl's vision for the flag, "Herzl's appeal was impressive. He was realizing that national identity - and national renewal - required a revival of the Jewish body and Jewish soul. To achieve that, Herzl proposed pragmatic steps and symbols - accompanied by speculative leaps. Writing to Baron Hirsch, on June 3, 1895, Herzl insisted a flag was not just "a stick with a rag on it... With a flag one can lead men wherever one wants to, even into the Promised Land. For a flag men will live and die; it is indeed the only thing for which they are ready to die in masses, if one trains them for it; believe me, the policy of an entire people - particularly when it is scattered all over the earth - can be carried out only with imponderables that float in thin air." Toggling between the hard-headed and the ethereal - "Dreams, songs, fantasies, and black-red-and-gold ribbons," Herzl noted, after all, "What is religion? Consider, if you will, what the Jews have endured for the sake of this vision over a period of two thousand years. Yes, visions alone grip the souls of men...."

Herzl saw the Israeli flag – although it hadn't been put together yet – as a symbol men could use to be inspired, even to give up their lives for if necessary. Rabbi Joseph Dov Soloveitchik published different talks he gave on Israel and Zionism. The work was called "Five Addresses," and in one of his talks Rabbi Soloveitchik gave a novel interpretation of the Israeli flag, "If you ask me, how do I…look upon the flag of the State of Israel, and has it any halachic value? — I would answer plainly… in the Shulchan Aruch it says: "One who has been killed by non-Jews is buried in his clothes, so that his blood may be seen and avenged… In other words, the clothes of the Jew acquire a certain sanctity when spattered with the blood of a martyr. How much more is this so of the Blue and White flag, which has been immersed in the blood of thousands of young Jews who fell in the War of Independence, defending the country and the population… It has a spark of sanctity that flows from devotion and self-sacrifice. We are all enjoined to honor the flag and treat it with respect."

For today's Zionist, the Israeli flag is a symbol of pride. It stands for the achievements of the Jewish people and the State of Israel over the past 150 years. After suffering through its worst tragedy in thousands of years the Jewish people didn't lay down and play victim. Instead, they put aside their tragedy, never forgetting their pain, but not allowing it to paralyze them, and rebuilt their nation step by step. What almost no other nation was able to achieve, rebuilding itself from the ashes, the Jewish people, with God's help, did. Like the flag flying above the tribes in the desert, and its ability to connect its tribe to the Cohen in the Tabernacle, the Israeli flag connects the Jewish people to its past. The flag also reminds the Jewish people not to get haughty with its success, and to always remember its humble past.

CHAPTER
THIRTY-FOUR

Unity Must Take Priority

The Western Wall, the Kotel Ma'aravi, has always been a place of high passions and emotion. When trying to describe the almost instinctual attraction that many Jews have to the Kotel, many Jews find it hard to put their feelings into words. In 1930, the British Empire released a report on the rights to the Western Wall. In the report they wrote the Jews had specific demands about the wall.

The Jews wanted the British to give recognition to the immemorial claim that the Western Wall is a sacred place for the Jews, not only for the Jews in Palestine, but also for the Jews of the whole world; They wanted the British to decree that the Jews shall have the right of access to the Wall for devotions and for prayers in accordant with their ritual without interference or interruption; In addition, the Jews wanted a decree stating that it shall be permissible to continue the Jewish services under the conditions of decency and decorum characteristic of a sacred custom that has been carried on for many centuries without infringement upon the religious rights of others, and to decree that the drawing up of any regulations, that may be necessary as to such devotions and prayers, shall be entrusted to the Rabbinate of Palestine, who shall thus re-assume full responsibility in that matter, in discharge of which responsibility they may consult the Rabbinate of the world;

The British responded that from numerous statements in the works of travelers, historians, geographers, etc., it is clearly evident that when the Jews were allowed to approach the Wall, which was not always the case, they restricted themselves to lamentations and made no attempt to hold actual religious services. Moreover, at certain periods, the Jews did not lament even at the Wall but outside the city instead. The fact that the Muslims in the course of time have come to tolerate Jews going to weep at the Wall under the same conditions as they have permitted the other inhabitants of Jerusalem and foreigners to go there, does not confer upon them any right whatsoever, either proprietary or that of enjoyment of the privilege in the future. In any case, the Commission cannot allow the Jews more than the privilege of paying simple visits to the Wall.

The British tried to squelch the Jewish passions for the Western Wall, but they failed. Today, the Western Wall is packed with worshippers and has become the symbol of Jews around the world for Israel and Jerusalem. For two thousand years the Jewish people were mostly kept out of Israel and away from the Kotel. With the return to Israel, the emphasis on the importance of the Kotel is a relatively new focus for the Jewish people.The focus on the Kotel is important, but shouldn't be the most concerning worry of the Jewish people.

Some people erroneously claim that "The Western Wall is Judaism's most sacred holy site," but this isn't true. The Kotel and its relatively newly built plaza isn't a sacred space, it is at best considered to have the sanctity of a Synagogue. It is the Temple Mount behind the Kotel that is sacred to the Jewish people. The Temple Mount is where Cain and Abel gave their offerings, where Noah's Ark landed, where Isaac was almost offered by Abraham, and where Jacob had his dream. The Temple Mount is where the two Temples sat, and where the third Temple will sit one day soon. It is an eternally sacred place, and where the Divine presence rests.

The Temples were destroyed because of division-led hatred between Jews. The Talmud tells multiple stories of the baseless hatred, driven by arrogance and ego, that allowed external enemies to penetrate Jewish security, defeat the Jewish people and send them into a 2,000-year long exile. The Jewish Sages explained that all evil that befalls the Jewish people comes from that original exile. It is easy to blame the Babylonians, Romans, Spaniards, Germans and countless other enemies throughout the long Jewish exile, but it was the Jewish divisions that brought on exile and the ensuing tragedies that came along with it.

Debate, disagreement and differences are healthy among the Jewish people – division and hate are corrosively destructive. Each year Jews mourn over the destruction of the Temple for three weeks and fast four times. Jews don't mourn and fast over something that occurred 2,000 years ago, in the words of Rambam, Jews fast, "To arouse our hearts and initiate us in the paths of repentance. The fasts serve as a reminder of our wicked conduct and that of our ancestors, which resembles our present conduct and therefore brought these calamities upon them and upon us. By reminding ourselves of these matters, we will repent." The division and hate Jews display today is the continuation of two millennia of divisiveness and hate.

The increasing divisions in the Jewish people should be the most concerning fear of Israelis today. Israelis have a right to be scared; they're surrounded by enemies who want to annihilate them. Yet, the most concerning issue for Israelis shouldn't be Hamas and Hezbollah's rockets, a Palestinian terrorist infiltrating an Israeli town and committing an attack, or even Iran's nuclear weapon program. The most concerning issue for Israelis shouldn't be an external enemy who hates Israel, it's the corrosive internal divisions among the people of Israel. Many Jews around the world and many Jews in Israel have strong opinions about many different issues in Israel. As strong as they feel about these issues, they should be less concerned about them than about the division of the Jewish people.

The Jewish people won't reach unity, perfection or closeness to God by praying in one area or preventing someone from praying there, if it comes at the cost of division and hate. Jews didn't wait two thousand years to return to Jerusalem to reestablish the hatred that caused their exile in the first place. Jews need to spend less time focusing on who is right and who is wrong and focus more on how they can bridge the gaps between their diverse communities. No space on Earth is worth internal hatred among the Jewish people. There must be a different way to present a viewpoint and advocate for its position without it resulting in division and hate. Pray for the peace of Jerusalem.

CHAPTER
THIRTY-FIVE

If there was no Zionism

When compared to the rest of Jewish history, it is evident that the times we live in are magical. The Jewish people are safe, they govern their homeland, the land of Israel, and they are exceedingly successful. Besides enjoying one of the best economies in the world, operating one of the best militaries in the world, Israelis are consistently ranked among the happiest nations of the world. The Jewish people spent thousands of years dreaming about returning to the land of Israel, but they never imagined the return would be this wonderful.

Many argue that this generation of Jews has been spoiled by living at a time when there is a State of Israel. To an extent, the generations that suffered the exile and saw the birth of the State of Israel are able to appreciate the state more than the people of the current generation born into an already existing state. The people born into the already existing Jewish state can't understand what life was like before there was a Jewish state.

Zionism provided the Jewish people a state where they were afforded a refuge from their enemies. It also created a state where Jews could actualize their rights to their own state and land. The State that Zionism created was a place where the Jews spread throughout the four corners of the land could return and gather in one place. On a spiritual and cultural level, Zionism has been a boon to the Jewish people. Zionism has created more Torah study than at any previous point in Jewish history - even at Mount Sinai! Jews from around the world who didn't even know the other existed have united as a people in Israel. It isn't uncommon to see Jews from Russia, America, Ethiopia and Yemen all mingling together in Jerusalem's Machaneh Yehuda

Marketplace. Maybe most importantly, for the first time in thousands of years Jews can raise their heads high. They are the elite of the world today.

If there had been no Zionism and no movement to reclaim Jewish rights to their homeland, none of this would have come to fruition. Jews would forever have been victims, left to the violent and antisemitic whims of their Gentile and Arab neighbors. Jews wouldn't enjoy the right to determine their own future, to protect themselves and afford themselves the means to prosper as a nation without the efforts of early Zionists and their movement. Jews would still be divided, unable or unwilling to unite together.

At its inception Zionism was a source of division and concern among the Jewish people. Many Jews of Eastern Europe were concerned a Jewish national movement would stir antisemites to take action against the Jewish people. Western European Jews thought a Jewish nationalist movement would generate accusations of dual loyalty - just as Jews were beginning to successfully assimilate into German, French and English upper society. Rabbinical scholars felt that Zionism would cause Torah to be forgotten as Jews traded their mitzvah observance for Zionist aspirations. In the back of all Jews' minds was the thought that a Jewish state could weaken Diaspora Jewry and put the Jews outside of Israel in a weakened position.

A hundred and fifty years after Zionism began picking up steam in the Jewish world, it is clear that the overwhelming amount of Jews support Zionism today. The reasons for overwhelming Zionist support are clear, without Zionism the Jews would be in a much worse place, with Zionism, they are in a much better place. Whatever reservations Jews had about Zionism, even those that might've come true, it is clear the benefits of Zionism and a Jewish state far outweigh what Jewish life would be like today without a Jewish State in the land of Israel.

CHAPTER
THIRTY-SIX

500 Skittles, Ukraine, and Zionist Values

"Many immigrants are horrible people, and I don't want them to come to Israel. Let me explain; if you had a bowl of 500 Skittles, and three of them were poisonous, would you eat any of the Skittles? Of course not. It's the same as immigrants, even if most are good people, the risk of one criminal immigrant should dictate we don't let any of them into Israel."

This was a participant's answer to an educational discussion about Israel, refugee Aliyah, and Zionist values. The Zionist student discussions were tackling issues that demonstrate Zionism's relevance in today's times. Israel has a policy of not allowing criminals to immigrate. The conversation centered around whether Israel's policy of suspending its usual criminal background checks at times of crises for Jewish refugee immigrants was consistent with Zionist values.

The young student didn't think of the answer themselves; they were quoting an American anti-immigration argument. The argument resonates with many people, especially those who place security as their top priority, but it doesn't reflect Zionist values. "The state of Israel will be open for Jewish immigration and for the Ingathering of the Exiles," reads the Israeli Declaration of Independence. Israeli Prime Minister David Ben Gurion stated, "Our daily efforts are dedicated to the ingathering of exiles, the absorption of the immigrants."

Aliyah, immigration of Jews to the land of Israel, has always been a Zionist priority. Former Israeli Knesset member and Ambassador to the United States, historian Michael Oren, wrote, "Far beyond the professional, educational, and military benefits brought by olim, Aliyah was and remains a central Zionist tenet. Without it, we are in danger of devolving into just another developed country concerned only with sealing its borders to immigrants. Precisely at a time of rampant anti-Semitism, Israel will fail to fulfill its primary historical mission of providing shelter for oppressed Jews worldwide."

Israel's Law of Return guarantees that every Jew who desires to settle in Israel can move to Israel unless they are engaged in an activity directed against the Jewish people; or they're likely to endanger public health or the security of the State. In 1955, the law was amended slightly to specify that dangerous criminals could also be denied that right. The exceptions built into the law of return play a crucial law in ensuring the safety of every Israeli, but they are exceptions, not the foundation of the law. Israel was built on putting national energy into having Jews move back to Israel, not keeping them out of Israel.

As multiple crises unfold around the world, more and more Diaspora Jews are put at risk. Millions of Jews have become refugees or been displaced because of wars raging through their country. Jewish citizens are just as affected as other war zone refugees. Zionism doesn't maintain Jews have a right to the land of Israel so that Jews will have a place of refuge, the Jewish right to their ancestral homeland stands irrespective of Jewish safety and security. Yet early Zionists urgently advocated for a Jewish state to secure a place of refuge for Jews in danger. Jewish safety and security were so paramount to early Zionists, they even considered founding the Jewish State in Argentina or Uganda until the land of Israel could be secured for the State of Israel.

The founding fathers of Zionism and the State of Israel knew that as long as there were Jews in the Diaspora, antisemitism and danger would be a constant reality. They recognized the importance of ensuring Israel would always be ready to welcome Jews in danger from around the world. The failure of world Jewry to secure safe refuge for the Jews of Europe during the Holocaust created a resolve among Israelis to guarantee there would never be such a colossal failure again. Whether it was Yemenite, Ethiopian or Soviet Jews, Israel opened its borders and arms for Diaspora Jewry in trouble who needed a place of refuge.

Israel deserves to be applauded for easing restrictions to ease the way for

Jewish refugees to find shelter in Israel from the war raging in their country and they should be encouraged to do whatever it takes to get our Jewish brothers and sisters home to Israel as fast as possible. The Israeli people, from those opening their homes to displaced families, to the volunteers dancing at the airport greeting new arrivals, to the thousands of donors giving to people they've never met before, have shown their true colors. Zionism was built on strengthening our nation, and today's Zionists are coming through strong.

There is a risk that a few of the refugees entering Israel will pose a danger to Israeli society. Israelis have always been a people willing to take risks for a greater good. Under "normal" circumstances, when war isn't raging, people aren't sheltering or running for their lives, and proper immigration procedures can be followed, it makes sense to filter prospective immigrants. But when emergencies occur, it is appropriate to suspend the usual rules and guarantee the Jewish people can find shelter in their homeland. Opening the doors for Jews to find a safe home is a Zionist value and priority.

CHAPTER
THIRTY-SEVEN

When did the peace process turn into the Two State Solution?

As a passionate 16-year-old I was electrified by the promise of the Oslo Accords. I had been to Israel twice and spent a considerable amount of time in a relative's settlement. I had been struck by the community's need to carry guns to Shabbat prayer services. I stared at the seven foot high bullet blocking concrete barriers that lined the side of the town that faced the nearby Palestinian Arab village. The potential to end the need for security and stop the bloodshed spoke to me and I couldn't understand people's resistance to Oslo.

Less than two years later I was studying in a yeshiva outside of Jerusalem and experienced Prime Minister Rabin's assassination, constant Palestinian Arab terror attacks, and the breakdown of the Oslo Accords. The history of ups and downs, Israeli offers and Palestinian Arab rejectionism, including the launching of a second intifada is well known. With the defeat of Ehud Barak and election of Ariel Sharon, the intermittent revival of talks gave little hope of an achievable peace. Over the last decade skepticism has overtaken promise and peace between Israel and the Palestinian Arabs seems a distant dream.

At some point over the past decade Palestinian Arabs and their advocates have pulled off a masterful trick. The Oslo Accords and the quest to end the Israeli-Palestinian conflict had been known as the "peace process." Over the past decade the focus switched from being about peace to the creation of a Palestinian State. The "two state solution" replaced the "peace process" as the vehicle to end the conflict. The exact point of the switch is debatable, but it is undeniable that the current quest to end the conflict is more about a Palestinian State than establishing peace.

After Prime Minister Rabin signed the Oslo Accords, he was asked if he supported the notion of creating a Palestinian State. His advisor responded, "The prime minister is of the opinion that there is no room for a Palestinian state." Rabin's successor, Shimon Peres continued this policy, as his advisor Uri Savir wrote, "It was the current government's policy to reject the creation of a Palestinian state." The Oslo Accords, much to revisionists' attempts to establish the contrary, were about creating peace not a Palestinian State.

In the world's eyes, the creation of a Palestinian state has become so imperative that its establishment has taken priority over peace between the Palestinian and Israelis. Instead of peace being the priority and a Palestinian state being a vehicle or reward for the cessation of Arab terror, peace is a hoped for, but not guaranteed product, of a Palestinian state. The abandonment of the goal of peace is tragic and creates an atmosphere of distrust among Israelis. In a blatant declaration of the insignificance of peace, Mahmoud Abbas, Arafat's successor in the Palestinian Authority, has stated, "In a final resolution, we would not see the presence of a single Israeli - civilian or soldier - on our lands." In the Palestinian's eyes, the two state solution is completely divorced from the end of the Israeli-Palestinian conflict.

How did peace take a backseat to the two state solution? Palestinian advocates created a fictional injustice of Palestinian Arabs being robbed of their land and Israel being the impediment to their state. A cursory examination of Arab reactions to the offer of a state will find their repeated rejections to all offers. Whether it was the 1930's Peel Commission, the 1947 UN partition plan, Oslo, or Annapolis, the Palestinian Arab community has rejected all offers of their own state. Fraudulent doesn't begin to describe the claim that 80 years after their first rejection Israel has prevented Palestinian statehood. In blaming Israel, Palestinian Arabs have shirked culpability for unfailing dedication to terror and violence.

With the replacement of peace with the two state solution, any hope of ending the Israeli-Palestinian conflict has been impeded. Israelis will always prioritize their security over Palestinian statehood. The pullouts from Lebanon and Gaza have taught Israel the harsh lesson that ceding land without peace doesn't bring peace. Until the focus returns to peace, the end of the Israeli-Palestinian conflict will continue to be delayed.

CHAPTER
THIRTY-EIGHT

The Isolated Echo Chamber

A few years ago, I was asked to speak about Israeli settlements in Judea and Samaria, (the area the world calls the West Bank) at a Jewish organization on an American Ivy League campus. University students are privileged to hear from top experts about the Israeli-Palestinian conflict. Ambassadors, Israeli-Palestinian negotiators and even former leaders regularly speak on college campuses around the world. I have never been involved in high level negotiations and I hold no official position in the Israeli government. I "just" teach high school and college students about Israel; I was puzzled about why they wanted me to speak?

I frequently speak to groups from around the world in my home in Mitzpe Yericho and across America about my life as a Zionist and a "settler." As a settler, educator and political activist, I have an unique viewpoint on life in my neck of the woods. Many assumptions are made about Israelis and Zionism and groups are generally surprised to hear a viewpoint that doesn't conform to their expectations. The students at this organization wanted to hear an Israeli's perspective on the current Israeli-Palestinian conflict.

A few weeks before my scheduled talk one of the students called to warn me that there were some objections raised at this organization's board meeting about my talk. Although no one had reached out to me, my opinions were assumed and found objectionable. One week later, this same student called to tell me that I had been banned from speaking at this organization's building and my talk had been moved to the university's Chabad house. Although I wasn't privy to the discussion and vote that led to this decision, I was told that I was excluded due to my political positions. I found this curious;

after all, no one from the organization was in touch with me to ask about my political positions. Based on my friendship with some politicians and Tweets praising these politicians, I was deemed untenable for organization. I had good company though; a few weeks before my scheduled talk, former Israeli Deputy Foreign Minister Tzipi Hotevely was also banned from the same organization at a different Ivy League school and spoke at the Chabad house.

I felt sorry for these students. I felt sorry for the students who wouldn't have the opportunity to hear a perspective they aren't exposed to at their usual meetings at this organization's building. I felt even worse for the students who refused to listen to opinions that differ from their own. The corrosive isolation into the echo chambers of our own opinions had extended to the academic sphere of an Ivy League Hillel.

Had the students listened to my talk they would've been pleasantly surprised to hear my plea for peace and dignity for the Israeli and Palestinian people, my explanation about why I signed a piece of paper that forces me to lose my house and its value for the creation of a Palestinian State, and my theories why Israelis and Palestinians aren't finding a peaceful path.

In rejecting my talk, this organization's student board silenced a moderate voice in Israel. If we don't expose ourselves to other viewpoints, if we don't listen to those we disagree with, if we demonize "the other," we will never think critically of our own views.

By spending more time finger pointing and less time listening, we do ourselves more harm than those silenced. I hope other student groups, and especially this organization, invite those to the left and right of their current positions to speak. I hope they hear different viewpoints, re-examine their own positions and find conviction based on proper analysis, not assumptions developed in an isolated echo chamber. I'll gladly come back when they call.

CHAPTER
THIRTY-NINE

Is chutzpah a bug or feature of Israeli life?

Israel has the chips stacked against it when it comes to economic success. Unlike the other nations in Israel's neighborhood, Israel has no national resources to bolster its economy. While other nation's treasuries overfill with oil money, 60% of Israel is covered by empty desert. Besides being bare of natural resources, Israel was surrounded inside and out by enemies who tried and are trying to annihilate it. Israel's survival is considered by many to be miraculous; Israel's success is inexplicable.

In their book "Start Up Nation," authors Dan Senor and Saul Singer took an innovative approach to explain Israeli hi-tech companies' considerable success in the global marketplace. Senor and Singer pointed to Israel's mandatory military service and the culture of Israel and its defense forces as they key to Israel's success. The close to three years of mandatory military service every Israeli serves (women serve less time) combined with the annual reserve duty every male serves shapes and forms the Israeli population. Soldiers learn teamwork, courage, and most importantly for the roles they'll be playing in civilian life, how to be innovative.

Senor and Singer discussed the factor that makes the Israeli Defense Forces different than all other armies and most contributes to how the army shapes Israelis to be successful in the hi-tech world. Most armies have a strict regiment of discipline with high-ranking officers giving orders to lower ranking officers in a one way road with no room for lower ranking officers to inject their opinions. The Israeli Defense Forces run differently. Lower ranking officers are not only allowed to offer their opinions, but they are also encouraged to do offer their ideas if they think it'll be advantageous to their mission.

The lack of formality in the Israeli Defense Forces can seem outrageous to experienced soldiers from other militaries. They sometimes say there's only one word for it – a unique Yiddish word that has made it into the English lexicon – chutzpah. It's the allowance of chutzpah in the Israeli military that encourages an attitude of pushing the best ideas forward first. The chutzpah inspires boldness of thought, creativity, and self-confidence. On the battlefield these traits can make the difference between harrowing rescues like the 1976 rescue at Entebbe, Uganda. In the hi-tech world, the traits that result from chutzpah advance the best ideas and create groundbreaking apps like Waze.

This chutzpah spreads to realms outside the battlefield and marketplace. Most non-Israelis who have watched a Knesset (Israel's parliament) debate is shocked by the raucous lack of decorum. Knesset members yell at each other, interrupt speakers mid-sentence, and even mock each other. If chutzpah at its best creates apps that change the world, chutzpah at its worst manifests in a Knesset that resembles an out-of-control kindergarten more than a world class parliament.

The lack of decorum in the Knesset isn't only attributable to chutzpah but to a general lack of formality and sensitivity in Israeli society. Israeli drivers seem to almost wake up angry and honking their car horns every morning. Traffic lights barely turn green and cars three or four back in line already start honking their horns. There's little to no consideration for the angst this causes other drivers or the noise pollution that disturbs entire neighborhoods every morning. This lack of decorum creeps into every aspect of Israeli life. Store clerks are more likely to scold and refuse to help than offer customer service and government workers are obstinate and create bureaucratic quagmires that seem insurmountable.

Anglo immigrants to Israel from countries like England, Australia, South Africa, and America struggle the most with Israeli chutzpah and lack of formality. The constant honking grates on their nerves, the lack of customer service befuddles them, and the government bureaucracy upsets them to levels where they almost want to find Theodore Herzl and convince him to keep at his job as a journalist instead of creating Zionism. When talking to Anglo immigrants in Israel, complaints about these aspects are frequently heard along with wonderment why Israelis and Israeli society can't act with more refinement and civility like America and England.

The immigrants who strive to improve (in their eyes) Israeli society by bringing American patience, courtesy, and politeness to Israeli society fail to recognize that Israel could only have succeeded because of the chutzpah and lack of formality that is a feature of today's State of Israel. Herzl and other early Zionist activists' audaciousness in attempting to convince the world to give the Jewish people their historic homeland and allow them to create a state could only have happened with an overloaded dose of chutzpah. When the British turned their backs on the Jewish people with their White Paper, the Jewish people's chutzpah led them to fight the British instead of giving up their dreams of their own State.

An argument could be made that refining Israeli life to look more like Anglo countries could disturb the entire culture of Israel's successful society. Chutzpah and the lack of formality in Israel isn't a bug of Israel, it is a feature. Israel's triumph is directly tied into its culture. The army didn't create this lack of formality, it is inherent in Israeli life. It was forged in the swamps that early Zionists cleared of malaria, in the fields the Haganah and Irgun fighters sat in when they defended the early Yishuv, and in the study halls Holocaust surviving Torah scholars built to recreate their old communities in a new Eretz Yisrael. As long as Israeli chutzpah persists, Israel will continue to overcome the impossible odds it constantly faces.

CHAPTER
FORTY

The most important difference between secular and religious Zionism

The latest discourse in Israel has centered around the rising role of religion in the policies of the Israeli government. In a state without a separation of "Church and State," the role of religion in government life has always been a point of discussion in Israel. Israel has never fully clarified the lines of where religion plays a role in national policy and the ambiguity of religion's role has led to robust debate among Israel's citizens.

Zionism has a rich diversity of both religious and secular members. The blending of these two populations' different values and priorities have created a dynamic nation that stands united in strengthening the one and only Jewish state. While there are occasional disagreements between secular and religious Zionists, they are rare and the shared values of the two communities has been the loudest of the voices in Israel.

There are many differences between secular and religious Zionism. There is one unique difference between the two forms of Zionism which overshadows all others. Secular Zionists maintain the only way the Jewish people can ensure their safety, security, and success is by the Jewish people taking matters into their own hands and working towards Israel's advancement. Secular Zionists maintain that Jews taking responsibility for themselves has, is, and will always be the only way the Jewish people can guarantee a homeland for themselves. They maintain that the success of today's Jewish state is due to the Zionist's efforts of draining the swamps, developing the land, and creating the infrastructure that led to the successful place the Jewish people are today.

Religious Zionists agree that it was Zionists that created the State through their backbreaking labor and admirable courage. They agree that it is today's Israelis who take responsibility for Israel's future that are ensuring Israel's security and success. Religious Zionists maintain the most important factor in Israel's past, present, and future success isn't human effort, but rather God's Providence. The factor that has, is, and will lead to Israel's success is the strength of the relationship between the Jewish people and God. When the Jewish people observe God's Torah by fulfilling the Mitzvot and acting consistently with Halacha, God will providentially protect the Jewish State and her people. It is only with God's blessing can the State of Israel continue to succeed.

The difference between secular and religious Zionists manifests itself in each community's approach to Israel's future. Both religious and secular Zionism stands for the need for a strong military and economy to keep the Jewish State secure and successful. Secular Zionism maintains the future of Israel depends solely on the State of Israel taking the necessary steps to keep the army and economy strong. Religious Zionism is more optimistic. It maintains that God, and the Jewish people's relationship with God will be the ultimate deciding factor in the future of the Jewish State. They are less anxious about external enemies and international diplomacy than their fellow secular Zionists because unlike their secular brethren, they consider God the most decisive factor in Israel's future.

Religious Zionists maintain that the destiny of the Jewish people will be determined more by Divine Providence than the actions of human beings. That doesn't mean that Israelis and their advocates shouldn't take the necessary steps to ensure Israel's success and security. It means that while doing their part they must be cognizant that their actions will only be successful if they have God's help.

Religious Zionists also maintain that the destiny of the Jewish people is an upward trajectory of success and the greatest mistake that can sidetrack or ruin that destiny is the Jewish people breaking from God and Torah observance. Our enemies, whether physical or political, cannot adversely affect Jewish destiny on their own without an absence of Divine Providence. It's for this reason that religious Zionists don't give as much credence or worry about political enemies or opponents as much as their secular Zionist brethren.

As Zionists continue to celebrate 75 years of incredible Jewish success it's important to recognize the source of that success. In my opinion, while the Zionists that came before me deserve a great deal of credit for Israel's current success, as a Torah observant Zionist, I maintain Israel's success doesn't solely come from the power and might of our own hand. Israel's success is attributed first and foremost to the power and Providence of God. The Jewish people and the State of Israel's success has not come on its own, it God's providence that has provided the blessing to the Zionists that built this land. Remembering this will ensure our people's continued success.

CHAPTER
FORTY-ONE

Israeli Self-Determination and Independence

Many Americans believe in "American Exceptionalism," the belief that America is a unique and special country, unlike any other in human history. In one of his State of the Union addresses President Biden spoke of American exceptionalism. President Biden said, "We're a good people. The only nation in the world built on an idea — the only one... We're the only nation based on an idea that all of us, every one of us, is created equal in the image of God. A nation that stands as a beacon to the world."

President Biden wasn't the first President to claim America was unique and he won't be the last. American exceptionalism is a bipartisan belief. America's dedication to life, liberty, and the pursuit of happiness, set it apart from the tyrannical monarchies of other nations. America's dedication to individual rights became more apparent when it abolished slavery, established women's suffrage, and gave all American citizens equal civil rights. America's distinctiveness shown bright against a dark backdrop of Nazi Germany and Soviet Russia.

Many Jews are proud Americans, grateful for the nation that raised them. The freedoms Americans fought for in America's Civil War, 2nd World War, Korean and Vietnam wars, led to the liberation of many American Jews' ancestors from Germany's camps. American Jews volunteer for the American army and dedicate effort and a great deal of their time to the United States.

There is a downside to the belief in exceptionalism. The belief in self-exceptionality can oftentimes lead to an arrogance that blinds one to their own faults and allows one to believe they are better than others. This arrogance frequently manifests itself in ignoring the same faults one criticizes others for possessing. Those who believe they are exceptional can fall for the trap of lecturing those they feel are less exceptional.

The belief in "American Exceptionalism" can lend American government officials to the notion that America leads the world in best governance, leadership, and morality. America's ideals are to be emulated by all nations, but putting ideals to actual practice isn't simple. Today's America, like most countries, is facing internal challenges that have some calling into question the assumption that America leads the world as a leader in democracy, rights and morality.

There are specific challenges America faces that deserve highlighting. While America's laws provide equal rights for all, many of America's minority communities feel disenfranchised from the establishment. There are data points that support these communities' complaints that they face systemic discrimination. As a democracy, America stands for representation for all, but Washington, Guam, and Puerto Rico are only given non-voting representatives in Congress. American Samoa is a territory of America, its people are American nationals, not citizens. America retains the power to approve amendments, override the governor's vetoes, and its nomination of judges. In addition, America has allowed every one its leaders who has committed a crime to avoid prosecution. There have been 376 school shootings, with hundreds killed and almost 350,000 children exposed to gun violence in their schools. These are some of the examples that call America's leadership into question.

America's founding fathers designed their new nation to be exceptional, but it's debatable whether today's America is living up to the founding father's vision. American Presidents and State Department frequently prescribe to Israel's leaders what they consider better ways for Israel's elected leaders to govern Israel. They also frequently criticize Israel for issues America itself suffers from as well. America and Israel are the closest of allies and have an open relationship where shared advice is appreciated. There is a line between allied nations sharing concerns and advice and prescribing how their partner nation should govern themselves. Before prescribing and criticizing other countries about their governance, America's government officials should ask themselves if they're in a position to criticize other nations about governance, leadership, and morality.

During the demonstrations over the past four months, Israel has had much to be proud of in how it has handled itself. Unlike many American protests, Israeli demonstrations are largely peaceful, its elections are run efficiently and are without skepticism. Citizens carry guns responsibly and school shootings aren't an issue. In Israel, a criminal Prime Minister, President and Knesset members have been charged, convicted and jailed. Neither American not Israel is perfect, but Israel's seventy-five years of strong democracy calls into question whether it should be lectured by other countries.

Former Israeli Prime Minister Yair Lapid addressed American President Joe Biden on his recent trip to Israel and discussed the strong U.S.-Israel relationship, "Our relationship runs deep. It crosses party lines. It connects not only our governments but also our peoples. This friendship is one of the cornerstones of Israel's national security. It is moving, and it is certainly not taken for granted." President Biden responded in kind, saying, "Israel and the United States also stand together to defend the fundamental values and underwrite global security, prosperity, and freedom, not just for us but for many around the world." The U.S.-Israel relationship is strong and both nations' leaders respect each other.

Throughout Jewish history, the Jewish people have faced outside pressure, from both friends and foe to institute policies the Jewish people did not feel were in its best interests. Israel is a strong democracy with a talented citizenry that doesn't need to be prescribed to by other countries. As Prime Minister Netanyahu wrote, "Israel is an independent country that makes its decisions according to the will of its citizens and not based on external pressures, including our best friends."

CHAPTER
FORTY-TWO

Tikkun Olam and Tikkun Yisrael

Jews have never been a selfish people. Throughout history Jews have contributed not only to their own advancement, but to the progress of the entire world. There are Jewish scholars that teach that embedded in the spiritual DNA of the Jewish people is a gene that pushes each Jew to help their neighbor and the world at large. The popular term among the Jewish people for this need to help others is "tikkun olam," or fixing the world. The term and its importance has become so popular, and therefore even lost its uniqueness, that one American presidential advisor told me that he strongly suggested the President stop using the term.

As popular as the term tikkun olam is, it isn't a new phrase. It was coined thousands of years ago, and probably first used in the Aleinu prayer. Aleinu reads, "May we speedily see Your mighty splendor, to cause detestable idolatry to be removed from the land, and the false gods will be utterly 'cut off', to takein olam – fix the world – under the Almighty's kingdom." Early scholars used the term as well, Maimonides wrote in his commentary to a Mishna in Pirkei Avot, "Through wisdom, which is represented by Torah, and the elevation of character, which is represented by acts of kindness, and observing the Torah's commandments, which are represented by the Temple offerings, one continuously brings tikkun olam, and the ordering of reality."

A more cynical person might look to other Rabbinic literature to show how widely used the phrase tikkun olam was used – and not in the feel-good way it's employed today. The standard of evidence required for a Jewish court of justice to carry out an execution was impossibly high. The Rabbis wrote that a death penalty conviction was so rare in a Jewish court that any court that executed a criminal even once in seventy years was considered a murderous court. This impossibly high standard of evidence allowed for murderers to walk free – something dangerous for society. The Jewish king was given the authority to extrajudicially execute criminals the court didn't convict. The Rabbis called the royal judicial insurance tikkun olam.

Today tikkun olam has taken on a life of its own. In an essay titled "Why Advocacy is Central to Reform Judaism," Rabbi Marla Feldman quoted Rabbi Eric Yoffie's February 1998 speech to the UAHC Executive Committee, "Reform Jews are committed to social justice. Even as Reform Jews embrace ritual, prayer, and ceremony more than ever, we continue to see social justice as the jewel in the Reform Jewish crown. Like the prophets, we never forget that God is concerned about the everyday and that the blights of society take precedence over the mysteries of heaven. A Reform synagogue that does not alleviate the anguish of the suffering is a contradiction in terms." Rabbi Feldman wrote, "It has become axiomatic that to be a Jew is to care about the world around us. To be a Reform Jew is to hear the voice of the prophets in our head; to be engaged in the ongoing work of tikkun olam; to strive to improve the world in which we live."

There's nothing wrong with social justice and improving the world is a great thing, but critics question whether tikkun olam is central to traditional Judaism. In a 2018 column defending tikkun olam, Andrés Spokoiny described the critics of tikkun olam, "The most strident critics — and the most politically motivated — say that Tikkun Olam is not a Jewish idea at all, but merely liberal politics masquerading as Jewish values. In a slightly conspiratorial tone, they surmise that lefties hijack the communal agenda and make it subservient to progressive goals. For them, the "Tikkun Olam movement" makes a marginal idea of Judaism into its core value. Jews, they imply, have responsibility for themselves, not for the world. "True" Judaism is deeply conservative instead of liberal, and Jews should abandon their cosmopolitanism to go back to our tribalist roots. These critics accuse the left of taking an obscure mystical term, changing its meaning, and crowning it as the ruling principle of Jewish experience."

Tikkun olam has a similar idea in traditional Judaism - tikkun Yisrael. This is the notion that the Jewish people are charged to help each other and improve the Jewish nation. The idea of chesed – showing kindness – is tikkun Yisrael. Maimonides wrote that chesed is directed towards fellow Jews, "It is a positive commandment of Rabbinic origin to visit the sick, comfort mourners, to prepare for a funeral, prepare a bride, accompany guests, attend to all the needs of a burial, carry a corpse on one's shoulders, walk before the bier, mourn, dig a grave, and bury the dead, and also to bring joy to a bride and groom and help them in all their needs. These are deeds of kindness that one carries out with his person that have no limit. Although all these mitzvot are of Rabbinic origin, they are included in the Scriptural commandment "Love your neighbor as yourself." That charge implies that whatever you would like other people to do for you, you should do for your friend in Torah and mitzvot." Acts of chesed aren't directed towards the global community but to fellow Jews, they are acts of tikkun Yisrael.

The Talmudic principle of "*Kol yisrael arevim zeh bazeh*," meaning all of Israel are responsible for each other, is another expression of tikkun Yisrael. The biblical prohibition of not standing by while your brother's blood is being shed is yet another traditional Jewish principle of Tikkun Yisrael. This prohibition does not allow one Jew to stand idle and not save their fellow Jew from physical, financial, or emotional harm.

Tikkun Yisrael is an aspect of Judaism that focuses on improving the Jewish people, while Tikkun olam focuses on helping the entire world. In a discussion on a podcast Rabbi Leor Sinai juxtaposed tikkun olam and tikkun Yisrael, and advocated putting tikkun Yisrael before tikkun olam. Rabbi Leor's point makes sense, and I've been thinking about it ever since our discussion. Tikkun olam is an important aspect of Judaism, but it hasn't traditionally been central to Judaism's focus.

The Zionist movement was built on ensuring a safe and secure place of refuge for the Jewish people. The Zionist movement was built on an ideology of tikkun Yisrael, Jews looking out for their fellow Jews. The Jewish people have sufficient resources to help the global community while advancing the Jewish cause, and the two aren't mutually exclusive. The problem becomes when the Jewish community begins to think that in order to achieve one form of tikkun it has to come at the expense of the other. The Jewish people can advance their own people and assist the world as well.

CHAPTER

FORTY-THREE

Miracles are the norm in Israel

The van flipped over on Israel's Highway One in late March, 2000. It was close to midnight on a Saturday night and the van my wife and one year old daughter were riding in was full of children. The van was traveling from Zichron Yaakov to Kiryat Arba, with a stop to drop off my family in Mevaseret Zion. I was asleep at home, suffering from a virus and having stayed home and not joined my family in Zichron Yaakov for Shabbat. The driver of the car behind the van fell asleep, pushed down on the accelerator, and slammed into the van. The van was lifted into the air and immediately flipped onto its roof. My wife and infant daughter were ejected out of the van onto the highway, and narrowly missed being run over by another driver.

Aliza and my daughter were rushed to the hospital, I met them there. My wife had hip pain and the doctors wanted to do an X-ray. They discreetly asked her if she was expecting and she said she couldn't definitively tell them, so they gave her a pregnancy test which came out positive! Due to my virus and other factors, more tests had to be conducted and we were told there was a chance that the baby we only recently found out about would have to be aborted. The results would only be known in three days. Aliza was injured, I was ill, and our lives were a wreck. We prayed for three days and were told the good news; our new baby would be fine. When she was born in November, we named her Temimah (for perfect faith in God) Shira (for praise of God). Twenty-two years later, we were grateful to marry Temimah off this to a wonderful young man, Yehoshua Segal.

The above story sounds nothing less than miraculous, and miraculous is the norm here in Israel. Addressing a popular secular Israeli society who were skeptical of calling events miraculous, David Ben-Gurion, Israel's first Prime Minister, said, "A Jew who does not believe in miracles is not a realist." It is difficult to understand the events that have created the Jewish State in a purely natural manner. From Israel's rebirth of a nation in its homeland after largely being absent for close to two thousand years, to rekindling a dead language and culture, to winning repeated wars where its military was greatly outnumbered, the State of Israel has beaten the odds countless times.

Rabbi Shlomo ben Avraham ibn Aderet, widely known as the Rashba, was a medieval Torah scholar who lived in Spain. He taught that the verse, "[Eretz Yisrael] is a land the Lord your God, cares for; the eyes of the Lord your God are continually on it from the beginning of the year to its end," was teaching that the land of Israel is run by specific Divine providence and events in the land of Israel don't occur purely because of cause and effect. He wrote, "Since the Jewish people are the chosen people and Eretz Yisrael is the chosen land of God, He is not going to leave the people or the land to an angel as God did for the other nations of the world. Rather God's "eyes" are on the land and all that occurs in the land occurs under God's providence."

The prophet Jeremiah consoled the Jewish people as they suffered their first exile and were taken to Babylonia, he said, "Again there shall be heard in this place, which you say is ruined…in the cities of Judea and the streets of Jerusalem that are desolate, without men, without inhabitants and without beasts - the sound of joy and the sound of happiness, the voice of the groom and the voice of the bride, the voice of those saying, "Praise the Lord for the Lord is good, for His mercy endures forever…" Jeremiah placed Divine redemption in the context of the joy of a bride and groom because they represent the building of the future, and the future we pray for is a redemptive future.

For two thousand years Jews dreamed of returning to Eretz Yisrael. In the early 1900's Zionist pioneers began moving back to a largely desolate land of Israel. It was full of swamps and malaria, and the early Zionists broke their backs making the land inhabitable. These early Zionists weren't working so they could enjoy the land. They had their children and future generations in mind. Could a farmer, draining a mosquito-filled swamp in 1923 ever dream of today's booming and successful State of Israel? I'd like to think these early pioneers were minor prophets who understood the significance of their work and that it would be felt a hundred years in the future. Much like today's Israelis who work tirelessly to make Israel better for their children, early Zionists worked hard to create a Jewish State for their children.

The Talmud draws a parallel between finding a suitable mate, and the difficulty in splitting the sea. The Talmud related that matching two people together is as hard as splitting the sea - *kasheh l'zavgan k'krias yam suf.* The Talmud taught that ever since the six days of creation God sits and matches up couples. The Talmud says this work is as hard for God as splitting the sea.

The Talmud's lesson speaks to the difficulty of finding a spouse. God doesn't normally interfere in the events of the world. God set the world to run on general Divine providence, which we perceive as cause and effect. There are unique times when God deems it fit to interfere in events of the world. This is when God stops running the world on general Divine providence and uses specific Divine providence. This interference is called miraculous. This teaching of the Talmud would suggest that God interferes in each and every matching of spouses. Hundreds, if not thousands of people find their spouses every single day. If the Talmud's contention that God sets up every match is to be taken literally, God interferes at a higher frequency than is commonly thought by early Torah scholars and philosophers. After all the teachings that limit the frequency of miracles, it is difficult to believe miracles occur as often as people find their spouses.

Israel is the land of the impossible and one of those impossibilities are frequent miracles. From winning wars, to creating a start-up nation, to marrying off one's children, in Israel the miraculous looks like the mundane and the mundane looks miraculous. These past three months have caused people to be skeptical of Israel's future, but I caution the skeptics, don't bet against Israel, it's been counted out many times, and it's always bounced back strongly.

CHAPTER

FORTY-FOUR

Zionists must define Zionism

One of the most noticeable differences between Jewish practices in Israel and the Diaspora comes during the Chanukah season. Traveling around Jerusalem as the stars come out during Chanukah one sees the streets lit up with Chanukah lights in every doorway. While the practice in the Diaspora is to light Chanukah lights indoors – a practice that began in fear of Gentile persecution – the practice in Israel has returned to the original institution, lighting Chanukah lights outside in the doorway. There is no fear of Gentile persecution in Israel and no reason to light as if we are scared.

The Chanukah candles being placed inside out of fear of persecution is a manifestation of a tragic phenomenon of the 2,000 year long Jewish exile. During the Jewish people's forced exile from Eretz Yisrael, the Jewish people all too often had to hide their Judaism and squelch their pride. To survive Jews had to abandon their identity and adopt the narrative of other nations. 2,000 years of hiding the Jewish peoples' story has had an adverse effect on Jewish pride and awareness of the Jewish narrative.

During its estrangement from the land of Israel the Jewish people tried to fit in with the nations around it. The Jewish people were forced to try being more German than the Germans, more French than the French, and today more American than Americans. The consequence was the loss of the "Malchut Yisrael," the sense of Jewish majesty. Subsequent Jewish generations – to no fault of their own or their ancestors – lost the sense of pride of being part of the royal Jewish nation. Forgetting their own splendor, they didn't have the dignity to boast their own narrative.

Many Jews became embarrassed of their identity. They looked to escape the shame of being Kikes, infidels and Christ-killers, and changed their names, language and dress to fit in with the world around them. Their efforts rarely worked – Jews weren't accepted, and their final failure was Hitler's insistence that being a Jew was genetic and it couldn't be erased by even conversion to Christianity. Instead of boasting of our illustrious history and rights, Jews buried them.

With the establishment of the State of Israel in 1948, Jewish shame should've been a tragedy of the past – but it wasn't. Instead of reclaiming Jewish glory, Jews assumed with its new autonomy the world would welcome them into the "league of nations." As Jews, now once again called Israelites, missed an opportunity to tell their story, their enemies told it for them. Zionism was declared racism and Jewish autonomy became known as oppression and apartheid. Instead of world acceptance as an independent nation like all other nations, Israelis were ostracized as colonizers of a land not their own. Silence once again damned the Jewish people – in the vacuum of an absent Jewish narrative, opponents filled the gap, slandering Jewish validity.

When the Jewish people didn't tell their own story, the world never heard the historical Jewish connection to Eretz Yisrael. They never learned that the Jewish people are the indigenous people of the land of Israel. The world didn't recognize the Jewish people's rights to self-determination in their historic homeland. The world never understood that the Jewish people spent 2,000 years yearning to return to its homeland.

As the world listened to the Jewish nations' enemies tell the Jewish story, they began to believe the Jewish narrative was illegitimate and its people's efforts to return to its land unjustified and demonic. They failed to recognize that Zionists' enemies only found their legitimacy by delegitimizing Zionist legitimacy, their own righteousness in demonizing Zionism, the justice of their cause by declaring the injustice of Zionist efforts to reclaim their historic homeland.

Jews began to claim that nationhood and our homeland were not core elements of Jewish identity. They began to believe the Jewish people were more religion than nation, that a Jewish historic homeland was ancient folklore and Jews had no national rights of self-determination. Along with the nations of the world who readily agreed with these positions, they denied the Jewish people their rights and fought Zionism. The Jewish majesty that had turned to Jewish shame now transitioned into hostility and opposition.

It is time the Jewish people reclaimed Jewish majesty. The time has come for Jews to tell their own story and tell their enemies their slander will no longer be tolerated. The Jewish people have enough reason to be proud of their past, boast of their narrative, and demand their rights without having to resort to their enemies' tactics of delegitimization and demonization. The Jewish narrative is legitimate, righteous and just – and it is time the world heard it, listened to it, and recognized it. Just as Israeli Jews light the Chanukah lights outside, proud of our story, it's time Zionists told their story as well, outside and with pride.

CHAPTER
FORTY-FIVE

White Sneakers, Army Boots and Zionist Dreams

As a child of late 1980's and early 1990's America, I grew up a Michael Jordan fan. I wasn't your run of the mill "Be Like Mike" fan, I was named Nike's Air Jordan Flight Club's third greatest Michael Jordan fan in the United States. I would beg my parents to buy me the newest version of Air Jordan sneakers every year, so it's only fitting that my 13-year-old son is now putting me through the same torture and begging me to buy him the same overpriced sneakers. I tried explaining to my son how irrational it is to buy sneakers at a premium price, not for quality, but image - our talk got me nowhere, he still wanted the Air Jordans. I relented, but not without a fight. I challenged my son that if he earned a perfect grade on his next Talmud test, I'd buy him the pair of sneakers of his choice.

My son met the challenge, earned his perfect grade and went with his mother shopping for sneakers. I was a proud father; I had successfully motivated my teenager to get off his computer, study and earn a high grade on a test. I also knew that my son's inner genius was being revealed! I was more than a little disappointed when I saw the sneakers he had chosen. Although he lives in a desert that can muddy any sneaker, he had chosen purely white sneakers. While bemoaning to friends how his sneakers would be ruined within a day, and maybe my son wasn't the forward thinker I thought he was, Robin, a friend, commented that I should allow him to enjoy his sneakers because soon he'll trade them in for army boots.

Robin's comment turned a slightly humorous incident into an opportunity to reflect on raising a child in Israel. I haven't had a child serve in the Israeli Defense Forces yet, my three oldest children opted for national service. There is a unique pride parents of IDF soldiers experience. There is also a much less talked about fear these same parents suffer. When I look at parents whose children are serving in the army, I can't pretend to imagine the combined worry and pride they feel. Although I don't know what it means to have a child serve in the army, I'm anxious nonetheless knowing the day will come.

It's ironic that Zionist parents worry about their children in the Israel Defense Forces. Zionism aimed to establish a means for Jews to defend themselves in strength. No longer would the Jewish people be at the whim of their hosts; Jews would defend themselves from their enemies. The image of a strong sun-kissed Israeli soldier standing guard over the Jewish homeland was a dream early Zionists felt was tangible – if only they worked hard to achieve it. Now that we've established our state, formed an army, and successfully fended off our enemies multiple times, we would think parents would only experience joy and pride at their children serving. Any Israeli parent will tell you the joy is tempered by worry of the unknown and the unthinkable.

In his description of Israeli memorial day juxtaposed with Israeli Independence Day (the days follow each other) Israeli battle veteran and former Minister of Communications, Yoaz Hendel wrote in "Zionism, not Cynicism" (April 2015), "The link between sorrow and joy is part of the complex story of life in Israel, of what we are – a part of what allows Israelis to be patriotic and critical in the same breath, to wear army boots on reserve duty and flip-flops to work the next day. A foreigner wouldn't get; I'm not even sure that we do."

The confused desire of the Jewish people to have their own army while simultaneously fearful of their children serving in harm's way can seem like cognizant dissonance, but it's the embodiment of the duality of the Zionist dream. Zionism spoke to the Jewish aspirations of a land all our own, where Jews can live in peace, and wear their foolish white sneakers. This was the Zionism of dreams. The other Zionism was the realist Zionism; where soldiers would need to wear boots, put themselves in danger, and defend their homeland. These dual notions of Zionism exist simultaneously. The Israeli Declaration of Independence stated, "The State of Israel will be based on freedom, justice and peace as envisaged by the prophets of Israel," and former Prime Minister Ben Gurion also stated, "Our security lies in constantly building up our strength in every area and on all fronts."

The Zionist goal of a free, safe and peaceful Jewish State belonged to the dreamers and the realists, and the two don't contradict. Having a state that exists on two contradictory planes simultaneously is the miracle of today's State of Israel. It is a land of dreams bolstered by the reality of the dangers that surround it and the security required to ward off those lurking dangers. This miracle isn't just the Israeli people's accomplishment. It is only with God's help, the special Divine Providence promised to the Jewish people and on their land, that can fully explain the miracle of modern Jewish existence.

I am cognizant, but not really understanding, that one day my son will have to remove his sneakers and trade them in for IDF issued boots. I know this will be a transformation for him, for me, and our family. I am also aware that he'll be lacing up his IDF boots in order to make sure another Israeli boy can study for his Gemara test, earn a perfect score and buy his own ridiculous white sneakers. I'm living the Zionist dream, and while it might be confusing at times, it is a 2,000-year-old dream fulfilled and I'm grateful for every moment.

CHAPTER
FORTY-SIX

Israel's success comes from taking responsibility

At the entrance to the Auschwitz concentration camp, and many others like Auschwitz, was a large gate with the German phrase, "Arbeit macht frei," meaning "Work sets you free" engraved into the gate. It was a cruel phrase that teased Auschwitz's inmates into thinking there was a chance they could earn their freedom. As a death camp, there was no amount of work that could earn an inmate freedom from the camp. Five years after the Holocaust ended, and the German antisemites had suffered defeat, the Jewish people had established their own state. Ironically, the Jewish State of Israel was built on hard work. No one gave the early Zionists a fully developed land for their state. They needed to build it themselves.

The most essential aspect of Zionism wasn't about Israel, it was about the Jewish people no longer waiting for a miraculous salvation but taking their destiny into their own hands. For two thousand years of exile the Jewish people assumed they'd only be redeemed and brought home with some sort of Divine sign. The Jews in Egypt had the ten plagues as their sign. The Jews in the Purim story had Esther's turnaround against Haman as their Divine sign. The assumption was that this last exile would also end with a Divine sign. Over the course of the long Jewish exile small groups of religious Jews made their way back to Israel, but they were a tiny minority of the Jewish people. Secular Jews eschewed returning to Israel, preferring to try to fit into the countries they found themselves in during the exile.

Rising antisemitism combined with rising nationalism encouraged a small group of Jews in the late 1800's to think of Jewish destiny in an entirely different way. The idea was revolutionary, break free of gentile rule by establishing a Jewish state in the land of Israel. Ironically, a movement that was built to achieve Jewish self-determination needed Gentile consent to realize its goal. The Jews didn't wait until they received Gentile and Arab permission to take back their homeland. While Zionist leaders lobbied foreign leaders for their support of a Jewish state, Jews from around the world began returning to Israel and putting in the hard work required to make the land livable once again. Although the British tried limiting Jewish immigration into Palestine, and the Arabs violently attacked the early Zionist pioneers, they couldn't stop the Jews.

As the Jews became more successful in British Mandate Palestine, the Germans began their extermination campaign against the Jews. Now, more than ever before in their 2,000 year exile, the Jews needed their own state where their most persecuted could be rescued from imminent destruction. After the Holocaust ended, the British still refused to allow Jews to return to Palestine, and although Europe had just committed a Holocaust, its people were harassing and murdering surviving Jews. It would've been easy for Jews to claim perpetual victimhood and claim eternal refugee status. The Jews refused to play victim. Instead, they went to work building their future Jewish state.

For hundreds of years the land had laid fallow. The local Arabs, themselves migrants to the land from the Arabian Peninsula, had mostly fled the land to population centers in Damascus and other Arab cities. In a visit to Ottoman controlled Palestine in the mid 1800's Mark Twain wrote, "The land was empty. Riding on horseback through the Jezreel Valley, Twain observed, "There is not a solitary village throughout its whole extent – not for 30 miles in either direction. There are two or three small clusters of Bedouin tents, but not a single permanent habitation. One may ride 10 miles, hereabouts, and not see 10 human beings. Of all the lands there are for dismal scenery, I think Palestine must be the prince... Can the curse of the Deity beautify a land? "Palestine sits in sackcloth and ashes. Over it broods the spell of a curse that has withered its fields and fettered its energies."

The Arabs of Palestine refused to invest in the land's infrastructure. In his book, "Both Sides Now" noted Israel critic Reuben Slonim quoted his thoughts in a column he wrote in the 1950's, "The way to serve the Arabs is to teach them that one throws off the shackles of national bondage by working, toiling on the land and reclaiming it with honest sweat. The Arabs will find their way to peace with the Jews if, like them, they adopt a great program of soil reclamation and expend the necessary energy to achieve it." Slonim was essentially suggesting the Arabs take on the Zionist's work ethic. They have yet to follow his advice.

In a private letter American President Herbert Hoover wrote to Zionist Lewis L. Strauss to commemorate the anniversary of the Balfour Declaration, boasted, "I have watched with genuine admiration the steady and unmistakable progress made in the rehabilitation of Palestine which, desolate for centuries, is now renewing its youth and vitality through the enthusiasm, hard work, and self-sacrifice of the Jewish pioneers who toil there in a spirit of peace and social justice." President Hoover recognized it was the industriousness of the Zionists that was leading to their taking control of the land.

A hard work ethic, never being reliant on others, and refusing to play victim, are all traits of the Jewish people. Early Zionists used these traits to settle the land of Israel and build a state that finds itself in the top ten of all nations economically, militarily, and even on the happiness index. Seventy-five years after its founding, the State of Israel is successful and thriving. While the Jewish people's success has always been attributed to God's providence, the early Zionists taking their destiny into their own hands, refusing to wait on the approval of other nations, working hard to make their homeland hospitable and most importantly refusing to play victim were key factors in their success. For the State of Israel to continue to enjoy success it needs to stay loyal to the factors that got it to where it is today.

CHAPTER
FORTY-SEVEN

Criticizing Israel: The Ultimate in Zionism

"The Americans we constantly see criticize Israel, whether in Washington, on college campuses or on social media are nothing short of antisemites!" These exact words and their sentiments have been said repeatedly as the rise and rancor of criticism of Israel in America is becoming louder and more frequent. The pushback against the criticism, characterizing it as antisemitism is directly commensurate with the rise of anti-Zionist and anti-Israel voices throughout America. Many in the Pro-Israel community don't seem willing to allow criticism of Israel to go unanswered and are willing to go past refuting the accusations and call it antisemitism.

The International Holocaust Remembrance Alliance (IHRA) defined antisemitism as, "A certain perception of Jews, which may be expressed as hatred toward Jews. Rhetorical and physical manifestations of antisemitism are directed toward Jewish or non-Jewish individuals and/or their property, toward Jewish community institutions and religious facilities." The IHRA provided a few examples, "Manifestations might include the targeting of the state of Israel, conceived as a Jewish collectivity." If accusations against Israel include lies or if they are applied in a double standard, where only Israel is singled out, the IHRA defines that criticism as having crossed a line into antisemitism.

What about criticism of Israel that isn't levied against Israel in an unfair way? What if the criticism isn't being said by Americans who seem to despise Israel, but by Americans who deeply care about Israel and consider themselves Zionists? What if the criticism is levied by Israelis? How should critiques of Israel be viewed if they're delivered in a speech at the Knesset by a Knesset member who is a former war hero? Could criticism levied by Zionists, Israelis, Knesset members or war heroes be considered problematic or even antisemitic?

Is there a meaningful difference between an accusation against Israel and criticism of Israeli policy? An accusation is a charge that isn't definitively true; it might be true, or it might not be true, but the accuser is of the opinion that it is entirely accurate. Criticism is generally levied against a policy that all agree is true, but opinions differ whether the policy is proper or needs correction. Many in the Pro-Israel community would accept legitimate and fair criticism but not tolerate unfounded accusations against Israel.

Some people in the Pro-Israel community view all criticism, even if warranted, that stems from people living outside of Israel as unfair and shouldn't be said. They argue that without being in Israelis' shoes and standing in their place, a non-Israeli can't possibly fathom the experiences that fed the calculations that led to the Israeli policy under question. The criticism might be reasonable but the people delivering it don't have the right since they can't possibly understand all that went into the making of the policy.

There are others, both within and outside of the Pro-Israel community, that counter the argument that all criticism by non-Israelis is out of bounds by arguing that if the criticism is reasonable and accurate, there's no reason why it shouldn't be said. They add that if a Zionist is offering the criticism, it is being said in a constructive manner, and should be heeded. To this group, there is no such thing as fair criticism that is out of bounds.

The IHRA added to their examples of criticism of Israel the following caveat, "However, criticism of Israel like that leveled against any other country cannot be regarded as antisemitic." The IHRA would never reject fair and warranted criticism of Israel, (as long as it wasn't delivered within a double standard) no matter who was delivering it.

As in most cases of both accusations and criticism, the defining line of what makes the criticism fair or antisemitic is dependent on who is saying it, why they're saying it, what they're saying and how they're saying it. As mentioned earlier, some would also add where the person saying it is residing matters as well. The IHRA definition attempts to restrict the metrics of appropriate vs. inappropriate criticism to what is being said, the who, why, what and where it is being said are irrelevant to characterizing the criticism as antisemitic. There are Zionists who agree and disagree with the IHRA restrictions.

Zionists shouldn't be concerned or overly defensive when reading criticism of Israel. Although there is a tendency to perceive all criticism as a threat or a call to delegitimize Israel, Zionists should reject criticism that crosses a line as antisemitic but embrace criticism that is legitimate. Instead of shifting into defense mode and twisting themselves into pretzels to demonstrate the criticism might not be accurate, Zionists should admit Israel can make mistakes and work on improving them. Not only is defensive rejection of criticism rarely convincing, but it also doesn't allow for constructive advice to be heard and genuine growth to develop.

Criticism of government policy is not only the role of a nation's citizens, but it is their responsibility. Every citizen of a democracy, and Israel is a democracy, has a right to freely criticize the government without fear of persecution. A nation can't improve without an involved and critical citizenry that vocalizes their criticism to their leadership. A nation's leaders tend to live in an echo zone assuming their policies are correct, an informed and critical citizenry allows their leaders to hear opinions from outside their echo chamber.

A prime misconception about Zionism is that its primary objective was to create a Jewish state in the land of Israel. This misconception leads people to think that once the State of Israel was founded, Zionism no longer has a purpose. These people claim we're living in a post-Zionist time. This understanding of Zionism is incorrect. Zionism isn't about creating a state, Zionism is about developing the Jewish people to be much better. To develop a state that is constantly growing Israel requires criticism. When done correctly, criticism is the best form of Zionism.

Criticism of Israel's policies and government that is unwarranted or crosses a line into antisemitism is obviously out of bounds and unacceptable. Criticism by Israelis, meant to improve Israel and relayed constructively is not only acceptable, but is the key ingredient to successful Zionism.

CHAPTER
FORTY-EIGHT

A land of values

As I walked into the large room I was overcome with emotion. All around me stood, sat and crawled a mess of humanity organized into lines, waiting areas, and makeshift stations. It took a minute to recognize what I wasn't hearing – noise. For a room full of Ukrainian refugees going through the bureaucracy of Aliyah, I'd have expected screaming, crying and yelling. While there was the occasional baby wailing, toddler whining and adult questioning having to wait longer, the room and people were relatively quiet. The Israeli government officials processing the newly arrived refugees were efficient, kind and caring for the overwhelmed people sitting before them.

Former Israeli Prime Minister Naftali Bennett told the Ministerial Committee on Aliyah and Integration, "The State of Israel is a refuge for Jews in distress, this is our mission. We will meet this sacred mission this time as well. We must make sure that those Jews who flee from places of danger are received here in the State of Israel in the best possible way: that when they feel there is an open door and a warm home for them," he said. "The State of Israel has done this many times in its history, and we will meet this sacred task this time as well."

As I entered the makeshift processing center in Central Jerusalem that morning, I've never been prouder and happier seeing government in action. The facility had recently been partly taken over by Israeli government ministries and immigration officials. These workers, all Russian and Ukrainian speaking, were there to process Ukrainian refugees. These newcomers had escaped the war raging in their cities to come home to Israel. Every half hour or so, a staff member from the facility visited the newest Israelis with snacks, games or Israeli flags for the kids. I couldn't help taking frequent runs into the room and the waiting area outside, darting between the people looking for little children. These smallest of refugees were bored, sad and confused, and when I handed them a brand-new flag they'd break out into a smile. Each time their parents would explain to them what their new flag represented. The only word I could make out was "Israel," but each time I heard it I broke out into a smile. It was during those split seconds I realized these new Israelis from Ukraine were providing the people of Israel more than the people of Israel were providing them.

Former Israeli Prime Minister Ariel Sharon said, "Aliyah is the central goal of the State of Israel." Early Zionists saw the European countries where Jews lived as their peoples' past and the land of Israel as its future. When the founders of "BILU" began their movement they stated, "Your state in the West is hopeless: the star of your future is gleaming in the East. Deeply conscious of all the foregoing, and inspired by the true teaching of our great master, Hillel, 'If I do not help myself, who will help me?' We propose to form a society for national ends."

The connection between a national Jewish move back to Eretz Yisrael and the rebirth of our nation was a frequent theme of early Zionist thinkers. Nahman Syrkin wrote, "The Jews were historically the nation which caused division and strife; it will now become the most revolutionary of all nations. From the humblest and most oppressed of all peoples it will be transformed to the proudest and greatest. The Jews will derive their moral stature from their travel, and out of their pain of their existence will come a pattern of noble living. The Jew is small, ugly, servile, and debased when he forgets and denies his character. He becomes distinguished and beautiful in the moral and social realms when he returns to his true nature."

As war between Ukraine and Russia broke out and it became clear that thousands of Ukrainian Jews would be seeking refuge in Israel, Israelis debated whether to open our borders wide for the Ukrainian masses looking for shelter and a new home. Naysayers wondered where all these people would live, how Israel could absorb so many people so quickly, and whether it was safe to allow so many unknown people into the country. The naysayers quickly lost their debate; The Jewish State was created to shelter fleeing Jews. Israel as a place of refuge for fleeing Jews was written in Israel's declaration of independence, its laws and the very character of the State. More importantly, opening its borders for fleeing Jews was a fundamental value of Zionism.

The State of Israel is more than a refuge for the Jewish people of the Diaspora, the Jewish State has become a refuge for the values of the Jewish people. The nation of Israel is more than a collection of people that stem from the same ancestors or location – they are a people with shared ethos. Abraham, the first Zionist, taught his followers and descendants, our ancestors, the values of ethical monotheism, and they are still our values today. The Jewish people are a kind and generous people. Maimonides famously wrote that a Jewish community has never existed that didn't have a charity fund, a statement that holds just as true today as when he wrote it over 800 years ago.

As time progresses and circumstances change, it is only natural for a nation's values to transition to meet the new situation. Values that were once considered sacred are seen as ancient and irrelevant. New values are needed and quickly adapted. Over the past four thousand years the Jewish people's values have not changed. Varying different institutions have ensured the Jewish people's loyalty to their fundamental ethos. In our times, the State of Israel has become the vehicle for the Jewish people to express their values, especially of mercy and kindness. The State of Israel has become the open vault that keeps the Jewish people's values safe.

Our ancestors didn't just dream of a return to their land, they dreamed of a land living according to the values they learned from their parents. When I spend time with our newest Israeli citizens, I am not only happy to see Jews coming home to Israel, the admirable efficiency of Israel's officials or how Israel is fulfilling its mission of opening its borders and arms to Jews seeking shelter, but I'm happy and proud to see Zionist values revealing themselves out in our State. It's been seven decades since our founders declared our independence, and we're still loyal to our values. Israelis have much to be proud of, but we should be most proud that we're committed to the same values our ancestors held dear and passed down from generation to generation.

CHAPTER
FORTY-NINE

Conflicts start with a war of values

Conflicts are a frequent topic of analysis when a book, column, or social media post focuses on Israel; Among the many conflicts are The religious-secular conflict, the Israeli-Palestinian conflict, the Arab-Israeli conflict, the left-right conflict, Israel-Diaspora conflict, etc. The key to understanding conflicts, and working towards a solution, is understanding the values each side holds dear. Most conflicts are generated by a difference of values between the two sides of the conflict.

The common interpretation of many of the conflicts that Israel is a party to, explains them as conflicts surrounding land, religion or politics. These explanations focus on issues unique to the each conflict; whether it be disagreement over control of the land specifically between the Jordan River and Mediterranean Sea, the more than a millennia violence between Jews and Muslims that's spanned the globe from Iran to Spain, that has nothing to do with land, or the battle of control between Zionists and Arabs. Each of these explanations fits part of the conflict, but they miss the foundation of the conflict – a difference in values.

As an example, religious and secular Jews disagree over the role of religion in government policy. That's the surface of their conflict, but the foundation of the conflict is the difference in values over the role halacha, the Torah, and God should play in every Israeli's life. Religious Jews value Halacha and put it as a primary value of their life, guiding most, if not all, of their decisions. They prefer a State of Israel that encourages the keeping of Halacha. Secular Jews don't exclude halacha, the Torah, and God from their lives, they just don't give it the same weight as their religious neighbors. The religious and secular divide over how the country should incorporate religion is really a conflict of values.

Israeli and Palestinian leadership have fundamental disagreements over basic values. Many will say their conflict is over land, but it goes much deeper than just land. When Gilad Shalit was taken captive by Palestinian terrorists in Gaza, Israel's primacy of the value of life became clearly evident. In a trade that freed Shalit, Hamas demanded that Israel release over a thousand Palestinian terrorists for Israel's one soldier. Part of Jewish ethos is that preserving life takes precedence over almost everything else – including the sacred Shabbat. Israel made the trade to ensure Shalit's life was saved.

Palestinian leadership doesn't value life in the same way Israeli leadership values life. Their institutions, from government, schools, and communities, praise and incentivize terror. Their "pay to slay" program pays terrorists a monthly stipend based on the heinousness of their attacks. A Palestinian terrorist who has murdered a Jew receives six times the salary of a school teacher in Palestinian cities. Palestinian schools are named after terrorists, teaching children who their role models should be and what they should aspire to in life. Mothers praise their terrorist suicide bomber sons, and Palestinians place their rockets in schools and residential buildings – knowingly putting their innocent civilians in harm's way. On the other hand, when Israel wages war it does its very best to preserve innocent life - not just of their own citizens, but the innocent lives of their enemies as well.

For over two thousand years, Jews have prayed for peace three times a day. Peace plays a central role in Israel's Declaration of Independence, with a paragraph calling on Israel's Arab neighbors to make peace with Israel. On the other hand, Palestinians engage in terror, making violent "resistance" a central part of their culture. Palestinians have rejected peace offers from Israelis even before there was an Israel – when Zionists aimed to create a Jewish state at peace with its Arab neighbors. Since then, Arabs have started wars, Palestinians have started intifadas, and Palestinian terror groups have started rocket barrages against Israel. Palestinians have rejected tens of Israeli peace offers over the past eight decades and have never once countered with their own.

In 1947 the United Nations proposed the partition plan as the solution to the Israeli-Arab conflict. The Arabs rejected it outright. The Jews, although giving up on over 75% of what they considered their historical heritage, agreed to compromise. The Arabs opposed the compromise and went to war – repeatedly. Over the course of the next seven decades, Jews would continuously suggest their own compromises and accept those suggested by others, to end the conflict with their Arab and Palestinian neighbors. Arabs have continuously rejected compromise. Even while putting on the show of willing to compromise they've been disingenuous. The division in the conflict is one of values.

All too often people project their values on to others and assume they share the same values. American diplomats have repeatedly made the mistake of presuming the people across the table from them, whether they be Russians, North Koreans, Iranians or Palestinians, share their values of life, liberty, and the pursuit of happiness. Americans become frustrated when countries turn down their generous offers with no rational reason. They don't – or refuse – to recognize their counterparts don't share their values and therefore don't see American offers as valuable.

While land, policy, and politics play a role in many of the conflicts Israel is involved in, they are not the foundation of each of these conflicts. To understand any conflict, and especially conflicts involving Israel, one must peel away the outer core issues of the conflict and look deeper at the values that are dividing the two sides. Trying to find solutions to the conflict without addressing the differing values that make up the conflict is futile.

CHAPTER
FIFTY

American aid to Israel helps America and promotes peace

Israeli Air Force "Captain S." is a 26-year-old female fighter jet pilot. She is the only female pilot in Israel to fly one of the Air Force F-35I stealth fighter jets and was recently appointed deputy commander of the 116th "Southern Lions" F-35 squadron. The F-35 jet that "Captain S." flies was manufactured at Lockheed Martin Aeronautics in Fort Worth, Texas. The company has made more than 500 F-35's since 2011. Israel has ordered over fifty F-35's at a cost of $110 million each, for a total order of over $5 ½ billion. Lockheed Martin Aeronautics in Fort Worth employs 16,4000 Americans; Israel's order of F-35 fighter jets contributes to many of those jobs.

After Israel's victory in its War of Independence, Israel applied to the U.S. for economic aid to help absorb immigrants. President Truman responded by approving a $135 million Export-Import Bank loan and the sale of surplus commodities to Israel. Since then Israel has received over $100 billion in economic and military aid from America. This includes President Nixon's emergency weapons airlift during the Yom Kippur War which saved Israel at its most needy time. In September 2016 a memorandum of understanding was signed between Israel's Prime Minister Netanyahu and American President Obama which assures Israel of $3.8 billion of annual military aid – Israel no longer receives economic aid. It guarantees Israel a qualitative military edge over similar hardware its enemies purchase from America. President Trump increased that amount during each year of his presidency. President Biden has done the same.

Critics maintain that American foreign aid to Israel is a waste of American taxpayer funds. At a time when America is in debt and Americans are suffering an economic downturn they claim that food, housing and healthcare are more important than bloated defense budgets and funding foreign militaries. These critics maintain that Israel defense contractors compete with American contractors and by giving Israel military aid, America is essentially helping foreign contractors outmaneuver its own businesses. The more dishonest among the critics maintain that Israel uses American foreign aid to mistreat Palestinians, deny them human rights, and govern the Palestinians through a system of oppression and even apartheid. The critics want America to end its foreign aid to Israel.

What these critics don't understand is American foreign aid to Israel strengthens and expands the U.S.-Israel relationship in ways that enhance the security of the United States and Israel. It is in America's best interest to help ensure that the Jewish state remains safe, strong and secure. The U.S.-Israel relationship is a mutually beneficial partnership that reinforces America's moral values and strategic interests. Israel is a reliable, stable, democratic ally that advances American interests in a highly volatile and strategically important region of the world. American support for Israel promotes peace and helps deter regional conflict by making clear to potential foes that they cannot defeat the Jewish state.

The United States provides security assistance to Israel because it advances American interests and regional objectives. Given growing security threats to Israel, it is essential that America maintains its commitment to the Jewish state. U.S. assistance helps ensure that Israel has the means necessary to defend itself—by itself—against growing threats. For decades, both Republican and Democratic administrations have provided security assistance to Israel.

Under the current memorandum of understanding signed between President Obama and Prime Minister Netanyahu, American foreign aid to Israel is spent in America. It creates American jobs, like in the F-35 fighter jet plant in Lockheed Martin Aeronautics of Fort Worth, Texas. America and Israel partner in intelligence, health care, scientific studies, energy and water sustainability challenges, military defense, border security, maritime security, biometrics, cybersecurity, and video analytics which help keep both countries safer.

Scholar Yair Rosenberg wrote, "The relatively small investments America makes in overseas foreign aid rebound to America's benefit in the form of a more stable and advanced world, diplomatic leverage over other countries, better collective efforts to fight global threats like disease, and in the case of military aid spent in the US, allies and technological advances funded by the aid money."

CHAPTER
FIFTY-ONE

Israel will grow unimpeded

God wrote, "You shall possess the Land and you shall settle in it, for to you have I given the land to possess it." (Numbers 33:53) In his comments to this verse, Nachmanidies wrote, "In my opinion, this verse expresses a positive command. We are commanded to settle and dwell in the land for it was given to them, and we cannot reject (me'us) the nachalat Hashem (the portion of God). If it would ever occur to us to go and capture the land of Shinar or the land of Ashur, or anything like it, and to settle there, one would be violating this positive command." In this comment the Nachmanidies stated his well-known opinion that one of the 613 mitzvot is to live in Eretz Yisrael. In truth there are two laws taught by Nachmanidies; the law to settle the land and the law for the individual to reside in the land.

The Jewish people began living in the land of Israel as a nation at the time of Joshua, some three thousand years ago. They experienced two exiles after their conquest of the land: the second lasting two thousand years. The last exile was devastating to the Jewish people for it spread them throughout the world, opening them to persecution. Yet there was always a small Jewish community in Israel. Even during the harshest times in Eretz Yisrael over the past two thousand years, there was always a Jewish presence in the land of Israel.

With the founding of the Zionist movement 150 years ago Jews in the exile began to earnestly return to Israel. Over five initial large "Aliyot," tens of thousands of Jews left their homes in Europe and moved to Israel. As Zionism became more and more popular, Jews from all over the world, and in greater numbers, uprooted themselves from lands as far as America,

Yemen and Ethiopia and moved to Israel. When Israel was declared a State, Arab countries evicted their Jews and 850,000 Jews moved from Arab lands to Israel. With the collapse of the Soviet Union, a million Jews fled their homes and moved to Israel.

Over the past two thousand years there have been many hindrances to Jewish development in Eretz Yisrael. Romans, Crusaders, Mamelukes and the Ottoman Empire all prevented the Jewish people from actualizing their destiny and building Eretz Yisrael. More recently, the British Empire ruled over Palestine and inhibited Jewish immigration and settlement in Israel. Today, even though Israel is an independent country, international forces pressure Israel not to build where it deems best for the country. Countless plans to build all over Israel, even in Israel's capital Jerusalem, have been stymied due to international objections. It isn't only Israel's enemies that have prevented Israel from building, even some of Israel's best friends have levied insurmountable pressure that has barred Israel from development.

Since its founding as a modern political movement, Zionism has faced more opposition than enjoyed support. At first opposition came internally; Jews, scared of antisemitic backlash to perceived double loyalties, hesitant because of religious beliefs in waiting for the messiah before establishing a third commonwealth in Israel, or a refusal to invest in a questionable project, opposed Zionism. Zionism wasn't only opposed internally, Zionists faced violent opposition from Arabs living in the land of Israel and Arab armies neighboring Israel. Zionism was also opposed by Western forces. There was opposition within the British government to Zionism because some of the English wanted to retain control of Palestine. Within the American government many argued that access to Arab oil, put at risk by Zionist "aggression," was more important than American Jewish votes.

With all the opposition Israel faced before, during and after its founding, Israel has still flourished. Each time an opponent has tried to limit Israel's area of settlement, Israel has broken free and enlarged its borders. War after war, each presenting another existential threat, were won by Israel, and provided Israel reason to grow. On the diplomatic front, resolutions accusing Israel of violating international law, of Zionism equals racism, and calls for Israel to abandon its land were ignored by Israel. Through tens of thousands of terror attacks and two intifadas, Israel continued to develop, build, and grow. As opposed to stopping Israel's growth, it almost seems that opposition to Israel's development furthers Israel's growth.

While many nations and forces have tried to stop the Jewish people and Israel from growing, Zionists are resilient and can't be stopped. Pressure from other nations have caused delays in Zionist plans but have never completely held Israel back from thriving. Zionism was started by brave Jews as a healthy response to two thousand years of persecution. They were sick and tired of being dictated to by hateful Gentiles. Israel is a successful country that determines its own future. No one will stop it from continuing to build and thrive.

CHAPTER

FIFTY-TWO

It's the people that makes Israel so special

There are various factors that make Israel special. There almost seems to be no end to the list that can be generated of aspects that makes the Jewish homeland unique. There is the feeling a Jew gets when they walk the streets, knowing they're stepping the same steps as their ancestors, there's the sanctity of the land, and the feeling a Jew has knowing that while in Israel, they're home.

Today's Israel is a truly unique place. It is the only country in the world that hosts an ancient people who once called their land home, were exiled, and have now returned to their ancestral homeland to restart its nation. I'd like to recount three short stories to explain what I think makes this land so special – the people.

In 2014 our family went viral. On a trip to Alabama we found seven pairs of tefilin in a store that sold items people lost on airplanes. The tefilin were lost to their owners, who never expected to get them back. We bought the seven pairs of tefilin, posted pictures of the seven pairs on Facebook and asked people to share them until the pictures reached the owners.

Within one week of posting the pictures we had found six of the seven owners. The last pair of tefillin had no name on the bag, and no one claimed it. There was a sticker on one of the boxes from a tefillin store in Israel. A friend of mine in Israel took the initiative to drive to the store, show the owner a picture of the tefillin bag and ask if he knew the owner of the tefillin. He did, and the tefillin were returned.

A few years later, our family had been living in Israel for a few years and Aliza and I took a day off and went to Tel Aviv. We took a taxi from the Port to a museum and we left Aliza's wallet in the taxi. We had no way of tracking the taxi down and figured the worst. Later that night Aliza got a call from the taxi driver that he had her wallet and would deliver it the next day.

The taxi driver had opened the wallet, found Aliza's ID card and saw she lived in Mitzpe Yericho. He called the phone company and asked for a Pilichowski in Mitzpe Yericho's phone number – but we don't have a home phone. Using ingenuity, he asked for Moshe Cohen in Mitzpe Yericho's phone number. He figured every town in Israel must have a Moshe Cohen, and our Moshe Cohen would know Aliza's cell phone number. There is a Moshe Cohen in Mitzpe Yericho and he knew Aliza's phone number and gave it to the taxi driver. Aliza had her wallet back in one day.

This year our son Moshe found a bus card on the street and he knew when you see a lost object you can't just look away, you need to pick it up and find the owner. The chances of finding the owner didn't look good. Moshe and I went into a Sefarim store and asked the man behind the counter if he recognized the person on the card. Not only did he say he didn't know the owner, but told Moshe to just throw the card away; everyone loses their bus card.

Moshe didn't agree with the Sefarim store clerk and kept the card. He took it to school, gathered his friends and asked them to come up with a plan. Wouldn't you guess it, only in Israel, but the card owner was one of Moshe's friend's cousins! A few phone calls later and the card owner knew not to get a new card, and his card was returned to him.

These three stories mean the world to me because they demonstrate the uniqueness of today's Israel. What makes Israel so special is its people. These stories could've happened in New York, Paris or Moscow – but these stories rarely happen as often as they do in Israel. The combination of a small country, people closely related, and the unusual being usual here makes stories like these almost likely.

Israel's first Prime Minister, David Ben Gurion famously said, "In Israel, in order to be a realist you must believe in miracles." This is truly a land of historic and contemporary miracles; while almost all miracles are Divine in nature, many of today's miracles in Israel are man made. I'm not referring to Israel's military victories, I'm discussing the miracles of unlikely odds like the returning of the tefillin, wallet and bus card. It's the Israeli people, the miracle makers, who make this land so special.

CHAPTER
FIFTY-THREE

A Presidential Visit to Israel

On a hot summer June day, President Richard Nixon stepped down the stairs of Air Force One onto the tarmac of Israel's Ben Gurion Airport. Israel was reeling from its latest war less than a year before. Victorious, the Yom Kippur War, had taken a toll on Israel's people and their morale. President Nixon wasn't doing much better himself. This foreign trip to numerous countries was designed to distract from the Watergate scandal that would ultimately bring President Nixon down in disgrace. President Nixon's trip wasn't a distraction for Israel; It was historic. This was Israel's first visit by an American President. In 24 hours of hard work, President Nixon and Israeli Prime Minister Rabin signed multiple agreements forging an even stronger US-Israel relationship.

Before President Biden's Presidential trip to Israel, the White House announced that President Biden would take his first trip to the Middle East as President. The announcement stated that he will stop in Israel and Saudi Arabia and his trip would start in Israel on July 13. This was far from President Biden's first trip to Israel; what made this trip so special is his arrival as President of the United States. An American Presidential visit is more than just a visit, it is an honor with great significance. In the words of Israel's Foreign Ministry, a Presidential trip "Symbolizes the unique relationship, the common heritage and the close and historic ties that have long existed between the United States and Israel."

Presidents Nixon, Carter, Clinton, George W. Bush, Obama and Trump have all visited Israel on official Presidential trips. Trips have been scheduled to sign historic agreements, bestow honor, celebrate milestones and for tragedies, as President Clinton's 1995 trip to eulogize Prime Minister Rabin and President Obama's 2016 trip to eulogize President Shimon Peres. President Biden made the twelfth Presidential visit to Israel.

Prime Minister Naftali Bennett invited President Biden to Israel when Bennett visited Biden in the White House the previous April. President Biden met with President Herzog, Prime Minister Bennett, Foreign Minister Lapid and Defense Minister Ganz. He visited Yad Vashem and an Iron Dome battery to highlight the extra one billion dollars in funding America recently provided to restock the Iron Dome missiles.

While most of the focus of the trip was centered on the politics of the trip and the analysis focused on the Biden Administration's treatment of Israel, there is an aspect of the trip that speaks to larger meaning. Aside from whatever was achieved during President Biden's visit to Israel, the Israeli people should be excited about the visit for what it represents for the US-Israel relationship.

American Presidents have taken their travel very seriously. While President Washington spent a month traveling through New England to demonstrate to Americans how the Presidency differs from a Monarchy and President Taft averaged 30,000 travel miles a year, nineteenth-century presidents never left the country. In November 1906, President Theodore Roosevelt was the first President to travel outside America on official business when he sailed to Panama to inspect the construction of the Panama Canal. While it seems like international travel is no big deal, with Air Force One, the Presidential motorcade and the host countries shutting down their cities for Presidential movement, making the President as comfortable as possible, these trips take months to plan and cost tens of millions of dollars. Multiple planes make the trip, carrying the President's limousine, ambulance, helicopter, advisors, staff, security, and journalists. Advance teams come weeks in advance to plan routes and hundreds of locations, each with their own significance, are considered and most rejected.

The decision to visit a country is a statement by the President that he considers the country he is visiting important to the United States of America. Certain Presidential trips are made to visit allies, others to make security arrangements and some to bestow honor on a country that has partnered with the United States. Presidential trips to Israel are made for a combination of all three reasons.

Israel, following its Zionist values, has quickly become America's best friend in the region. It partners with the American government on intelligence, security and industry. Its friendship with the United States is founded in the values the two nations share. Both countries view Iran as a threat to their own national security as well as global peace. President Biden discussed the Iranian threat with Prime Minister Bennett. The choice to visit Israel is a way of President Biden honoring Israel and Israelis should celebrate the honor.

In May 1948 a serious debate waged between President Truman's advisors whether it was in the best interests of the United States to recognize a Jewish State. It wasn't clear that siding with the Zionists was in America's best interests. Secretary of State George C. Marshall urged President Truman not to recognize Israel, as he feared Arab backlash against the United States would hurt America's access to Arab oil. President Truman made the correct decision and recognized Israel. I imagine that not many in the President's office that day would've believed how impressive a state the early Zionists would build and how many Presidents sitting in Truman's chair would pay homage to Israel by flying thousands of miles to visit the Zionist State. All Zionists should be proud of the State they've built and commit themselves to making Israel even better.

CHAPTER

FIFTY-FOUR

Reinvigorating Israel Advocacy with Zionism

The Jewish people are worried about attrition of the next generation's connection to Israel. This has spurred the birth of multiple organizations and programs aimed at capturing the hearts and minds of Jewish teenagers and bringing them back into the Israel fold. There isn't one solution to Jewish teenagers moving away from Judaism and Israel. Each teen is different and will react differently to the messages they hear. Some messages will resonate, others will not.

One proposal frequently suggested to bring the Jewish teen community back into the fold is to change the narrative that Israel's opponents frequently spread. If the Jewish community marks success as changing the narrative, they're setting themselves up for failure and will never succeed. The global narrative won't change because there are no metrics for the narrative. It's impossible to know which narrative is being spread at any one time and which new narrative spread will be effective. Creating counter narratives to combat opposing narratives is no better than "shooting in the dark."

I've seen activists and advocates criticizing establishment organizations for their efforts, claiming they aren't effective. Criticizing other Israel advocacy and educational organizations isn't helpful to the cause. There isn't a teenager in the world who will become a stronger Zionist and draw closer to Judaism by hearing a chorus of infighting within the Jewish community. Zionists are in the "battle" together, each take a different direction, and each covers a different segment of the population. Different messages resonate with different teens.

A lazy accusation is that "wokism" has infected Jewish teenagers with a distorted set of values. It's too easy to claim all teens share the same woke and progressive values, and it's those values leading them away from a connection to Israel – but it's not true. Teens don't all see the world the same way and aren't all woke progressives. While many progressives take anti-Zionist positions, there is nothing mutually exclusive about progressive and Zionist values. There are many Zionist progressives. Indicting all progressives as anti-Zionist is not only unhelpful, it's dishonest.

Addressing all teenagers the same way instead of offering differentiated learning, assures turning off a large percentage of teenagers to Israel and Judaism. It risks whatever lesson that was going to be taught to them becoming irrelevant to the teenagers. When an Israel educator makes this mistake, they risk turning the teenager off from Israel – the opposite result they're trying to achieve. Lessons must be individualized and differentiated to be successful.

There's a tendency to simplify world conflicts, but the Syrian civil war, the Ukrainian-Russia war and the Israeli-Palestinian conflict can't be simplified. To teach these conflicts and for our students to understand them, nuance must be employed. All too often in an attempt to make things easy to understand for students, teachers paint complicated issues as black and white, when they're anything but clear cut. Teachers need to have confidence in their teenage students and trust they can understand the complexities of Zionism.

In an effort to simplify the complex, win the narrative, and engage Jewish teens, some advocate for abandoning our core values in the hopes that a new approach will win the day. New approaches that lack a foundation of values fall empty. Zionism is the core value when it comes to teaching Israel and its conflicts. To succeed in connecting more Jewish teens to Israel we must reinvigorate our Zionist education and advocacy with Zionism's values. Zionism doesn't stand for changing narratives, creating division among Zionists, demonizing political movements, or simplifying the complex by omitting nuance. Zionism is a movement that stands for the Jewish people's rights. It is a proud movement that doesn't cower from others, need shifting philosophies, or attacks to distract from opponents. The best way to bring Jewish teenagers back to Zionism is by reinvigorating their Israel advocacy with Zionism.

CHAPTER
FIFTY-FIVE

Renewing Our Zionist Vows

There was a thought in the late 1940's and immediately after the founding of the State of Israel that the Zionist movement could now come to an end. Beginning in the mid 1800's, the Zionist movement aimed to achieve two objectives. The first was to create a Jewish State that would provide a place of refuge for persecuted Jews. The second goal of the Zionist movement was to actualize Jewish rights to self-determination in their historic homeland, the land of Israel. With the creation of the Jewish State, the Zionist movement had achieved its goals and it was suggested that it could put itself to rest and concentrate on State building.

Instead of evolving into a movement solely focused on improving the new Jewish State, Zionists began diverging into different focuses. One of them became defending the rights of the Jewish State in international forums. While Arab armies were trying to wipe the State of Israel off the face of the map through military means, the world had begun trying to use public discourse to delegitimize the Jewish State. Zionists have shifted from trying to convince world leaders to create a Jewish State to convincing the world of the Jewish State's legitimacy.

Zionists have fought the legitimacy battle for 75 years and it hasn't really convinced those looking to delegitimize the Jewish State. Zionist arguments largely fall on deaf ears. Universities have become the base for anti-Israel ideology and the streets of the world's capitals host protests calling for an end to Zionism and Israel. Even the World Cup, the biggest sporting event of the year, featured anti-Israel protestors decrying the illegitimacy of the Jewish State.

Many Zionists fight the battle of Israel's legitimacy arguing over the big issues like Israel's right to exist, the Jewish people's right to a State, and the Israel Defense Forces right to defend itself against its enemies. But the day-to-day nitty-gritty of Israel's issues tend to distract Zionists from their core values. Instead of focusing on building and improving the Jewish state by taking an aggressive offensive stance, Zionists have digressed to playing defense. They have begin trying to invalidate every critique made against Israel. Instead of playing defense, Zionists must return to their core values and go back on offense to improve the Jewish State.

One of the prime values of Zionism was Aliyah. Moving to Israel has never been considered a lateral move for the Jewish people. The word "Aliyah" means to "go up," because moving to Israel has always been seen as an improvement for a Jewish person. The Zionist movement's first calls were to Jews to relocate and go up to the land of Israel to make their new homes. Unfortunately, many Zionists take offense at calls for Aliyah today. They somehow perceive a call to move to Israel as invalidating the Diaspora as a home for the Jewish people – but it is far from it. The call to move to Israel isn't looking down at other places, it is a call to begin looking at the land of Israel as the Diaspora Jews' next home. It is time that Aliyah was once again strongly encouraged by Zionists.

Along the lines of encouraging Aliyah is the value of making Eretz Yisrael the home of all Jewish people – irrespective of their identity, gender, religious beliefs etc. All too often modern-day Israeli society is seen as a polarizing place as opposed to the early Zionist's vision of a State that welcomes all Jews. It is time for today's Zionists to redouble their efforts to erase any form of rejectionism and transform Israel into a place where all Jews feel at home.

To fully renew their Zionist vows, Jews must once again begin developing the land of Israel into a home for individuals and businesses. When Zionists first began moving to the Eretz Yisrael they focused on draining the swamps, plowing the fields, and building roads. It is time for Zionist pioneers to begin once again to envision what an Israel at 100 years old should look like to attract more people and business. Developing the State requires developing the land in a smart way.

Zionist must also commit to building a State that is inclusive and acts as a light onto the nations of the world. Early Zionists and the founders of the State of Israel always understood that the Jewish State wasn't going to just service the Jewish people but was going to be an exemplar of moral national policy and behavior. This hasn't been enough of a focus of Zionists. In the great distraction of playing defense, we forgot that just acting as we are designed to act is a sufficient enough offense to fulfill our mission of showing the world the way.

Playing defense against anti-Zionist false accusations hasn't advanced Zionist objectives. It is time that modern day Zionists renewed their Zionist vows and begin to return to the goals and values early Zionists set for the Jewish nation. Instead of trying to invalidate every charge against Israel, Zionists should renew calls for Aliyah, transform the State of Israel into a hospitable state for all Jews, and a place where commerce and individuals can thrive. Lastly, Zionists must focus on ensuring the Jewish State acts as an exemplar for the rest of the world. It is only by aggressively pursuing its objectives that Zionists can hope to achieve them.

CHAPTER

FIFTY-SIX

The difference between Zionism and Israeli policy

There are a few topics that will always be debated among Zionists; Should all Diaspora Jews move to Israel? Do Zionists demand that Israel be a land exclusively for the Jewish people? Is Zionism an aspect of Judaism or its own separate movement? One of the most debated topics among Zionists is whether anti-Zionism is inherently antisemitic or a legitimate critique of a popular movement. This is a heated topic; Jonathan Greenblatt, the Director of the Anti-Defamation League gave a groundbreaking speech where he stated, "To those who still cling to the idea that anti-Zionism is not antisemitism, let me clarify this for you as clearly as I can—anti-Zionism is antisemitism. I will repeat: Anti-Zionism is antisemitism." Many who had taken the side of the argument that anti-Zionism is antisemitism felt supported by Greenblatt's statement.

Greenblatt's position took on an air of controversy when critics of Israel fought back against Greenblatt's assertion. They argued that criticism of Israel's policies was legitimate protest against an oppressive Israeli rule that treated Palestinians unjustly. The two sides debated intensely and lines of civility previously uncrossed were breached. There were charges of antisemitism and tyrannical shutdown of free speech thrown at both sides and it seemed the debate that stemmed from Greenblatt's comments had caused a schism that wouldn't be easily repaired. This debate never had to reach this level of divisiveness – it was caused by a misunderstanding.

Greenblatt, and those who agreed with him were focused on those opposed to Zionism. They were characterizing the opposition to the ideology of Zionism as antisemitic. Those who disagreed with Greenblatt weren't addressing his actual comment, but rather chose to focus on Israeli policy instead. To the unfamiliar eye, the presentation of both sides would seem similar but there is a significant difference between the two sides of this conversation. To some the question of antisemitism focuses on opposing Zionism, while to the others, the question focuses on opposing Israeli policies.

Zionism and current Israeli policy are not the same. When the question of whether anti-Zionism is antisemitic is asked, a large percentage of the questions is actually asking if critiquing Israeli policy is antisemitic. Zionism is a four-thousand-year-old ideology that turned into a movement. Zionism stands for the right of the Jewish people to exercise self-determination in their historic homeland, the land of Israel. The Zionist ideology might inform current Israeli policy – in much the same way the values written in America's Declaration of Independence informs American policy – but the ideology does not dictate the policy of the Israeli government.

The best Zionists are some of Israel's strongest critics. Israel is a parliamentary government. It contains a coalition government and an opposition. Some of Israel's greatest Prime Ministers like Menachem Begin and Benjamin Netanyahu spent years in the opposition critiquing the Israeli government's policies. No one would dare suggest their criticism of Israeli policy should be characterized as antisemitic. It is perfectly legitimate to criticize Israeli policy. Israel is a Democracy that gives its citizens free speech and the right to criticize their government. Claiming that criticism of Israel is by nature antisemitic flies in the face of Israeli values and law.

Many Zionists grow concerned with the nature of the criticism directed at Israel. When the criticism contains forms of double standard, uses classic age-old antisemitic tropes or slanders Israel with fabricated facts and stories, it has crossed the line from legitimate criticism of a government's policies to rage-based antisemitism. When the criticism contains discrimination, it loses its legitimacy and becomes classic antisemitism. If the criticism of Israeli policy is honest, there is nothing wrong with it.

In contrast to criticism of Israeli policy, opposition to Zionism will almost always present as antisemitism. Opposing Zionism means opposing Jewish rights. Unless you oppose all nation's rights to self-determination and their historic homeland, why should the Jewish people be the only nation that doesn't deserve the rights all other nations deserve? It is hard to find a legitimate answer to that question. Almost all answers come back to antisemitism.

Not everyone understands the difference between current Israeli policy and Zionism. Their misunderstanding stems from ignorance of Zionism's actual axioms or a politically motivated refusal to recognize the difference between the two concepts. These people either see all criticism of Israel as a criticism of Zionism, and characterize both as antisemitic or see Israeli policy as somehow retroactively reflecting on Zionist ideology that was created over four thousand years ago. A current Israeli policy doesn't retroactively change Zionism, nor is it a direct consequence of Zionism. It has become unfortunately acceptable for Israel's opponents to conflate Israeli policy with Zionism; it's crucial that Zionists not allow themselves or their movement to become falsely tarnished by nefarious characters trying to besmirch the Zionist movement.

CHAPTER

FIFTY-SEVEN

The Need for Big Tent Zionism

In an address to the United Nations, former Israeli Prime Minister Naftali Bennett compared today's political polarization to the corona pandemic saying, "Both coronavirus and polarization can erode public trust in our institutions, both can paralyze nations. If left unchecked, their effects on society can be devastating. In a polarized world, where algorithms fuel our anger, people on the right and on the left operate in two separate realities, each in their own social media bubble, they hear only the voices that confirm what they already believe in. People end up hating each other. Societies get torn apart. Countries broken from within, go nowhere."

Zionism hasn't been immune to the growing partisan rancor that has infected 21st Century politics. Discussions and debates among fellow Zionists that were once respectful and polite expressions of differing opinions have become bitter and resentful. Friendships have ended, and families have broken up over differing political opinions.

While religious Zionists consider Avraham the first Zionist, and the charge of "Go to your land," the first Zionist charge, Zionism is a political movement. As a modern movement, Zionism began in the late 1800's when Theodore Herzl began inspiring Jews to return to Israel to create the first Zionist state in 2,000 years.

The modern Zionist movement advocated for self-determination of the Jewish people. It promoted the notion that Jews should choose their destiny and not put their future in the hands of Gentiles who often persecuted their Jews. Zionism wasn't satisfied with Jews determining their future in exile, it endorsed Jews returning to their historic homeland, Eretz Yisrael. Zionism also charged Jews to fulfill the prophetic promise of returning and gathering in the land of their forefathers. Instead of waiting for a Messiah's eagle wings to bring them home, Zionism demanded Jews take their future into their own hands and return to govern their land.

There are different camps in the world of Zionism, it is not a monolithic movement. There are Labor Zionists, Revisionist Zionists, peace Zionists, religious Zionists, secular Zionists, greater Israel Zionists, etc. Zionism was never given an official definition with boundaries that prevent variations from arising – an argument can be made that Zionism was purposefully designed to allow for variations.

Unfortunately, a phenomenon has developed where people dismiss others from the Zionist camp due to their political views on Zionism. Zionists with differing opinions can disagree and argue, but they should never "cancel" each other. I live in Judea and Samaria, but I still appreciate Zionists who maintain my neighbors and I must move to make room for a Palestinian State. There are religious and secular Zionists who see each other as opponents, and think their opponent is ruining the State of Israel - but they can still recognize that both are still Zionists. The Zionist camp is diverse, and each side must welcome the other.

Jews rarely agree – in fact the entire Talmud is based on disagreements between Jewish scholars, and disagreements about other scholars' disagreements. To be a good Jew is to be involved in never ending disagreements. The excitement of Talmud study is the examination of opposing opinions. Each opinion is scrutinized and appreciated – even if not followed. Zionism is a prism of many different opinions. Opinions considered anti-Israel by American Zionists are given voice by Zionist legislators in the Knesset every day.

Although every Zionist imagines the tent of Zionism is small and only includes people that agree with their brand of Zionism, the truth is Zionism is a big tent that includes many people. Zionism is too small of a club to be exclusionary. Every Zionist thinks their opponents' positions puts Israel in danger, but a plethora of opinions - strong opinions - is healthy. 73 years after the realization of the Zionist dream of creating a free and Jewish state, we've demonstrated that all the positions we thought were dangerous and existential threats to Israel, weren't really that dangerous. Israel is thriving and the healthy debate about the best steps forward didn't take away from Israel, but rather added to its success.

Some may argue that enlarging the Zionist tent weakens Zionism's potency, but the opposite is true. The larger we expand Zionism's tent the stronger it becomes. Whether it's in the IDF or the hi-tech boardrooms of Herziliya, Israel has always flourished with differing opinions. It's important we keep the Zionist tent as wide open as possible.

CHAPTER
FIFTY-EIGHT

The Shortfalls of Zionism

While Zionism has achieved a great deal, it has also fallen short of its original goals: People often confuse the focus on Zionism's shortfalls as criticism of Zionism or even antisemitism, but that's an erroneous take. Pointing out areas of required improvement isn't being unfairly critical, it's a demonstration of care and concern. Zionists needn't be embarrassed about these shortfalls; Zionists must identify them and address them. It's only in correcting Zionism's shortfalls that it can improve.

Zionism originally encouraged a geographic shift of the Jewish people from the four corners of the world to the Jewish people's historic homeland, the land of Israel. Zionism aimed to inspire a change of the Jewish people's language, culture, and calendar from their Gentile neighbors' culture to a modern renewed Jewish society. Zionism was thought to be a uniting force that would heal the divisions plaguing Judaism. While the divisions among secular and religious Jews, or even among religious Jews looked insurmountable, Zionism's ideal of the Jewish people coming together was thought to be the remedy for Jewish disunion. Religious Jews saw Zionism as the movement that would begin the steps to the ultimate redemption, heralding in a messianic era. With all the Jews gathered from the four corners of the world to the Jewish people's historic homeland, how could the Messiah not arrive?

As the Zionist movement took off, objections to Zionism began to be heard throughout the Jewish world. From the different communities and groups of Jews Zionism began to be demonized. Jews were worried that the Jewish focus on establishing their own state in their own land would call into question each nations' loyalty to their current nation. The dual loyalty charges would increase antisemitism throughout each nation Jews currently made their home. Other Jews saw that Zionism represented a sort of alternative approach to Jewish peoplehood. This new alternative approach was disturbing and broke the traditional understanding of what made the Jewish people.

Religious Jews had their own objections to Zionism. They understood that the Torah was the defining character of Judaism. Zionism, especially as a movement, came to erase or replace Torah as the defining character of Judaism. Religious Jews, especially the Ultra-Orthodox communities saw Zionism as a threat to traditional Torah based Judaism and opposed it. Other more mystical Jews saw Zionism as trying to preempt a messianic era. In their understanding, only observance of the Torah could bring the Messiah. Trying to shortcut the system and bring the Messiah early by encouraging the exiles to gather in Eretz Yisrael and create our own state was bound to have disastrous effects.

150 years after the modern political Zionist movement began the question of whether Zionism has achieved its goals and is still relevant is a frequent conservation among Zionists. While many Jews have moved to Israel, almost half of world Jewry isn't considering it. The Aliyah rates, while shockingly high at times like the influx of Jews from Arab lands, Russia and Ethiopia, has been disappointingly low from countries that are hospitable to Jews. Israeli culture hasn't taken off as such a strong force that it's replaced the culture and language of Jews throughout the world.

Contrary to Zionism's goal of uniting global Jewry an argument can be made that Zionism has exacerbated divisions among the Jewish people. The Religious and Secular divides among Jews both in and out of Israel have gotten wider, louder, and more pronounced. Arguments between Orthodox, Conservative and Reform Jews over the policies of the Kotel, conversions and marriage have also intensified over the past three or four decades. The question of who qualifies as a Jew has brought people to strong arguments and disunity. The conflict between Jews and Arabs, and the growing disparities between the two communities have become a symbol of Israeli dysfunction. Although debatable, it can be argued that Zionism has increased antisemitism, not lowered it. While a Teshuva movement began in earnest, Religious Jews are still greatly disappointed by the amount of secularism in modern Israeli society.

Moving forward, Zionists must take steps to address its shortcomings and improve its accomplishments. The repeated elections have created an ecosystem that forces elected leaders to view issues in a shortsighted manner; Zionist and Israeli leaders must look past the next election and address fundamental points and issues. Zionism won't address the issues that truly determine its long-term success.

Israel must begin to reach out to the Diaspora in a new way. Israel must fundamentally change its relationship with Diaspora Jewry. Instead of Israel looking to the Diaspora for support, it needs to offer Diaspora Jewish communities support and becoming the giver, not the taker. Israeli society must look to heal divisions, not exasperate them. Instead of standing on principle, always looking to preserve old customs for fear of change undermining the fabric of Zionism, Israel must put peace among the Jewish people first and foremost. The Israeli separation, or lack of separation, between "Church and State" must be redefined. A priority of the Ministry of Religious Affairs must be to make halachik Judaism attractive, not burdensome, especially on non-observant Judaism.

Zionism is a spectacular movement that has fundamentally changed the Jewish world. It has proven itself eternally relevant. From Abraham's journey to Israel to Ben Gurion's declaration of Israel's independence and everything in between and afterwards, Zionism has become a force for good, improving Israel and the Jewish people. As Israel head's to its 100th year – it'll be here sooner than we imagine – it must take the steps to address its shortcomings and achieve the few objectives it has yet to accomplish.

CHAPTER
FIFTY-NINE

Vacationing in Israel

I stared in shock at the full two-page advertisement. I was perusing a Jewish magazine on Shabbat over a cup of coffee and saw the left page of the advertisement quote a verse from the Torah, "Build me a sanctuary and I will dwell amongst you." Curious, I wondered what was being advertised. The facing page was even more surprising, the text stated, "There's nowhere you'd rather be..." could this be an advertisement for building the Temple in Jerusalem? Where else would any Jewish person, reading a Jewish magazine, want to be? I was shocked when I realized it was an advertisement for a bungalow colony in the Catskills! In a time when all Jews can move to Israel, is it appropriate to be building our sanctuaries in Upstate New York? Are the Catskills where all Jews really want to be over the summer? I certainly didn't want to be in the Catskills, I wanted to be in Israel this summer.

I've always preferred to vacation in Israel than go to Europe, Asia, or America. This isn't just a personal preference, it is in line with our traditions and Jewish law; Maimonides wrote, "It is forbidden to leave Eretz Yisrael except to study Torah; to marry; or to save one's property from the gentiles. After accomplishing these objectives, one must return to Eretz Yisrael. Although it is permitted to leave Eretz Yisrael under these circumstances, it is not pious behavior." There are plenty of great Torah scholars who permit leaving Israel for vacation, the Chafetz Chaim maintained it was permitted even to visit a friend, but I prefer not to leave the land, even for a short period of time.

When our family vacations throughout Israel we travel Israel's history on five levels: Biblical times, Mishna times, Talmudic times, exile times, and modern Zionism times. The people and events of these times left a mark on the land. There are places one can visit that are unique to only one time period and others where events occurred from one, two or even all the time zones. Simply traveling the land allows learning the events of our past in a way that history books and even master educators can never teach it. Touching the rocks, feeling the air, and walking the same roads our ancestors walked so many years before renews our connection to our history.

Israel isn't only a place of history; it is a land of fun and recreation as well. When it comes to fun in Israel, there are also five levels of fun. Israel offers its people hiking, culture, cuisine, fun and shopping. Each region in Israel offers a different terrain which lends Israelis a different hiking experience on each hike. The culture, whether one goes to a concert to hear music, visits a theater to see a play or visits the many museums, Israel's culture simply can't be beat. With immigrants from every corner of the world, Israel's restaurants offer the widest variety of food that can be imagined. Kibeh from Syria, falafel from Iraq and Kurdish shamburak will ensure you never forget your vacation. The fun doesn't stop there; ride banana boats on the Kinneret, ATVing in the Judean Desert or skydiving over the Mediterranean coast, the adventures really never stop in Israel. Lastly, whether it's art, clothes or Judaica, Israel's shuks, stores and malls offer incredible shopping and souvenirs to remember your trip.

On a Palestinian television program called The Supreme Authority, Riyad al-Aileh, a Palestinian political science lecturer stated, "The Jews claim that they were in Palestine 2,000 years ago, If we look at the history, we will see that they were not in Palestine in the past, but rather only as invaders less than 70 years ago." Some opponents of Zionism claim the Jewish connection to the land is more contemporary by nature and was invented by modern Zionists. As a Zionist educator vacationing in the land of Israel I couldn't help noticing that every few feet there are signs (literal and figurative) of the Jewish people's connection to the land. Ignoring the Jewish connection to the land of Israel is ignoring reality. Early Zionists didn't choose the land of Israel randomly from a spinning globe. The Jewish connection to the land of Israel goes back thousands of years, and the Jewish people have never given up hope of returning home.

Whenever circumstances force me to travel abroad, I stand at the departure gates of Ben Gurion airport wondering if I've lost my mind. For two thousand years my ancestors waited for the chance to see this land, and now that we finally have it, I'm going to leave it? Of course, I have valid reasons to leave Israel, but even so, how can I leave a place we've been praying to return to for so long?

Living the dream of our ancestors in Israel has many great benefits, but one not talked about often is vacationing in Israel. Whether you're a hiker or shopper, an eater or a skydiver, vacationing in Israel is simply the best. Vacationing in Israel delivers the opportunity to relax, have fun and eat a great meal, all while getting a sense of the land and the Jewish connection to Eretz Yisrael. I'm aware that Israel can feel cramped and claustrophobic and that it can be more expensive to vacation in Israel than to fly to resorts in Europe, Cyprus, or Dubai. I don't judge anyone for taking a vacation outside of Israel, I'm just fascinated by the land we've been given and want to enjoy every moment I'm blessed to be on the land.

CHAPTER
SIXTY

Who would ever have thought?

Israelis take wondrous events for granted every single day. These events and phenomena would seem miraculous to our great-grandparents and they barely cause us to turn our heads. From Hebrew street signs to thousands of yeshivot, our ancestors would never have dreamed of the multiple wonders that today's Israel boasts. Join me as I list 75 wonders of Israel and ask - Who would ever have thought?

Who would ever have thought,

1. A nation exiled from its land, would return to it after 2,000 years?
2. A people who had stopped speaking its ancient language, would revive it?
3. Israel would become the center of the Torah world again so soon, with more people studying Torah today in Israel than ever before in Jewish history?
4. Jews could freely visit Ma'arat Hamachpielah in Hebron and pray at the graves of the "Mamas and the Pappas?"
5. Jews could "go up" to the Temple Mount, pray and study Torah again? (yes, we do!)
6. Shemittah, Terumah and Maasrot, and all the other mitzvot that can only be done in Israel would become just as practical as putting on tzitzit and lighting Shabbat candles?
7. At the end of the Passover Seder, we'd have to explain to our children what, "Next Year in Jerusalem" means, because they're already sitting

in Jerusalem?

8. Our tragedies would be the past, our celebrations are the present, and our future is brighter than ever?
9. Jerusalem would be filled with the sound of joy of brides and grooms in our day?
10. The flag of Israel would fly high over the land of Israel?
11. Israel would invent "ReWalk," an exoskeleton that allows paralyzed people to walk again?
12. Jews from all over the world have the right to return to their homeland whenever they want, and Israel will pay for the plane ticket?
13. Israel would win wars in 1948, 1956, 1967, 1973, 1982 and many more after that?
14. The Jewish people would rule over their land in a third commonwealth in our lifetime?
15. The Jewish army would be one of the most powerful in the world?
16. Masada, a mountain of great Jewish tragedy, would transform itself into a symbol of Jewish triumph?
17. Israel would develop peace with nations formerly sworn to annihilate Israel?
18. Israel would be the world's strongest country's ally, partnering with the United States in hundreds of areas?
19. Jews would furiously debate what form of Hallel should be said on Israeli Independence Day?
20. There would be an Israeli Independence Day?
21. Israel would invent a pill with a camera, helping doctors see internal problems without conducting surgery?
22. Street signs would be written in Hebrew?
23. Israel would be the destination of over a million Soviet Jews, when they were freed?
24. Israel would discover and save Ethiopian Jews, long thought lost to the sands of time?

25. Israel could pull off a daring rescue 900 KM away from its land when its people were hijacked to Entebbe?
26. Israel would reunite its divided capital, Jerusalem, swearing to forever keep it united?
27. The Israeli people would boast some of the best and brightest noble prize winners?
28. A Jewish nation would develop farming technology that would save the world from famine?
29. The world would look to Israel for help when it suffered natural disasters and tragedy?
30. Israel would have one of the first female leaders in the world?
31. Israelis would invent the first instant messenger?
32. Jews would fight militarily as a nation to reclaim and then defend their land?
33. Israel would make the desert bloom in seemingly impossible ways?
34. Israel figured out how to grow dates from seeds that are 1400 years old?
35. More than half of Israel's land mass is desert, but it boasts some of the most efficient farms in the world?
36. An Israeli, Shari Arison, started Good Deeds Day, and led over 4,000,000 people in doing good deeds?
37. Israel would develop over 300 wineries, some of them producing world famous wines?
38. Denied at first, Israel would reclaim Judea and Samaria in a daring war in 1967?
39. Israel would draw over $10 billion in global investment, as business leaders around the world want to partner with Israel?
40. There would be more yeshivot and kollelim in Israel than ever were in Europe or Bavel?
41. Israel would create BioBee, a system that protects crops from bugs, without using harmful pesticides?

42. City streets in Israel would be called Ramban Street, Ibn Ezra Street and Jabotinsky Street?
43. The Israeli Baseball team (!) would make the Olympics?
44. Over three million Jews would move to Israel?
45. The Foreign Ministers of multiple Arab countries would meet, at a Conference, with an Israeli leader, in Israel?
46. American Presidents, the leaders of the free world, would come to Israel to visit?
47. Israel's Parliament, the Knesset, would have 120 seats because it's modeled after the Second Temple-era Anshei Knesset HaGedolah (the Great Assembly)?
48. Israel's weekly second free day would be Friday, and not Sunday, so that Jews can prepare for Shabbat?
49. When Jews are in trouble, whether under rubble in Surfside, Florida or fleeing war in Ukraine, it is the Israeli flag they see when they're first rescued?
50. During Passover in Israel, it's illegal for stores to sell chametz?
51. Israelis would create a social and community-based navigation system the whole would use, called Waze?
52. Israel is approaching ten million residents and the majority of the world's Jews live in Israel?
53. The noise of Sukkahs being built can be heard once again throughout Eretz Yisrael in the days following Yom Kippur?
54. In Israel, the Jewish calendar date can be used on contracts, legal documents and checks?
55. Israel has figured out how to make it rain from the air?
56. Jews would combine their cultures; Ashkenazim eat mufletas after Pesach and Morrocans eating herring on Shabbat morning?
57. Israel figured out how to make honey without bees?
58. Israel has more museums per capita than any other country in the world?

59. Foreigners, even in Arab lands, would learn Hebrew so they could talk to Jews in their own language?
60. Israel's economy is so strong it made a law that it can't accept economic aid from foreign countries?
61. An Israeli would discover quasicrystals?
62. An Israeli woman would be known as Wonder Woman all around the world?
63. The glue on Israel's postage stamps would be marked Kosher, and so would its army?
64. Israel wants Jewish babies so badly; it pays for the first two in vitro fertilization sessions?
65. Israeli cows produce more milk than cows anywhere else in the world?
66. Muslim Arabs would serve as soldiers and pilots in a Jewish army?
67. Some of the best restaurants in the world would be opened in Israel?
68. Luscious fruits and vegetables would once again grow in Israel, even before Moshiach arrived?
69. Israel would have its own airline and it would have minyanim and Torah reading mid-flight?
70. Jews from all four corners of the world would study Torah together in Israel and serve together in its army?
71. Zionism, once equated by the world to racism, would be a movement whose adherents loudly proclaim a massive success?
72. Israel grants religious freedom to all the world's religions?
73. Jewish festivals are Israeli national festivals, and dairy sales rise before Shavuat, donut sales rise before Hanukkah and mattress sales rise before Sukkot?
74. Israel is a diverse land, where you can ski and lay on the beach, all on the same day?
75. Israel, a tiny country with few natural resources, would last more than 75 years and become the thriving success story we're so proud to call home?

As I drive through Jerusalem each morning from my Torah study session with my son Moshe to my office, I frequently think of my great-grandparents, murdered in the gas chambers of Auschwitz. Could they have even dreamed of the life their descendants live? I don't think they could've even imagined it, and if they saw it, they wouldn't believe it. As we celebrate Israel, let's be grateful for the dream we live every single day!

CHAPTER
SIXTY-ONE

Israel Needs Strong Leaders

The art of survival politics is compromising for fear of losing popularity, while the art of leadership is taking bold stands without fear of popular approval. Israel needs to be led by strong leaders willing to take strong stands. Before the founding of the State, Menachem Begin bid his time as Irgun leader, second to the Haganah. He wouldn't compromise his principles of fighting the British in order to gain popularity by being within the Haganah circle of influence. He waited until the Haganah recognized Begin was correct, and only then did he partner with the Ben Gurion led Haganah.

After Israel's founding Begin ran for office, hoping to be Prime Minister. He spent thirty years as head of the opposition. It would've been easy for him to compromise on his principles to gain popularity and rise up the ranks to succeed Ben Gurion and other Prime Ministers. Begin refused to compromise and lost eight straight elections. He waited until the Israeli people would recognize the virtue of his positions and then he led Israel based on his convictions.

As Prime Minister, Begin took consistently unpopular positions because he felt they were correct. Knowing his base would be upset that he was pulling Israelis out of Yamit and other Sinai Desert settlements, Begin made the decision to do so because he felt they weren't part of Eretz Yisrael and peace with Egypt was more important than keeping the new towns. He risked losing his base to make a decision he felt was correct.

When Begin found out that Iraq was building a nuclear weapons program and that the only way he could stop it was by bombing the reactor, he made the decision to bomb it. He was risking failure, the death of Israel's treasured pilots and the inevitable wrath of the international community, including Israel's biggest supporter, America and its new President, Ronald Reagan. The bombing raid was successful, but Israel was condemned by the United Nations and President Reagan withheld American assistance to Israel.

Prime Minister Begin maintained the Golan Heights was part of Eretz Yisrael and Israel should control it eternally. He led the passage of a law in the Knesset that extended Israeli sovereignty over the Golan Heights. Begin knew the international community would rise against him and Israel. He was well aware that the world would never accept Israel's sovereignty over the Golan. Begin also knew extending Israel's sovereignty over the Golan was the correct decision for Israel, and he did it. The international community still refuses to recognize Begin's decision and it was only President Trump, thirty years later, who was the first American President to recognize Israel's sovereignty over the Golan.

Israel needs a Menachem Begin style leader who will take bold stands even at risk of popularity. What happened to the Israelis raised in a Begin led Israel? Where is the courage they saw as their political philosophies were being formed? In a now famous interchange, Menachem Begin told then-Senator Joe Biden he wouldn't be intimidated by Biden's threats and he was no "weak-kneed" Jew. Today's Knesset members and Israel's future leaders need Begin's courage to tell American Presidents and world leaders Israel's positions and take the bold steps necessary to ensure Israel's success.

CHAPTER
SIXTY-TWO

Zionism has made the world a better place

Zionism isn't just a Jewish movement – it is a movement that contributed to the benefit of the entire world. The identity of the earliest Zionists is a matter of debate; many consider Abraham following God's command to "Go from your birth land to a different land," to be the seminal moment of Zionism, others point to the first Zionist Conference in Basel, Switzerland to be the start of Zionism. Those moments focused on bringing the Jewish people to Eretz Yisrael, but the movement itself was never designed to only assist the Jewish people. Zionism raised the level of social rights, justice and morality in the world.

Thousands of years ago the Jewish people were charged with a vague command – to be a light unto the nations. This command inspired early Zionists to ensure they contributed not only to the Jewish people, but to the welfare of all people, Jewish, Arab, Muslim, Christian, that live in Israel. In its Declaration of Independence, Israel declared, "The State of Israel will foster the development of the country for the benefit of all its inhabitants; it will be based on freedom, justice and peace as envisaged by the prophets of Israel; it will ensure complete equality of social and political rights to all its inhabitants irrespective of religion, race or sex; it will guarantee freedom of religion, conscience, language, education and culture; it will safeguard the Holy Places of all religions."

For two thousand years an injustice existed in the world. The Jewish people were prevented from returning to their homeland, and it was the nations of the world that often violently prevented the Jewish people's return to their land. This injustice was a stain on the soul of the world. Knowing the Jewish people remained homeless while people after people, including

Americans, Europeans and Arabs, established their own nations on lands throughout the world, justice was not only delayed, but injustice was perpetrated. Zionism gave the world the opportunity to restore justice to the Middle East by returning the Jewish people to their historic homeland.

Worst of all was the immorality of the world in their treatment of the Jewish people. Like all other people, Jews have the right to self-determination. The withholding of Jewish self-determination was an act of immorality to the Jewish people. Israel's Declaration of Independence referenced the consequences of denying the Jewish people self-determination, "The catastrophe which recently befell the Jewish people - the massacre of millions of Jews in Europe - was another clear demonstration of the urgency of solving the problem of its homelessness by re-establishing in Eretz-Israel the Jewish State, which would open the gates of the homeland wide to every Jew and confer upon the Jewish people the status of a fully privileged member of the comity of nations." Zionism fought to add to the morality of the world.

Zionism is a movement that seeks peace. In the same Declaration of Independence, Israel followed Zionism's values when it extended its hand in peace to Arabs both in and outside of Israel, "In peace we appeal, - in the very midst of the onslaught launched against us now for months - to the Arab inhabitants of the State of Israel to preserve peace and participate in the upbuilding of the State on the basis of full and equal citizenship and due representation in all its provisional and permanent institutions. We extend our hand to all neighboring states and their peoples in an offer of peace and good neighborliness, and appeal to them to establish bonds of cooperation and mutual help with the sovereign Jewish people settled in its own land. The State of Israel is prepared to do its share in a common effort for the advancement of the entire Middle East." It was on the foundation of Zionism that the State of Israel was led to make peace with Egypt, Jordan, The UAE, Bahrain, The Sudan and Morocco.

The world has greatly benefited from Zionism. Zionism is a value-driven movement that strives to build the perfect society. Never satisfied with the status quo, Zionists are always looking to improve the world around them. Zionism stands for justice, morality and peace, all values the world could use more of right now. While Zionism focuses on advocating for the Jewish people to determine their own destiny in its historic homeland, its values have improved the world.

CHAPTER

SIXTY-THREE

Bringing God back to Zionism

As he stood at the podium in front of a joint session of the United States Congress, Israeli President Isaac Herzog was more aware than anyone in the room of the historic nature of his speech. The Herzogs are the closest thing Israel has to a royal family. President Herzog's grandfather, Rabbi Yitzhak HaLevi Herzog, was the chief Rabbi of the British Mandate of Palestine and of Israel after its independence in 1948. President Herzog's father, Chaim Herzog, was an Israeli general and Israel's sixth President. In 1987, President Chaim Herzog became the first Israeli President to speak to Congress. It is rare for foreign leaders, especially ceremonial leaders, to be invited to speak in front of Congress.

As President Herzog spoke, he was aware that he was speaking to Congress and the American people, but also to Israelis back home. The messages he was sending were meant just as much for Israelis as the Americans. Herzog brought up many contentious topics including Iran's nuclear weapons ambitions, Palestinian terrorism, and Israel's current judicial reform debates. He courageously addressed the anti-Israel members of Congress and drew a line where anti-Zionism crosses into antisemitism.

I was taken by another aspect of Herzog's speech. While I am not familiar with his personal life, President Herzog isn't known as a religiously observant man. Yet throughout his speech President Herzog kept referencing God's role in the destiny of the Jewish people, the State of Israel, and even the United States. His references to God might have seem natural the day before when Herzog visited the Ultra-Orthodox Yeshiva Gevoah in Lakewood, NJ, but in front of Congress they were surprising to those who pay attention to the balance between religion and state in Israel and America.

Herzog's first mention of God was when he quoted his grandfather telling American President Harry Truman that it was, "Divine Providence that destined President Truman to help bring about the rebirth of Israel, after two thousand years of exile." President Herzog then spoke of Israel's founding, and instead of focusing solely on Israel's founding members' efforts said, "When the State of Israel was established in 1948, the land which the Almighty promised to Abraham, to which Moses lead the Israelites, the land of the Bible, of milk and honey, evolved into an exquisite land of democracy." When President Herzog discussed peace in his speech he talked about praying to God, "We pray for the fulfillment of Isaiah's prophecy, 'Nation shall not lift up sword against nation, neither shall they learn war anymore.'"

President Herzog spoke about the U.S.-Israel relationship and put it in the context of both nations' commitment to God, "We are so very proud of the true friendship we have forged. It is rooted deep in our respective declarations of independence. In the American Declaration of Independence, the founders appealed to the "Supreme Judge of the World." In the Israeli Declaration of Independence, influenced by America's, our founders placed their trust in "the Rock of Israel." Of course, President Herzog ended his speech by praying, "God Bless the State of Israel! God Bless the United States of America!"

Herzog's frequent association of God and Israel is conspicuous because it comes within a growing backlash against religion in Israel by secular Israelis. There is a growing suspicion that religiously observant Israelis have plans of imposing Halacha (Jewish law) on general Israeli society. Secular Israeli suspicion of religious Israeli plans has been morphing into growing resentment against the religious community. Unfortunately, this resentment has caused some secular Israelis to try and erase the contributions religious Zionists have made to the State of Israel.

Secular Israeli efforts to erase the contributions of religious Zionists to Israel isn't as nefarious as the effort by some Israelis to erase God from Israeli history and society. Giving all credit for Israel's founding, its survival, and its success to the efforts of Israel's leaders, soldiers, and citizens while omitting Divine providence ignores the obvious – it's impossible for the Jewish people to have regained their land, sovereignty, and succeeded against all their opponents without Divine providence.

President Herzog, a man steeped in Jewish culture, history, and traditions, might not be personally observant like his Chief Rabbi grandfather, but his view of Israel can not be separated from God's providence. His understanding of the Jewish connection to the land of Israel is based on God's promise of the land to the Jewish people. Israel's destiny is tied to the vision of the prophets, especially the prophet Isaiah's vision of peace and Israel's continued success is based on "the Rock of Israel's" blessing.

Recognizing God's providential contribution to the success of the State of Israel doesn't require religious observance or a change in Israeli law. Choosing to be secular isn't a denial of God, it's an objection to state coerced observance. For secular Jews, there is nothing mutually exclusive between a secular lifestyle and maintaining that Israel's success has come with Divine providence. Israeli society is enriched by including God in Israeli national and personal life. It was for this reason Israel's mostly secular founders mentioned God in Israel's declaration of independence.

In citing God throughout his speech President Herzog was setting an example for how Israel should relate to its success. From its President and Prime Ministers to its children in school, Israelis must put God back into Zionism and national discourse. Mentioning God requires humility and distances a nation from the hubris that all too often brings down empires. When the Jewish people realize and keep aware that it's only with Divine Providence they can succeed, they'll be more open minded to different paths and not as obstinate about constructive criticism. It's time Israelis brought God back into the national dialogue and Zionism..

CHAPTER
SIXTY-FOUR

Balancing ideological and practical Zionism

When Theodore Herzl began peddling his idea of reestablishing a Jewish State in the land of Israel, many Jews agreed with his ideology but thought his idea was impractical. The Ottoman Empire was a Muslim Caliphate, Jews were spread throughout the world, and Palestine, as it was known then, was a desolate wasteland. Most of world Jewry opposed Herzl's Zionism as not only impractical, but dangerous ideological thinking that could cause others to look at their fellow Jewish citizens having suspicious dual loyalty.

The modern political movement of Zionism is based on an ideology that is more than 3,000 years old. Abraham was told by God to leave his birth land and travel to a land that God was to give him and his descendants. The Jewish people entered the land of Israel as one nation thousands of years ago after being emancipated from a 200-year long slavery. They ruled this land for over a thousand years under a theocratic monarchy of their own royal leaders. Exiled over two thousand years ago, the Jews spread throughout the world, but never forgot about Israel and their homeland. Although foreign Christian and then Arab conquerors exiled almost all remaining Jews from Israel, the Jews always looked to return to Israel.

For the duration of their 2,000-year exile, there was always a strong, albeit small, Jewish community in the land of Israel. These Jews ensured a continuous three thousand year long presence in Israel. Throughout their exile, most Jews never thought there was a chance of their return to Israel without a Messiah coming to bring them home. It wasn't until a few forward thinkers, with Theodore Herzl at their lead, began envisioning a modern Jewish state, that Jews believed a return to Israel was possible. These Jews based their movement on the ideology of their ancestors' view of Israel as their homeland.

Herzl's Zionism injected a healthy dose of practical strategizing to the ideology of the grand Jewish return to Israel. Using a combination of encouraging emigration to Palestine, establishing Jewish cities, farms, and towns in Palestine, and the start of a shadow government, the modern Zionists began to form the foundations of the Jewish state they hoped to create. As Zionist leaders traveled the world lobbying leaders of different countries for their support of a Jewish state in the land of Israel, the Zionists in Israel carried out the groundwork to make the land inhabitable for the millions of Jews who would migrate to Israel once a Jewish state was formed.

While Herzl was initially rejected by over 90% of world Jewry as being impractical and starting something dangerous, as time went on, global Jewry began to view Zionism as more pragmatic than ideological. The Zionist leaders doing the political work, and the on the ground Zionists doing the backbreaking labor demonstrated that a Jewish state was a real possibility. Slowly, world Jewry began to come around and support the creation of a Jewish state. After the Holocaust exposed the dangers of not having a Jewish state, over 90% of American Jewry became dues paying members of different Zionist organizations.

The Zionists that worked hard to form a Jewish state created a model for the future leaders of the State of Israel. They showed them that ideological thinking doesn't have to give way for practical strategy, and that practical strategy should always be grounded in the Jewish people's traditional ideology. Zionists never lost sight of Israel as the Jewish people's historic homeland, and never allowed ideology to interfere with their practical planning.

A keen example of the proper balance of ideology and pragmatism was Israel's founder's decision to accept the United Nations partition plan. The plan only gave the Jewish people a small portion of the land they claimed as their homeland. There were many reasons for the Zionist leadership to reject the partition plan, including a real worry over Jewish safety with so little land and the forfeiture of most of the Jewish homeland – including its heartland and capital, Jerusalem. Zionist leaders thought practically, and recognizing they weren't going to be able to meet their maximalist ideological goals, still accepted the first realistic opportunity for a Jewish state to be founded on the land of Israel in close to two-thousand years.

It is important for Zionists to remember Israel's founder's balance of ideology and practicality as they make decisions for Israel's future and set policy for the Jewish state. It is easy for leaders to avoid difficult decisions by standing behind a shield of ideology, but as Ben-Gurion and his colleagues showed, leadership requires practical compromises to ensure the State moves forward. Moving towards either extreme, by becoming too ideological or too practical, will ruin the balance that has led to Israel's success.

CHAPTER SIXTY-FIVE

American support for Israel is solid

"This threatens to end the support the American people give the State of Israel." This fear has been expressed countless times over Israel's existence. Israeli operations, incursions into Arab populations and policies vilified as oppressive, have all caused Zionists to worry whether Israel was risking a significant drop in the American people's traditional support of the Jewish state. Besides the loss of Presidential and Congressional support of Israel, Zionists constantly fear the loss of the American people's support of Israel. Current events in Israel are complex and require analysis and nuance to grasp. All too often Americans rely on superficial and biased reports to form opinions about Israel. This is an unfortunate reality and often leaves Americans asserting inaccurate criticism of Israel.

Zionists' worry about a drop in American popular support frequently comes along with rocket-based conflicts with Hamas, Palestinian Islamic Jihad, and terrorists in Gaza. Responding to Hamas rockets fired at Israel from Gaza, Israel bombs Hamas strongholds and rocket positions. The anti-Israel narrative quickly spreads on social media and spread to traditional news outlets and was even given voice a few months later, on the floor of Congress. Zionists the world over, but especially American Zionists, were worried if this widespread false narrative about Israel was the start of something more ominous, specifically a change in popular American perceptions of Israel. The fear of popular American support isn't truly about "Joe in the Street," but about elected officials sharing negative views about Israel and a drop in American military and diplomatic support for Israel. Israel enjoys over 4 billion dollars in annual military aid from America and the American veto at the United Nations Security Council. The fear is that support could disappear if American popular opinion about Israel shifts against Israel. American policy, the thought goes, is influenced by public opinion.

Young Americans between the ages of 18-30 cause particular concern to Zionists. Showing only 36% support for Israel in a recent Gallup poll, many Zionists are claiming they're losing the younger generation to Israel's opponents. Academic boycotts, BDS student resolutions, and "Apartheid Week" on campuses throughout America only cause more concern. Zionists spend millions of dollars on student advocacy programs designed to give Pro-Israel students the tools they'll need to counter anti-Israel narratives spread by professors, students, and activists on the college campus. Yet, few are asking the question if the fear of losing American popular support is really warranted or is this an industry talking point and nothing more?

Zionists don't have as much to fear as they've convinced themselves. Things aren't as bad as they seem, or better yet, to put it in truly neurotic Jewish terms, it's always been this bad. The fear Zionists express is that in polls measuring how favorable American public opinion is towards Israel, the favorables are low and assumably dropping. This is worrisome as long as the numbers are actually dropping and that American public opinion about Israel influences American government policy towards Israel. Looking at past polls, tracing numbers and policy demonstrates three things; poll numbers aren't low, poll numbers have been consistent from past polls until today and when poll numbers have fluctuated, they've had little to no influence on American government policy towards Israel.

In a 1997 Gallup poll 42% of Americans above fifty years old and older favored Israel, in 2018 that number had risen to 54%. In that same poll, 40% of Americans between the ages of 30 and 49 favored Israel, and in 2018 that number stayed stable at 34%. 32% of Americans between the ages of 18 and 29 favored Israel in 1997 and in 2018 that number had also stayed stable at 36%. While below 50% numbers might seem low, in American polling these numbers are actually healthy. Polls are greatly dependent on the question being asked. When asked if their sympathies lie with Israelis or Palestinians, in 2001, 51% of Americans said Israelis and 16% answered Palestinians. When that same question was asked in 2021 58% of Americans answered Israelis and 17% said Palestinians.

The biggest comfort to worrisome Zionists should be about American youth. Contrary to the widespread belief that American youth are moving away from Israel, two factors show the opposite. First, the poll numbers of favorables towards Israel have been consistent for the past twenty-five years. Second, if a low number of American youth favored Israel twenty-five years ago, we would expect to see Israel's favorable among middle aged Americans (the same youth, just older) drop twenty-five years later. It turns out, as American youth mature, they develop a more favorable impression of Israel and the U.S.-Israel relationship.

There are a few examples of times where poll numbers on favorables towards Israel have fluctuated and yet they've had little to no influence on American government policy. This is true whether the numbers have risen or dropped. During the first Persian Gulf War, favorables towards Israel was at its highest ever point and yet even though the United States had previously agreed to provide Israel $10 billion in loan guarantees to help Soviet Jews resettle in Israel, President Bush said that the United States would not issue those guarantees until Israeli prime minister Yitzhak Shamir agreed to halt its settlement building in the West Bank and Gaza and enter a peace conference with the Palestinians. Israel's favorable numbers were the lowest in May 2021 and yet Congress and the administration overwhelmingly supported Israel and its right to defend itself. It's clear public opinion plays little role in how the President and Congress decides to support Israel.

American government support for Israel has rarely been based on public opinion. The President and Congress have supported Israel based on American national security interests and shared values. It's in America's best interest to have a strong relationship with Israel. Israel's intelligence, research, and technological innovation all contribute to America's increased national security. In the dark neighborhood of oppressive Middle East regimes, Israel's values of freedom and equality shine bright. Americans see Israel as a country like their own and naturally gravitate towards it. When support for Israel dips in polls, Zionists should realize it's part of the usual cycle and has little effect on American government policy.

CHAPTER
SIXTY-SIX

What is the role of Diaspora Zionism?

The accusation that you can't be a Zionist outside of Israel is often levied at Diaspora Jewry, but does the accusation have merit or does it misunderstand Zionism at its core? Understandably, many Diaspora Zionists find the notion that their Zionism is lacking because they don't live in Israel to be offensive. Diaspora Zionists believe in Zionism's principles and love Israel and her people just as much as anyone living in Israel, why should their Zionism be discounted?

Some of the greatest Zionists never lived in Israel. After being Divinely punished with being prohibited from entering the land of Israel, Moses begged God to be allowed to enter Israel. God refused Moses's multiple requests and Moses never walked in Israel, let alone lived there. He wasn't the only Zionist to never live in Israel, Theodore Herzl, Leon Pinsker, Louis Brandeis and Max Nordau, the who's who of early Zionists, lived their entire lives outside of Israel. The argument that the founder of modern political Zionism, Theodore Herzl, had a faulty Zionism because he never lived in Israel is untenable.

The "negation of the Diaspora" (Shlilat Hagolah) in Zionist thought became popular among early Zionist thinkers. As Professor Shalom Ratzaby wrote, "This new perception of Exile was based on three premises: First, Exile has no purpose and serves no mission. Second, Exile is a negative phenomenon that causes suffering for the Jewish people, places the Jewish nation in existential peril, and distorts the nation's way of life thereby causing harm to the authentic creative potential of the nation and its individuals. Third, the existence of a Diaspora is untenable in the age of modern nationalism."

As Ze'ev Jabotinsky wrote, "Eliminate the Diaspora, or the Diaspora will surely eliminate you."

150 years after the first "negation of the Diaspora" arguments were forwarded, and 75 years after the creation of a Zionist state, it is evident that Diaspora Zionists have added to Jewish life and supported the State of Israel. Even early in the Zionist movement, as European and Palestinian Jews spread the idea of negating the Diaspora, American Jewry never considered it and saw a strong Diaspora Zionism as an asset to the Zionist movement and an eventual Jewish State.

Dr. Jonathan Sarna offered a novel idea for the place of Diaspora Jewry, "My own suggestion is that we not only abandon shlilat ha-golah, (negation of the Diaspora) but that we actually embrace, nurture, and encourage a spirit of friendly competition among the great contemporary centers of world Jewry so that each seeks to create a society where Jews and Judaism might flourish. Such competition, as we have seen, has long existed somewhat furtively, without official recognition or legitimation, between the Jewish communities of Israel and the United States."

When Jacob was to meet his brother Esav, the brother who had promised to murder Jacob in revenge for his having stolen Esav's blessings, he prepared in three ways. He sent Esav gifts to appease him, prayed to God for peace and split his camp in two just in case Esav came in violence. The same benefit is an argument made by Diaspora Zionists to explain why the Jewish people cannot all be located in one place. If God forbid the Jews of Israel faced tragedy, the Diaspora Zionists would be safe.

In any scientific experiment in a laboratory, the introduction of a new variable greatly changes the results of the experiment. The idea of negating the Diaspora was initiated before the creation of the State of Israel when anything was possible and every Zionist idea was being considered. The notion of not having a Diaspora community was just as possible as having one. Once the State of Israel was founded, it became the ultimate variable and result changer. 75 years later the Diaspora community hasn't been negated. The founding of the State ended all practical discussions of the negation of the Diaspora.

There are valid arguments on both sides of the Diaspora Zionism argument. There's no easy end to the debate. Zionism is about taking control of the Jewish people's destiny and not leaving it to global forces. As much as early Zionist leaders imagined a future Jewish state that would gather in all the Jewish exiles from all over the world, ending the Diaspora's existence, "Man plans and God laughs," and the Diaspora is still strong. The future is an open book whose pages aren't written yet. It'll be up to the Jewish people to determine where our people will find themselves and the role of the Jewish Diaspora.

CHAPTER
SIXTY-SEVEN

Investor vs. Stakeholder Zionism

It has become in vogue for some Israelis, and especially some people who moved to Israel, to look down upon Jews who live in the Diaspora as lesser Zionists. They criticize their Zionism as less serious and lacking in the commitment of those who live in Israel. They reason that Zionism was a movement focused on creating a Jewish State populated by the Jewish people. A Zionist who only partially buys into the vision by supporting Zionism but not actually heeding the call to move to Israel themselves, must be a minor Zionist. If they were serious about their Zionism, they'd fully "buy-in" and move to Israel. Noting differences between people doesn't make one greater than the other. There is a significant difference between Israel based Zionism and Diaspora based Zionism. Each type of Zionism has its own advantages and disadvantages. It is important to note the differences so that Zionism in all its forms can be better understood.

From its very inception, Zionism was a Diaspora based movement. Whether one maintains Abraham, Moses or Herzl were the first Zionists, each of them were outside the land of Israel when they began their quest to move and establish their people in the land of Israel. Although he ended up in Israel, Abraham began his life outside of the land of Israel (then called Canaan) when God told Abraham to leave his homeland and travel to Israel. Moses never got to see the land of Israel. He brought the Jewish people all the way to the Jordan River and passed away before bringing the Jewish people into the land of Israel. Herzl also passed away outside the land of Israel before seeing the creation of the Jewish State. It would be more than thirty years after its founding before an Israeli-born citizen would become

Prime Minister of Israel. The passion to create a Jewish state was born outside of Israel.

Zionists inside of Israel can be considered stakeholders in the Jewish State. They haven't only invested in the Jewish State, but they've staked their lives on the State. They've moved to the State, raised their families in the State, and declared their futures depend on the success of the State of Israel. The decisions Israel makes, the policies it implements and the direction it follows will have a direct impact on the Jews in Israel. The reality of Zionism and Israel having an immediate and direct effect on a person's life makes the issues more impactful than issues that are of importance, but do not affect, a person's future.

Zionists outside of Israel can be considered investors in the State of Israel. An investor cares deeply about their investment. They sink their efforts, resources, and concerns into their investment. If their investment is big enough, they'll check on it multiple times a day, and continue investing more of themselves and their assets into it. They'll lose sleep when their investment is at risk and celebrate when it succeeds. Their happiness and well being is greatly dependent on their investment. Diaspora Zionists sink their lives into Israel and put forth effort day and night to ensure Israel not only survives but thrives.

Diaspora Zionists are also able to call together means not available to Israeli citizens for the benefit of the Jewish State. American Zionists can take advantage of their American citizenship to show fellow Americans, especially elected decision makers, the importance of Israel to American national interests. Hearing from fellow Americans, specifically constituents, about the importance of the U.S.-Israel relationship sounds different than when hearing it from an Israeli. Diaspora Zionists can harness resources not available to Israelis to help the State of Israel.

There are countless examples, starting in the decades before the State of Israel was founded, to the founding of the State, to wars the Jewish people faced, to the continued tourism and a successful economy that can be directly traced to the help and efforts of the Jewish Diaspora. Whether it was Eddie Jacobson convincing President Truman to support the State of Israel against his staff's advice, Secretary Kissinger talking to President Nixon about resupplying Israel in the middle of the Yom Kippur War, or the inspiring daily efforts of AIPAC members and staff to strengthen the U.S.-Israel relationship, the stakeholders of Diaspora Zionism have made significant contributions to the success of the Jewish State.

What are the differences between Zionist investors and stakeholders? As emphasized above, there is a difference in the effects on the Zionists. While Diaspora Zionists care deeply about the events, decisions, and policies of the Israeli government, unlike Israeli Zionists, they aren't directly affected by those decisions. When Israelis advocate for their Knesset members and military to take a specific approach, they have an additional worry that their Diaspora Zionist partners don't share – they need to worry about how their lives and the lives of their families will be changed.

There is no need to explore which of these two kinds of Zionists are "more" Zionist than the other. There is no scale which measures higher or lower Zionism. The important lesson to be taken from the differences between Israeli and Diaspora Zionism is to note the contributions of both sides to the success of Zionism and the future of the State of Israel. Each side must appreciate the roles of the other and be grateful for them. Without stakeholders in the State of Israel putting forth the effort to ensure the success of the Jewish state, Diaspora Jewry wouldn't be able to invest in the future of the State of Israel. Without the contributions and efforts of the Diaspora investors, ensuring a successful Israel would be much more challenging for Israeli stakeholders. While Israeli Zionists eagerly await the "Aliyah" of their Diaspora brothers and sisters, they wait patiently, knowing that they are working hard to ensure Israel's success.

CHAPTER
SIXTY-EIGHT

Is Diaspora Zionism necessary?

It was one of his most inspiring speeches in Israeli history and it was delivered to Mapei party youth. Future Israeli Prime Minister David Ben Gurion, less than five feet tall, spoke toweringly about Jews in exile and the need to gather in their own homeland. "Exile is one with utter dependence - in material things, in politics and culture, in ethics and intellect, and they must be dependent who are an alien minority, who have no Homeland and are separated from their origins, from the soil and labor, from economic creativity. So we must become the captains of our fortunes, we must become independent - not only in politics and economy but in spirit, feeling and will."Ben Gurion was following a trend of thought called, shlilat ha'golah, the negation of the Diaspora.

In today's Israel, feelings are divided towards the Diaspora. Many Israelis appreciate the support from Diaspora Jewry. Israelis recognize the love, dedication and feelings of commitment Diaspora Jewry have towards Israel. Long distance relationships are never easy, and Israelis are often surprised by the strong feelings Diaspora Jewry has towards Israel. On the other hand, many Israelis are perplexed by Diaspora Jews who identify as Zionists. From their perspective, a Zionist who believes in the State of Israel lives in the State of Israel. It is difficult for them to understand how a Zionist would choose to live outside of Israel. It's not that these Israelis aren't appreciative of the support they receive, they just don't understand their Diaspora siblings.

At the founding of the State of Israel, the fledgling nation was struggling economically, socially, and challenged by a myriad of security threats. Israel needed the help from wherever it could secure it. Diaspora Jewry answered

Israel's call for help, sending it much needed funds. As Israel matured, it developed into its own, becoming mostly self-sustained. It overcame its security challenges by defeating its enemies on the battlefield. It met its social challenges by creating a quick melting pot that gathered global Jewry together into one cohesive nation. As a start-up nation, Israel's hi-tech sector brought economic prosperity to the only Jewish state. With a modern and successful Jewish State that is almost completely self-sufficient, is there still a necessity for a Diaspora for the Jewish people?

Although many have asked the same question about the necessity for a Diaspora for the Jewish people, and some Israelis question the Zionism of their Diaspora brethren, there are still great benefits Diaspora Jewry provides to the Jewish people. The support the Diaspora Jewish community lends to Israel is unmatched. While it is true that Israel's survival is no longer dependent on that support, it is still beneficial to the Jewish people. The benefit of a strong Diaspora extends past the financial support it provides Israel and its institutions. Diaspora Jewry advocates for diplomatic support for Israel among the international community. Diaspora Pro-Israel organizations like AIPAC and the Conference of Presidents of Major American Jewish Organizations ensure the support for support of the local elected leadership.

The baseless assumption many make about the third commonwealth of the Jewish people is that it is guaranteed to last forever. Just as the first two commonwealths were destroyed, so too the third can be destroyed as well. If Israel's enemies were able to annihilate the Jewish state, the only thing saving the Jewish people would be a robust Diaspora. It would be foolish for the Jewish people to put all of their eggs in one basket. In a worst-case scenario, a strong Jewish Diaspora could be the salvation of the Jewish people.

There are valid arguments on both sides of the question of the necessity of a Jewish community in the Diaspora for the Jewish people. It isn't reasonable for any one side of the debate to confidently claim they're correct to the exclusion of the other side of the debate. One thing can be stated about the debate - It will not be up to the Jewish community in Israel to decide if a Diaspora Jewish community is necessary. Only Diaspora Jewry will determine whether they are a necessity for the Jewish people.

CHAPTER
SIXTY-NINE

Zionists, pro-Israelis are honest about what they want, just listen

In his book Power, Faith and Fantasy – America in the Middle East from 1776 to the Present, historian, scholar and statesman Dr. Michael Oren wrote of the long history of Zionism in America. His thesis is that the American desire to restore the Jewish people to their homeland predates Herzl's modern Zionist political movement by a century. Today's strong American Zionist community is a manifestation of the long American tradition of Zionism.

Folklore tells of two questions politically minded American Jews asked each other to measure their motivation to help Israel: First, do you believe in a strong state of Israel and second, should America support it? As the tale goes, if your answer to these questions is yes, then getting involved with pro-Israel political activism is for you. While many people get distracted by the petty partisanship of today's politics in both Israel and America, it behooves the pro-Israel community to remember that we can't lose sight of the fact that there's only one Israel.

The American pro-Israel community is learning that supporting Israel in the 21st Century looks different than it ever has in their lifetimes. America is Israel's most important ally and solid supporter. America experiences major transitions of power: new speakers and party leaders. This change in leadership can present challenges to the traditional support Israel has enjoyed from America. Thanks to the American pro-Israel community, Israel has a strong relationship with both parties and can ensure support for Israel remains strong and bipartisan.

There is a six-decade-long tradition of strong bipartisan Zionist activism in America, especially its elected leaders. That relationship is robust, but it is beginning to be put at risk. For the first time, Israel and America are watching as voices without strong support for Zionism get louder, gain support through social media, and run for Congress at an increasing rate. The American pro-Israel community cannot sit by and watch this group gain a foothold in Congress and adversely affect America's long history of Zionism.

Even a small group of representatives can upend the entire Congress. This isn't the first time a small group has been able to stop the majority of representatives from passing bills. In recent years America and Israel watched as a small group held up Iron Dome funding and then as a Senator did the same.

It's not hard to imagine a small group of representatives who oppose Zionism stopping the significant majority of those who vote for American security aid for Israel. It's not tenable for Israel or the benefits America receives from the relationship. In an America that is more concerned with internal affairs and a Congress where 75% of its members weren't in office just 12 years ago, ensuring Congress's long-standing support of Israel and Zionism is harder than it has ever been.

The greatest concern facing Zionists and the pro-Israel community today is Iran's race to develop a nuclear weapon and its terror proxies, Hezbollah and Hamas. These nefarious enemies of Israel don't care about whether Israel's prime minister is Benjamin Netanyahu or Yair Lapid and neither should those who support Israel. Zionism and Israel must survive past the politics of the day and constantly remind us that Israel is our home and that we must commit to protecting it. With an Iran that is aligning itself with Russia, peace has to come through strength. The American and Israeli partnership ensures the strength necessary to stop Iran's plans.

The Pro-Israel community can't take anything for granted. The American Zionist community has to be positioned to fight for what they believe and that means embracing those we may not agree with on all issues, as long as they will support Israel. It all returns to keeping your eye on the prize and driving American policy to be supportive of a strong US-Israel relationship.

In a changing world, Zionists can't insist on sticking to the same model and assume it will continue to work just because it was effective in the past. There are new strategies being employed by the American pro-Israel community. These new strategies were once eschewed by the pro-Israel establishment but are now being embraced in light of the new atmosphere. At the same time, the relationship-building and activism of the past are still important. Relationship building as a vehicle for explaining Zionism's values has always been key to the movement's success.

Twenty years ago, I was drawn to AIPAC by its message that any American Zionist can turn their passion into concrete support of Israel. Jew, Gentile, wealthy or poor, it made no difference as long as they were willing to put the time and effort into forming relationships with their elected officials and explaining Zionism to them. I am not a man of means but this opportunity to help Israel in a concrete way spoke to me.

I could call a member of Congress's office, make an appointment with a staffer, speak to them about Zionism and Israel, and by following up (lobbying once is an oxymoron), I could have an influence on that member of Congress's position on Israel. The more information I shared, the more grateful the staffer was for keeping them informed. At first, I made an appointment with members of the congressional staff and eventually, I had meetings with members of Congress, the Senate and even White House staff.

Of course, I donated to pro-Israel organizations, like AIPAC, and to political campaigns. I didn't have the means to give as other people gave but I gave what I could afford and to the elected officials I felt it was important to support because I appreciated their pro-Israel positions. As things change in the world and the pro-Israel community faces challenges they've never faced before, I commit to continue to give of myself, my resources and most of all, my energy. It's an entirely new world out there in the pro-Israel sphere. Helping Israel out concretely requires giving of ourselves and our resources more than ever. I consider it my responsibility and I hope you do, too. But never forget, at the foundation of all support of Israel is the decision to get involved and form the relationships that matter.

Zionism's opponents love beating up Zionists by accusing them of all sorts of evil activities and motives. Zionists believe that the Jewish people have the right to self-determination in their historic homeland, Israel. There is nothing nefarious about their objectives. Seventy-five years after the establishment of Israel, Zionists and the pro-Israel community have taken on the responsibility to make sure Israel is strong and secure. Zionists and the pro-Israel community have always been honest about what they are, the world just has to listen.

CHAPTER
SEVENTY

Things Americans say about Israelis

I was with my students in a Congressperson's office on Capitol Hill waiting for the Representative to return from a committee hearing and the Congressperson's chief of staff was addressing our group until her boss returned. Trying to connect to our group and show a familiarity with Israel, the chief of staff said, "It's understandable that during this latest wave of terror, Israelis are scared." I normally never talk in these meetings; my role is an educator and I want to empower my students to advocate, not me. I interrupted our speaker (politely) and said, "Israelis feel safe." I then stood back and allowed the chief of staff to continue. The next day I wrote to her and reiterated that Israelis aren't living in fear.

Americans care about Israel and their care manifests itself with many opinions about Israel. While some Israelis find American opinions about Israel annoying and intrusive, there are Israelis that understand American opinions as a sign of affection towards Israel and her people. Americans see themselves as semi-Israelis, with their destiny tied to Israel. Many Israelis appreciate American concern for Israel and look forward to hearing their perspective.

The assumption many in America have that Israelis don't feel safe stems from believing the media reports seen on television, the internet and social media. Videos of terror attacks posted everyday make it seem that Israelis face terror attacks everywhere and every day. After watching this constant stream of terror, the assumption that constant terror brings constant fear is understandable but incorrect. Israelis have been through many terror waves before. Israelis have survived wars, rockets and intifadas, and are prepared for our enemies attacking us and don't cower in fear from their attacks. Israel is a safe place. Terror attacks in Israel make headlines around the world but don't reflect the reality of life in Israel. Israelis are prepared to stop terror and keep themselves safe. The Israeli ability to stay aware keeps them from being scared.

I was visiting my American bank and a stranger asked me if I lived in the neighborhood. I told him that I did a while ago but had moved to Israel over seven years ago. He said, "You must love to fight, Israelis are always fighting." Not one to miss a teaching moment, I told him his comment was a generalization about Jews, was false, and was antisemitic. I didn't have time to sit and explain that Israel has repeatedly reached out in peace to both its Arab neighbors and the Palestinian Arabs within Israel. I would've loved to share with him the multiple peace plans Israel has suggested, and that Israel only goes to war when attacked or when it's about to be attacked. The Israeli army isn't called an army, it's called the Israel Defense Force, because their only task is to defend Israel, it has no ambitions of capturing land. Israeli Jews pray for peace three times a day, reflecting their value of peace. Israelis place peace as a top national priority, they've signed six peace and normalization treaties with Arab countries and are looking to sign even more.

"So many Israelis visit America, you must love coming back here!" I'm grateful to the United States for providing me a place to grow up, and shelter to my family both before and after the Holocaust. I enjoy taking my students to Capitol Hill and the White House where we fulfill our civic duty by lobbying for the issues that concern us. I also enjoy the creature comforts of America; the Big Gulp at 7-11, the Amazon two-day delivery, and the customer service. Yet, with all the things I love about America, Israel is home, and nothing beats being at home. Israel isn't just home because it's where my family and I live, but because Eretz Yisrael is my ancestral homeland. I enjoy America and feel comfortable there; my trips make me feel like I'm walking back into my childhood, but Israel is my actual home and I pine for Israel when I'm away from it.

Americans, and especially American Jews, understand Israel more than anyone else on Earth - except Israelis. Americans and Israelis share the same values of life, liberty and the pursuit of happiness. Israelis, like Americans are entrepreneurial, place a premium on safety and security and lead family centered lives. They both have a Western mindset featuring similar morals and ethics. Americans and Israelis understand each other intuitively and employ those intuitions to assume things about each other.

As much as American Jews visit, read and follow Israel, they aren't experiencing the feelings of an Israeli who lives in Israel. Some Americans tend to draw many assumptions of life here in Israel. They make assumptions of Israeli reality, feelings and day to day life in Israel. Many of these are correct, but some are flat out wrong. The only solution to incorrect assumptions is to be in Israel in person frequently or permanently.

American Jews should feel assured that Israelis are prepared for all threats, they aren't scared of Palestinian terrorists, and they feel confident and safe. Israelis aren't spoiling for a fight with Palestinians, Arabs or Iranians. Israelis dream of peace and await its arrival every single day. We go on vacation to all four corners of the Earth. Yet, no matter how many Israelis leave Israel for vacations, post army, and business trips, Israelis always find their way home.

CHAPTER
SEVENTY-ONE

What is a Christian, Muslim, and Buddhist Zionist?

It was a typical sweltering warm July Wednesday in Israel. Cleared of most air-traffic, Ben Gurion Airport in Lod, Israel was still a hive of activity. The twelfth American presidential visit to Israel was set to begin mid-afternoon when American President Joe Biden would land on a direct Air Force One flight from Saudi Arabia. This was to be President Biden's tenth visit to Israel, but his first as President.

As Air Force One landed and taxied to its spot of honor at the top of the red carpet, Israelis eagerly anticipated President Biden's opening remarks. President Biden had always reserved a warm spot for Israel in his heart and in speeches over the past forty years he had spoken warmly of his love for Israel.

As he stepped off the plane and began his remarks, he didn't disappoint. "My first visit was, as you mentioned, as a young United States senator from Delaware in 1973, [was] just a few weeks before the Yom Kippur War. I had the privilege of spending time with Prime Minister Golda Meir. I'll never forget — I was sitting next to a gentleman on my right, one of her aides. His name was Rabin. I look back on it all now, and I realize that I had the great honor of living part of the great history of this great — and I did say and I say again, you need not be a Jew to be a Zionist."

Many Israelis were surprised at President Biden's self-identifying as a Zionist, although they shouldn't have been surprised because it wasn't the first time he had boasted of being a Zionist. There were Israelis who weren't as surprised as President Biden calling himself a Zionist, or an American President calling himself a Zionist, but were surprised by a non-Jew characterizing themselves as a Zionist. These Jews had always understood Zionism to be a Jewish movement.

Zionism is a four-thousand-year-old idea that stretches back to God's promise to Abraham that the land of Israel would be inherited by his descendants. 150 years ago, a modern political movement of Zionism began that aimed to realize the Jewish people's right to self-determination on their historic homeland, the land of Israel. Some early Zionists were motivated by a fear of rising antisemitism and the need for their own land to defend themselves. Other early Zionists were motivated by the right of the Jewish people to return to their homeland. Either motivation was Jew-centric and didn't seem to make room for non-Jews.

Non-Jews had been interested in seeing the Jewish people return to the land of Israel hundreds of years before Theodore Herzl started the modern political Zionism movement. From President Lincoln to a young Winston Churchill, non-Jews have supported the idea of Jews returning to their historic homeland. With non-Jewish support of Jewish objectives came Jewish suspicion! Why would outsiders, non-Jews who usually persecuted the Jewish people, suddenly want to support the Jewish people?

Conspiracy theories about the true motives of non-Jewish Zionists spread fear through the Jewish community. Accusations of nefarious motives from wanting to convert all Jews to its only when all the Jews move to Israel that their Messiah can come, are thrown at non-Jewish supporters of Zionism and Israel. While undoubtedly, some non-Jews have ulterior motives, many do not. Many Israelis challenge the reason to even question non-Jewish Zionist motives – after all, what difference does it make to a Zionist why a non-Jewish Zionist supports Israel and the Jewish people?

Our Sages taught an interesting lesson that relates to the topic of non-Jewish Zionists, "If a person tells you there is wisdom among the nations of the world, believe him." Zionism is a movement that aimed to achieve justice for the Jewish people. Having been denied their rights to their homeland for thousands of years, justice demanded the situation be corrected with the creation of a Jewish State in the land of Israel. Once the Jewish people founded a State, justice demanded it be protected from the enemies trying to end it. A non-Jew who ascribes to the inherent justice of the Zionist movement shouldn't be suspected but lauded.

CHAPTER
SEVENTY-TWO

Our teenagers take Israel for granted

As hard as I try there is one lesson I try teaching Jewish teenagers today that never seems to sink in – today's Jewish people live in incredible times. I try to explain what Jewish existence looked like over the past 2,000 years of exile and that today's Israel is a privilege and luxury in comparison to our past. I ask them to think about what life was like for a Jew who couldn't even consider visiting or moving to Israel. I juxtapose their life, in which a plane ticket is all they need to enter Israel, with their ancestors lives a mere one hundred years ago who couldn't come to Israel. I usually fail getting the teenagers I'm teaching to recognize the privilege they enjoy by having a State of Israel. Admittedly, it's challenging imagining a different reality than the one they currently live in. There is a State of Israel today, and therefore that's the only reality teenagers can imagine.

Over the past 2,000 years Jews have suffered through exile and desolation. Starting from the Romans two millennia ago through the Germans during the Holocaust Jews faced enemies and antisemites who tried to annihilate the Jewish people. Even when the goal wasn't annihilation, antisemites killed tens of thousands of Jews during the Crusades and then pogroms. The Holocaust brought an already concerned Jewish world into frantic worry. It became imperative that the Jewish people have their own state.

Fifty years before the Holocaust, early Zionists, led by Theodore Herzl, were worried about a mass violent antisemitic event that would decimate European Jewry. The early Zionists couldn't envision an event as horrific as the Holocaust, but they knew something terrible was destined for European Jewry. The early Zionists' first priority, and main motivation, was to establish a Jewish state as a place of refuge and safety for fleeing European Jews.

Early Zionists also aimed to create a Jewish state specifically in the land of Israel. They understood the Jewish people, like all peoples, had a right to their historic homeland, and to practice self-determination in their land. They intended to change the course of Jewish destiny. Cultural Zionists hoped to create a state where Jewish culture would flourish. Religious Zionists wanted to recreate the Torah study houses of thousands of years ago. Zionism had a rich and diverse set of goals as it worked towards the creation of a Jewish state.

A hundred and twenty-five years after the start of the modern political Zionist movement it can claim success. The Jewish people have established a state of their own that provides refuge for countless Jews in need. It has a military that is one of the best in the world and has proven itself capable of protecting Jews both at home and abroad. The modern State of Israel is a center of Jewish culture and religious studies. Every major Israeli city has a theatre playing Jewish works. There is more Torah studied in Israel on any given day than at any previous time in Jewish history – including at Mount Sinai. Israelis are also the fourth happiest people in the world.

The headline of the Jewish people's story in the 21st century is "Renaissance." A downtrodden people, the Jews post Holocaust were missing six million of their people, refugee survivors were stuck in displaced person or internment camps, unable to restart their lives. It would only be a few years before millions of Jews living in Arab lands would face their own wave of persecution and need a place of refuge. The turnaround the State of Israel brought to the Jewish people in all areas of their existence is remarkable. The Jewish people have experienced a renewal that is unprecedented.

Teaching a comparison between the Jewish past and its present state of success leads me to the question of whether it's better for our teenagers to know how privileged they are by being aware of their traumatic history or to live in the bliss of ignorance and take Israel for granted. Judaism places a premium on remembering and Jews study their past much more than they plan for their future. One can't help but wonder if Jewish teenagers would be better off without knowing all the trauma of their past. Maybe it is healthier to have Jewish children lead the people without the burdens of our dark past. This way they can simply enjoy the wonderful world provided to them.

A life without trauma always seems more advantageous and attractive.

Yet it is specifically the Jewish memory that motivates the Jewish people to create a better future for their nation. Knowing the alternative to success isn't mere failure, but the very real possibility of annihilation as been demonstrated by every preceding generation of Jews, puts the importance of the Jewish state into perspective for Jews. Although it's challenging teaching Jewish teenagers the privilege of their current lives, it's necessary so they keep working hard to preserve the Jewish State and its success.

CHAPTER
SEVENTY-THREE

18 facts about Israel every 18-year-old American needs to know

As high school seniors graduate this month, their attention turns to starting college in the Fall. Unfortunately, American Universities have turned into bastions of anti-Zionism and anti-Israel lectures and activism. As the Anti-Defamation League stated, "The campus anti-Israel movement frequently denigrates Zionism as inherently racist and disparages pro-Israel students, at times invoking antisemitic tropes." These 18 facts about Israel are designed not to give American Jewish students the tools to defeat the campus anti-Israel movement, but to know the truth about Israel to identify the lies of those who slander Israel.

1. Israel isn't Dangerous

If all your knowledge of Israel came from the media, you'd assume Israel has been a war zone for all its 75 years. The media covers the most sensationalist stories, including the violent ones. While there is little violence in Israel, and statistically much more in any major American city, the perception is that Israel is a violent place. Israel is a calm and peaceful place – and a pleasure to visit!

2. Understanding Israel Requires an Open Mind, Intellectual Honesty, and Nuance

Today's partisan world prefers to box all subjects into black and white, and no greys – or any other colors! The world isn't that simple, it's very complex, and like the world, Israel is complex. To understand Israel in all its complexity, a person must have an open mind to accept facts and narratives they might never have heard before. They also need to be intellectually honest so they can be open to arguments they haven't heard before and recognize there are two sides to every story – which requires nuance.

3. You Should Visit Israel on Birthright, but Israel can't be Fully Understood on a 10 Day Tour

Soon you'll be eligible to visit Israel on Birthright, an almost completely free trip to Israel. The trip will give you a front row seat to Israel (and it's a ton of fun). Israel can not be understood without seeing it – studying Israel from 6,000 miles away isn't enough. At the same time it's important to recognize that ten days on a fun trip isn't enough to fully understand Israel. The more time one spends in Israel, the more they'll come to understand it.

4. The Media Presents an Inaccurate Picture of Israel

There are many theories suggested why the media generally presents a negative image of Israel in its coverage – but one thing is almost universally agreed upon – Israel is portrayed with a bias against it by most of the world's media. Their biased coverage is generally delivered without proper context. Israeli policies and actions are presented in a negative shade without Israel's side of the story. To understand events in Israel, always ask, "What's the Israeli side of this story?"

5. The Jewish People are a Nation, not Just a Religion.

An attack many opponents of Israel like to use to delegitimize the State of Israel is stating that Jews are a religion, and religions don't deserve certain rights that nations deserve – like land and self-determination. For over 3,000 years the Jews were known as a nation and they have a right to their historic homeland, the land of Israel.

6. The Jewish People have the Strongest Claim to the Land of Israel

Recently, Jews have been accused of being colonial imposters with no right or connection to the land of Israel. Historical records, archeology, and international consensus all demonstrate that the Jews have a longer connection to the land of Israel – more than 3,000 years - than any other people around today. Arabs only immigrated to the land 1300 years ago.

7. The Jewish People have a Right to Self-Determination

For the close to 2,000 years the Jewish people were in the exile and were controlled by the governments of the lands they lived in. While they had the right to exercise self-determination, no one would allow the Jews to determine their own destiny. Zionism was a movement that advocated the Jews determining their own future and the State of Israel is where they exercise that right today.

8. Jews have been in Israel continuously for 3000 years

Jews are not strangers to the land of Israel. While a modern political movement, Zionism, to reestablish a Jewish state is only 175 years old, Jews have lived in Israel continuously for 3,000 years. When millions of Jews returned to Israel over the past 100 years, they weren't moving to a new location, they were rejoining a three-millennium old Jewish community.

9. Jerusalem has been the Capital of the Jewish People for Thousands of Years

Almost 3,000 years ago, King David, the King of the Jewish people, inaugurated the city of Jerusalem as the capital city of the Jewish people. After the Jewish nation was defeated and exiled they spent thousands of years praying to return to Jerusalem and a reestablishing their capital. No other people had ever established Jerusalem as their capital. In 1948, the Jewish people did just that, and in 1967, they united the entire city under Jewish rule.

10. Anti-Zionism is Usually a Cover for Antisemitism

Zionism stands for the rights of the Jewish people to self-determination in their historic homeland, the land of Israel. Denying the peoplehood of the Jewish people, claiming they, unlike all others nations, don't deserve self-determination, and that they have no connection or rights to their own homeland, is nothing short of antisemitism. Anti-Zionism isn't a political position, it's hate.

11. Treating Israel with a Double Standard is Antisemitic

We've all seen the accusations made against Israeli policies. Most aren't reflective of the truth, many are made out of context, and even more hold Israel to a standard no other country is held up to when it comes to international standards. Judging Israel with a double standard is antisemitic and reflects a dishonest approach to analyzing events in Israel.

12. Not All Criticism of Israel is False, but Not All Criticism of Israel is True.

Criticizing Israel isn't absolutely antisemitic or slanderous, there are legitimate reasons to criticize Israeli policies. Yet many of the most frequent criticisms of Israel are made by Israel's enemies and aren't reflective of true Israeli policy.

13. Israeli Politicians and Leaders aren't All Angels, but they also aren't All Devils

Israel's critics love characterizing Israeli elected leaders as evil people who deserve to be arrested and jailed for crimes. Israeli politicians are like all other politicians – not the world's best actors, but they're nowhere near the evil Israel's enemies portray them to the world.

14. Israelis aren't Responsible for Palestinian Mistakes and Miscalculations

There are great inequalities between Israelis and Palestinians. These inequalities are not unjust inequalities that are Israel's obligation to correct. They are inequalities caused by the Palestinians' poor personal and political choices, including terrorism, rejecting peace deals, and intransigence.

15. Jews Treat Palestinians Well

The narrative of Israeli oppression is nothing but a fable. When the layers of lies are peeled away even a cursory survey of Palestinian Arab life under Israeli rule reveals a life with human rights, opportunity and fair treatment. Claims of a life of hardship are contradicted by the plethora of Arab owned late model luxury cars and mansions spread throughout Judea and Samaria. Jobs in Israel and joint industrial zones are available to Arabs and the health care and education available to Palestinian Arabs is among the highest rated in the Middle East.

16. It's Only Under Israeli Rule that Religious Sites are Open to all World Religions

When the land of Israel was under the rule of Christian Crusaders, Muslims, Ottomans, the British and the Jordanians, the religious sites were closed to one or two of the world's religions. It was only in 1948 and then again in 1967 when all religious sites in Israel came under Israeli rule that all people and religions were given the freedom to visit all religious sites in Israel.

17. The U.S.-Israel Relationship is a Partnership

The United States provides Israel with no less than four billion dollars a year in military aid. Many misunderstand this aid as charity that America gives its needy ally, Israel. American military aid to Israel isn't charity, it's an investment in the partnership that provides America with the highest intelligence, research, and technology available.

18. While many Consider Israeli Rule of the West Bank Illegal, America and Israel do not.

The international community, as reflected in repeated United Nations resolutions, considers Israeli rule of Judea and Samaria, the region the world calls the West Bank, inconsistent with international law, Israel and the United States do not agree. As former American Secretary of State Mike Pompeo said, "The establishment of Israeli civilian settlements in the West Bank is not per se inconsistent with international law."

CHAPTER

SEVENTY-FOUR

The Mitzvah of Living in Israel

Introduction.

The topic of living in Eretz Yisrael has taken center stage in the Jewish world over the past century. I would venture to say that there is hardly a more debated halachic topic in contemporary times. Due to this popularity, the topic of living in Eretz Yisrael has become emotionally charged. My goal in this essay is to "take a step back" and examine the role of Eretz Yisrael and the obligation to live there in halacha from a strictly rational standpoint.

The mitzvah to live in Israel is mentioned in a posuk in the Torah, but it doesn't fit clearly into any of the four categories of halachic obligations normally found in analysis of Jewish law. In this essay I will focus on the opinions of the Ramban and the Rambam on the mitzvah of living in Israel. Our goal is not to reach a practical conclusion – although it will be obvious as to what the Torah demands – but to understand how these two scholars understood living in the land of Israel.

Part I. The Four Categories of Jewish Law

All mitzvot can be divided into four categories: One of the 613 mitzvot, a law from the Torah (din de'oraita), a Rabbinic law (din d'rabanan), or a philosophical kiyum – a fulfillment of a goal of the Torah that was never legally legislated. These categories have subcategories as well.

Categorization has practical ramifications in Halacha. For example, one of the 613 mitzvot is to recite the shema twice a day, while a din de'oraita is to read the three parshiot of the shema. A Rabbinic law is to recite the blessings of shema when reciting shema. King David instructed us to "serve Hashem in happiness." While observing the mitzvot in happiness is an extremely important idea, it is not an obligation within Jewish law. Rather, it is a fulfillment of a philosophical idea. Thus one who read all three paragraphs of the shema and recited the blessings surrounding the shema, while feeling depressed would have fulfilled his Biblical and Rabbinic obligation, but would be lacking philosophically. The mitzvah of living in Israel doesn't naturally fit in this framework.

Part II. The Position of the Ramban

Hashem wrote, "You shall possess the land and you shall settle in it, for to you have I given the land to possess it."[1] Commenting on this pasuk, the Ramban wrote, "In my opinion, this verse commands one of the 613 mitzvot. We are commanded to settle and dwell in the land for it was given to the Jewish people, and we cannot reject the portion of Hashem. If it would ever occur to the Jewish people to capture the land of Shinar or the land of Ashur, or any land like it, and to settle there, one would be negating this mitzvah."

In this comment the Ramban stated his well-known opinion that one of the 613 mitzvot is to live in Eretz Yisrael. In truth there are two obligations stated by the Ramban, the national obligation to settle the land and the obligation for the individual to reside in the land. In this essay we will examine only the latter obligation.[2] The obligation to reside in the land is called dirat Eretz Yisrael.

The Ramban wrote that as fulfillment of this mitzvah, we cannot reject the land -for it was given to us by Hashem and is God's portion. In order to understand the position of the Ramban, we must explain the philosophical idea of the land being called "God's portion."

There is a teaching in the Talmud,[3] "Hashem irrigates Eretz Yisrael

---

1 *Bamidbar* 33:53

2 Evidence of there being two *dinim* here is clear from many different sources. The *posuk* itself "*V'Horashtem*" and "*V'Yishavtem*" reflecting both *dinim*. In addition in his proofs that *Dirat Ha'aretz* is a *mitzvah*, the Ramban leaves out what would seem to be the perfect proof, the *halacha* (Bava Kama 80b) that a Jew can instruct a non-Jew to sign his name on a contract on *Shabbos* – normally a Rabbinic prohibition – in order to purchase a home in *Eretz Yisrael*. The reason given is for "The settling of *Eretz Yisrael*." The *gemara* and the *poskim* do not write that the Rabbis allowed the instruction to the non-Jew in order to for the individual's settling himself in the land. It would thus seem that there are in fact two *dinim* to this *mitzvah*.

3 *Taanis* 10a

Himself, and the rest of the world by a representative." In his commentary on the homiletic portions of the Talmud, the Rashba[4] says, "Eretz [Yisrael] is called God's treasure, and God's "will" is within it. Eretz Yisrael, the chosen land, was given to Bnei Yisrael, the chosen people. Hashem did not give the land over to mazal or a sar of the nations, for Hashem has put His portion in us. The events in Eretz Yisrael are not directed by an angel or representative; all of the events occurring in Eretz Yisrael are always under the providence of Hashem Himself."

Thus, according to the Rashba the uniqueness of the land is that it is Hashem's chosen land. We cannot, in our limited knowledge[5], possibly understand why Hashem chose this land over all other lands, but we can explain the quality that separates the land of Israel from other lands. God relates to the land through specific providence, rather than general providence as He does in other lands. General providence is what we call nature, i.e. the regular set patterns under which the world operates. While created by Hashem, he does not dictate every individual act of nature. When specific Divine Providence operates, the subject of this providence is related to directly by Hashem.

All mitzvot help perfect a person either through improving one's character or adding to one's understanding of God. What benefit does living in Eretz Yisrael provide? According to the Rashba's explanation of the uniqueness of the land, how are we perfected by living in a place which is subject to Hashem's specific providence?

There's an analogy that can explain it well. There are two ways to gain understanding and insight into an idea or a topic. A topic can be studied or it can be experienced. A blind and a seeing person can both examine the nature and components of color. But the seeing person will have an advantage over the blind person in that they have experienced color.

Many wise philosophers, indeed some of Judaism's greatest scholars, have examined the area of Divine Providence. Many books and articles have been written explaining this idea. Yet one who has experienced specific Divine Providence has a much deeper, more profound, understanding than

4 *Peirushi Haggados*, ibid.

5 I am unsure if this knowledge is possible for a human to attain, but if it is, only a tremendous *chacham* could hope to understand why it is that this land was chosen.

even the scholar who has devoted much time to its study. This is the benefit that Eretz Yisrael provides. Eretz Yisrael allows a person to experience Divine Providence.

The Ramban supported his argument that living in Eretz Yisrael is one of the 613 mitzvot. First, the Talmud includes numerous glowing praises of the land that imply that there is an obligation to live in Israel.[6] The Ramban's other three proofs are inferences from various halachot. The first halacha Ramban quoted is the prohibition of leaving Eretz Yisrael. The remaining two are halachot that apply in the event where one spouse would like to move to Eretz Yisrael and the other does not. If the dispute results in divorce, the financial advantage is given to the spouse wishing to go to Eretz Yisrael. Specifically, where a husband wants to move to Eretz Yisrael, but the wife does not, they can divorce, but the wife loses her ketubah. In contrast if the wife would like to move to Eretz Yisrael and the husband would like to stay in chutz la'aretz, the wife receives her ketubah if they divorce.

The rationale of the Ramban requires explaining. The Ramban argues that if there were no mitzvah of living in Eretz Yisrael, then these halachot would not be obligatory. There is a difference between one of the 613 mitzvot and a din de'oraita. How can the two be differentiated? The Ramban provided us with an explanation. All halachot must be generated by one of the 613 mitzvot. It is impossible for a halacha to stand on its own. When these three halachot are stated, there must be a mitzvah that generates these halachot. To the Ramban, that mitzvah is living in Eretz Yisrael.

Part III. The Position of the Rambam

Many scholars have attempted to define the Rambam's position on the mitzvah of living in Eretz Yisrael. The Rambam's position on this mitzvah is a source of much debate. In this section of the essay I will offer my humble opinion on the Rambam's position.

It is crucial to note the Ramban's position was the Rambam did not maintain living in Israel was a mitzvah. Ramban criticized the Rambam for omitting the mitzvah of living in Israel from the Rambam's list of the 613 mitzvos. Based on the Ramban's critique of the Rambam and the Rambam's own words, the Rambam does not hold that living in Eretz Yisrael is one

6 K'subos 110a

of the 613 mitzvot. A simple reading of the Sefer Hamitzvot will show that Rambam did not include it in his list of the 613 mitzvot.

The Rambam stated[7] that it is permitted to live anywhere in the world except for Egypt. The language the Rambam uses for the allowance to live anywhere is "mutar" (permissible). In the Rambam's Mishneh Torah the word mutar is used to connote an ab initio framework[8], something which is more than just not prohibited, but indeed is permitted, as acceptable as any other alternative. The Rambam's codification of the halacha that a person can live anywhere is not coming to state that if one does not live in Eretz Yisrael he can live anywhere, rather a person can choose where he wants to live with Eretz Yisrael as one option among many. It would be contradictory for the Rambam to write that a person can live anywhere they want, but is obligated to live in Eretz Yisrael.

The Rambam quoted the Talmud's teaching[9], "A person should always live in Eretz Yisrael." It is this quote that has caused much confusion about the Rambam's position. It is clear from the Rambam's use of the quote that the Rambam understood that one *should* live in Eretz Yisrael, but what does the word "should" connote? In which of the four categories does the Rambam place living in Eretz Yisrael?

When quoting the directive to live in Eretz Yisrael, the Rambam uses the word "l'olam." Throughout the Mishneh Torah the Rambam used the word "l'olam" as a directive in only two ways. It is used to indicate either an everlasting prohibition or a philosophical kiyum (benefit). It is never used to imply an obligatory mitzvah. As an example of the former, the Rambam wrote, "One can never (l'olam) sell a Torah scroll, except under two circumstances."[10] The word l'olam is used to connote the prohibition's everlasting nature. An example of its use to indicate a philosophical kiyum is in Hilchot Deiot where the Rambam wrote[11] "One should always (l'olam) teach his students in a concise manner." A teacher who delivers a long-winded lecture hasn't violated a mitzvah or a law; the teacher has merely disregarded the advice of the Sages. Based on the fact that the Rambam never uses the word l'olam to refer to an obligatory command, neither from the Torah or the Rabbis, it is

7 *Hil. Melachim* 5:7
8 *Hil. Shabbos* 1:4
9 *Hil. Melachim* 5:12
10 *Hil. Sefer Torah* 10:2
11 *Deios* 2:4

conclusive the Rambam maintained that living in Eretz Yisrael is beneficial for a person, but is not an obligation. The Rambam maintained that living in Eretz Yisrael isn't a mitzvah but rather a philosophical kiyum.

The Ramban stated four proofs that living in Eretz Yisrael is one of the 613 mitzvot. How would the Rambam counter these points?

The Ramban posited that by the Talmud's praise of one who lives in Eretz Yisrael and its criticism of those who live outside the land[12] imply that living in Eretz Yisrael is one of the 613 mitzvos. The rationale of the Ramban is that only an actual mitzvah would be given this much attention. The Rambam would argue that philosophical benefits also warrant praise from our Sages, and the Talmud's language is not a proof of its status as one of the 613 mitzvos.

The other three proofs of the Ramban were derived from halachot that the Ramban held are generated by the mitzvah of living in Eretz Yisrael. The proof, again, was by inference. What other category of mitzvah could have generated these halachot if not one of the 613 mitzvos?

The first two laws mentioned by the Ramban are cases of spouses arguing whether to live in Eretz Yisrael or not. The spouse that desires to live in Eretz Yisrael gains financial advantage over their spouse in any divorce settlement. While the Ramban held these halachot are generated by the obligation to live in Eretz Yisrael, one could posit that anytime a husband or wife desires to improve their relationship with their Creator, and their spouse attempts to prevent that growth, financial advantage is given to the spouse looking to grow, for no spouse has the right to hold back the growth of their spouse. This position is supported by a parallel halacha. When one spouse demands to move to Yerushalayim – even from another area within Eretz Yisrael - the dissenting spouse loses financial advantage. If the Ramban was correct that halachot must be generated by a mitzvah, there must be a mitzvah to live in Yerushalayim which generates this halachah as well. But neither the Rambam nor the Ramban includes a mitzvah to live in Yerushalayim in their list of the 613 mitzvot.

The last proof of the Ramban is derived from the prohibition against leaving Eretz Yisrael, if there is no mitzvah to live in Eretz Yisrael, how

12 *K'subos* 110a

could there be a prohibition to leave Eretz Yisrael? In order to suggest how the Rambam might refute this proof, we must first explain a conceptual disagreement between the Ramban and Rambam.

Part IV. Explaining the Conceptual Argument between the Ramban and Rambam

The Ramban supported his argument that living in Israel is one of the 613 mitzvos by citing existing halachot that imply living in Eretz Yisrael is one of the 613 mitzvos. What makes an injunction one of the 613 mitzvot and what makes something a philosophical kiyum? The Rambam started his Sefer Hamitzvot with 14 rules of qualifications for the 613 mitzvot, but let us investigate the matter conceptually.

The benefit of living in Eretz Yisrael is unique in that it is indirect. Most mitzvot help one develop character or improve one's intellect. As the Rashba explained, the benefit that Eretz Yisrael provides is that of experiencing specific Divine providence.

In the Rambam's understanding of mitzvos, the Torah only commands the Jews to take advantage of direct benefits. The Torah identifies and recommends actions which confer indirect benefits, but the Torah never obligates Jews to fulfill them. This is consistent with the view of the Rambam that we do not recite a bracha on a hechsher mitzvah[13], for how can we say "asher kidishanu b'mitzvotav" (that God commanded the Jewish people) regarding an action God did not command the Jews to perform?

The Ramban, in contrast, entertains the notion that God did command the Jewish people in an action that provides an indirect benefit. Hashem said, "kedoshim tihi-yu"[14], you shall be sanctified. Although the Ramban agrees that this is not one of the 613 mitzvot, he does use the language of command when explaining the idea of kedoshim tihi-yu [15].

The disagreement between the Rambam and the Ramban over whether or not God commanded the Jewish people in an action conferring only an indirect benefit is the same disagreement they have in the mitzvah of living in Eretz Yisrael. The Ramban maintained that the Torah can command us in an

13 *Hil. Berochos* 11:8
14 *Vayikra* 19:2
15 Ramban *Al-HaTorah* ibid.

indirect benefit and thus commands us to live in Eretz Yisrael in order to gain the indirect benefit that experiencing specific Divine Providence provides. The Rambam maintained that God doesn't command us in indirect benefit, and so the Torah advises the Jewish people to benefit from the experience of living in Eretz Yisrael, but doesn't obligate us in such an experience.

Part V. The Prohibition Against Leaving Eretz Yisrael

The Ramban inferred an obligation from the Torah to live in Eretz Yisrael from the Biblical prohibition against leaving the land once there. How would the Rambam counter the Ramban's argument?

While the Rambam maintained that God does not institute a mitzvah in order to merely derive an indirect benefit, it does prohibit abandoning an indirect benefit which one is already experiencing. It is for this reason that the Rambam connects the prohibition of leaving Eretz Yisrael to the prohibition of leaving Bavel[16]. Bavel was the center of Torah learning, and thus the living there provided an indirect benefit to the individual. The same prohibition of voiding an already acquired benefit applies equally to Eretz Yisrael and to Bavel.

Stated differently, the Rambam could simply counter the Ramban's position with the argument that since there is a prohibition to leave Bavel[17], the Ramban should maintain there is a mitzvah to live in Bavel! Yet all agree that no such mitzvah exists.

The Rambam listed four circumstances allowing one to leave Eretz Yisrael. One can leave in order to study Torah, find a spouse, save one's self from non-Jews, or to save one's self from identifiable, dire financial strain. Do these cases create a situation where residing in Israel isn't considered residing in Eretz Yisrael, a rejection of the land itself or an actual fulfillment of living in Eretz Yisrael by living outside of the land?

When the optimal solutions to the four circumstances lie outside the land, the mitzvah of living in Eretz Yisrael can not be fulfilled even while living in the land. The cases of dire financial strain and threat of death from non-Jews fit this category, for living without the means to continue living is not living at all.

Alternatively, perhaps that living under these conditions is itself

---

16 *Hil. Melachim* 5:12
17 *K'Subos* 110b

a rejection of the land, and living under these conditions would violate a prohibition of rejecting the land! The allowance to leave the land in order to find a wife fits in this category. Without marriage, the continuation of the nation is put in jeopardy. Living in the land while not being able to fulfill the purpose of the land –advancement of the nation – is thus a rejection of the land itself. Accordingly, one is permitted to leave the land to marry.

Finally, perhaps under these circumstances living outside of the land is the equivalent of living in the land. If the purpose of the mitzvah of living in the land of Israel is to experience the portion of God, then another activity that is considered being in the portion of God might also fulfill the obligation. The Rambam wrote that when one dedicates his life not to trying to make a living, but to learning and teaching Torah alone, Hashem Himself is his portion[18]. There is an allowance to leave the land of Israel in order to study Torah because although fulfilling the pursuit of living in the portion of Hashem in the classical sense of living in Eretz Yisrael isn't achieved, through the study of Torah the Jew finds themselves in the portion of God.

Conclusion

Is living in the land of Israel one of the 613 mitzvos? According to the Ramban and many other early scholars, yes. According to the Rambam it isn't one of the 613 mitzvos nor is it one of the Torah or Rabbinic laws. The land of Israel provides the Jewish people with the opportunity to experience specific Divine providence. This is an opportunity all scholars agree a Jew should strive to achieve.

18 *Hil. Shemittah V'Yovel* 13:12,13

CHAPTER
SEVENTY-FIVE

Remembering the Temple as an act of Zionism

Although it was his dream to build a Temple, King David was only allowed to purchase the land and gather the materials to build the Temple. The land King David purchased as the location of the Temple from Araunah the Jebusite was a place of significance for the Jewish people. Jewish tradition stated that the rock from which the world was created lay on Mount Moriah, that Cain and Abel's sacrifice was offered on the same mountain, that Noah gave his first offering after exiting the ark on the mountaintop, and Abraham brought Isaac as an offering on the mountain as well. Eventually King David's son, King Solomon would build the Temple on that spot in 827 BCE, and hundreds of years later, a second Temple would be built on that same mountain. A tenet of Jewish faith is that a third Temple will eventually be built on that same mountain.

The Romans destroyed the second Temple in 70 CE and since then the Jewish people have mourned the Temple's destruction. Although some mistakenly think it is the Temple building the Jewish people grieve for, it is actually what the Temple represents that the Jewish people mourn. The Temple was more than a great edifice, it was the location where the entire Jewish people, and many non-Jews gathered to give offerings, pray, and connect to God. It was the place of Divine miracles that demonstrated to the Jewish people that God's providence was protecting the Jewish people. The Temple's destruction didn't just mean the Jewish people lost a building; it was a symptom of the loss of Divine protection. The Jewish people aren't mourning the loss of the Temple, they're mourning the decline of the special Jewish relationship with God.

The Talmud tells a series of similar interesting stories about weddings featuring well known scholars acting in strange ways. The explanation of each behavior was similar - the scholars saw too much joy at each wedding and wanted to ground the people into a more subdued attitude. The Talmud quoted Rabbi Yochanan who taught a prohibition he learned from Rabbi Shimon the son of Yochai, "It is forbidden for a person to fill their mouth with joy in this world." Rabbi Menachem Meiri explained the prohibition as stemming from the destruction of the Temples. As a demonstration of mourning over the two destroyed Temples we never want to become too joyous, even at a wedding. Rabbi Yona Gerondi understood it differently and as referring to a worry that a person will become too happy and forget to observe the Mitzvot of the Torah.

There are many practices Jews observe in memory of the Temple and recognition of the weakening in the relationship between God and the Jewish people. The Jews spend three weeks mourning the Temple each summer, fast four times a year, leave a portion of their house unfinished, a seat set but empty at the table, and based on the Talmudic teaching above, break a glass at a wedding. These practices are designed to inspire introspection with a correlation to improvement. The hope is that if enough Jews improve sufficiently, God will allow Jews to rebuild the third Temple.

The common practice of mourning over the Temples and the lack of a Temple today stems from a sense that the Jewish people aren't complete without the third Temple being built and the Divine Providence that comes along with the third Temple. Although there is no consensus position within Jewish tradition that the third Temple will only be rebuilt once a messianic era is inaugurated, and on a technical level Jews could build the third Temple without the Messiah's arrival, it is the traditional assumption that the third Temple will only be built once the Messiah arrives. Until then, the Jewish people remain incomplete, and all their achievements are marred by not having a Temple and the full array of Divine Providence.

People traveling the land of Israel today see a complete country. The State of Israel is older than half the countries of the world, its military and economy are among the top ten of the world, and its people consistently rank among the happiest in the world. It's challenging to reconcile the Israel of today with the customs of commemorating an incomplete country as the Jewish people mourn their Temple. As difficult as it is to perceive at face value, and even though the Jewish people experience great success, until the Temple is rebuilt and Jews enjoy Divine Providence, the nation and people are lacking.

Although mourning the Temple and recognizing our loss are generally considered religious obligations, there is a Zionist aspect to them as well. A four-thousand-year-old ideology, Zionism became a modern political movement in the mid 1800's. The spirit behind Zionism was the national memory of greater times in the past and a desire to recreate those remarkable times by forming a Jewish state in the future. Mourning the Temple acted as a reminder of the Jewish people's great potential and inspired the Jewish people to hope for a brighter future. Today, with a successful State of Israel, the continued mourning over our Temple reminds us that although times are much better, they haven't met their potential – yet.

CHAPTER
SEVENTY-SIX

Has the State of Israel lived up to Jewish values?

In early 1958 Rabbi Joseph Soloveitchik zt"l delivered a talk where he shared his concerns about the future emerging State of Israel. Rabbi Soloveitchik said, "The Jew has experienced prosecution and brutality. We never had a state, we never had political province. What if we had been a state in the Middle Ages? How would we have acted - just like the feudal lords, or would we have acted differently because of Jewish values? Who knows? Now with the State of Israel, the test has come, we are facing the test, will we behave like any other state ethically? Will we restrain ourselves from engaging in certain injustices, so-to-say praxis which are in conflict with basic Judaic ethics, or will we yield temptation?"

Rabbi Soloveitchik continued, "Here we have an opportunity, the Jews are the rulers, they legislate the laws, they are so-to-say the masters. Will we act like masters, or will we understand that Judaism doesn't know the concept of master and slave, victor and vanquished, powerful and weak? This is my problem with regards to the State of Israel."

"The whole of Jewish history will be interpreted in terms of what the State of Israel will do in the next 50 years. If the State of Israel doesn't live up to Jewish ethics, people will reinterpret Jewish history in a whole different light. The question is not whether Israel will defeat the Arabs on the field of battle... [but] whether we'll defeat our evil within our own community and be victorious in this field? To me this is the most important problem. "

Rabbi Soloveitchik focused on the Jewish history of being oppressed by Gentile rulers. Governing brings out the worst of human nature and rulers generally oppress their people. For the first time in 1900 years Jews have found themselves the rulers. Rabbi Soloveitchik taught the challenge facing the Jewish people with their newfound state was whether they'd remember their history and values and become benevolent rulers over their Arab minority or forget those values and become oppressive rulers.

70 years later the world slanders Israel and accuses Israel of failing Rabbi Soloveitchik's challenge and becoming oppressive rulers over their Arab minority and Palestinians. Slanderous voices claim there is rampant racism practiced by Jewish Israelis against Arab Israelis. Israel's adversaries accuse Israel of denying Palestinians freedom, treating them in apartheid like conditions and of occupying Palestinian land. Even some of Israel's friends decry Israel's treatment of Palestinians. They believe the narrative of the suffering Palestinian and hold Israel responsible for Palestinian suffering. They ask why Israel can't be more flexible, offer more generous solutions, and empathize with the Palestinian condition.

The accusations against Israel can be divided into two categories. First, the Jews stole Palestinian land. While Palestinian activists in America refer to the West Bank as the stolen Palestinian land, the Palestinians in the Middle East consider all the land from the Jordan River to the Mediterranean Sea to be Palestinian land. There is no room for a Jewish State. Is Israel ruling over the West Bank and greater Eretz Yisrael consistent with Jewish values? The Torah declares that all the land, whether it be Tel Aviv or Hevron, Jerusalem or Haifa, are all Jewish lands. Jewish values stem from the Torah. A primary Jewish value is settling our land.There is no Jewish value of abandoning Jewish ancestral land because others claim it is their land.

The second category of accusations against Israel claims Israel mistreats Palestinians. Israel's critics consider any behavior that upsets Palestinians or doesn't allow them the rights of Israeli citizens is oppression - and even apartheid. This accusation doesn't stand the test of reality. A careful inspection of Israel's policies against the United Nations list of human rights clearly demonstrates Israel doesn't deny Palestinians any human rights. Palestinian civil rights are the Palestinian Authority's responsibility. Israel isn't violating any Jewish values when Palestinian leadership oppresses their own people. Palestinian suffering isn't caused by Israeli policy, but by Palestinian Authority and Hamas policies meant to subjugate Palestinians.

Many of the Israeli policies towards Palestinians that even our friends criticize: checkpoints, restricted movement, refusing Palestinians entrance into Israel and Jewish areas, aren't a restriction on Palestinian rights and are borne of security needs. In a choice between benevolence towards Palestinians and Israeli security - and yes, those are the choices, Israel must choose the security of its citizens. It's not only Jewish values that dictate that decision, every country makes the exact same choice in its immigration policies. Israel's policies towards Palestinians are perfectly in line with Jewish values.

I wasn't a student of Rav Soloveitchik and I don't know how he would have judged Israel's actions. I think an honest assessment of how Israel has governed will show Israel isn't perfect but has governed in accordance with Jewish values. Israel has granted Arabs who stayed in Israel after 1948 full citizenship, with equal rights to Jewish Israeli citizens. Israeli Arabs have the highest standard of living of all Arabs in the Middle East, with full civil rights and health care that is the envy of most of the world. In 1967 Israel captured the Golan Heights and Judea and Samaria (West Bank). At the time, only four Arab cities in the West Bank had running water and there were few roads built. Since then, Israel has greatly improved the infrastructure of the West Bank. Palestinian population numbers, life expectancy and quality of life has greatly improved.

There's no doubt that many Arab-Israelis and Palestinians would rather the Jewish state disappear and they – for the first time – rule over the land from the Jordan River to the Mediterranean Sea. Israel's refusal to appease those Arabs and Palestinians doesn't make them oppressive rulers. Israel and the Jewish people have a right to rule their own land, and ruling Eretz Yisrael is consistent with Jewish values.If Rav Soloveitchik were alive today, I hope he'd be proud of how the government of Israel and its people have ruled their land.

CHAPTER
SEVENTY-SEVEN

Is God still knocking?

In 1956, a mere eight years after the Jewish people declared their Independence and the State of Israel was born, Rabbi Joseph Soloveitchik, the Rosh Yeshiva of Yeshiva University and a leading American Rabbi released an essay called, "Kol Dodi Dofek." The essay was groundbreaking for American Jewry because its central message was that Israel's Independence wasn't natural, but an act of Divine Providence and it required American Jewry to respond.

In King Solomon's Shir Hashirim (Song of Songs) he tells a parable of a lover who knocks on the door of his lover's home. His lover is tired and tells him to come back the next day. Her lover though gives up and doesn't return; she searches for her lover but he is not to be found and she has forever lost him because she didn't answer the knock. Rabbi Soloveitchik, known admiringly as "The Rav" to his students, compares the knocking lover to God and the lover who ignored the knock to American Jewry. The creation of the State of Israel was God's knock and by staying in America, the Jews of America were ignoring God's knock.

The Rav's first knock demonstrating the Divine providence that brought about the creation of the State of Israel was the agreement of the world's two rival superpowers, the United States and the Soviet Union to support the creation of Israel, "This was perhaps the one resolution on which East and West concurred. I am inclined to believe that the United Nations was especially created for this end — for the sake of fulfilling the mission that Divine Providence had placed upon it." The Rav's second knock was the IDF's surprising victories in war, "The tiny defense forces of Israel defeated the mighty Arab armies. The miracle of "the many delivered into the hands of the few" materialized before our eyes."

God's third knock was the refutation of hundreds of years of Christian doctrine that used the Jewish exile to prove God had abandoned the Jews and the Christians had replaced them. The creation of the State of Israel refuted their claims, "The theological arguments of Christian theologians to the effect that the Holy One has taken away from the Community of Israel its rights to the Land of Israel, and that all of the biblical promises relating to Zion and Jerusalem now refer in an allegorical sense to Christianity and the Christian Church, were all publicly shown to be false, baseless contentions by the establishment of the State of Israel." God's fourth knock was the State of Israel's ability to draw the assimilated Jewish youth back to their roots, "A seemingly unstoppable tidal wave stood over us and threatened to destroy us. Suddenly, the Beloved began to beckon to the hearts of the perplexed, and His beckoning, the establishment of the State of Israel, at least slowed the process of flight."

The fifth knock is the message to the enemies of the Jewish people that Jewish blood is no longer cheap and comes at a high price, "Divine Providence has amazed our enemies with the astounding discovery that Jewish blood is not cheap! If the antisemites describe this phenomenon as being "an eye for an eye," we will agree with them." The final and sixth knock was the availability of Jews from all over to find a place of refuge, "A Jew escaping from an enemy's land now knows that he can find refuge in the land of his forefathers. This is a new phenomenon in the annals of our history. Up to now, when a Jewish population was uprooted, it wandered in the wilderness of the nations without finding shelter and habitation."

After delineating the six knocks, Rav Soloveitchik challenged his fellow American Jews, "What was our reaction to the beckoning of the voice of the Beloved, to the munificence of His loving-kindness and miracles? Did we get out of our beds and immediately open the door, or did we continue to rest like the Lover in the story of the Song of Songs, and were we too lazy to get out of our beds?" Rav Soloveitchik answered his own question with a harsh criticism of American Jewry, "Let us admit our own faults and confess to our own derelictions. Among the Jews of America, Orthodox Jews bear the most blame for the slow pace of the conquest of the Land through settlement. It was for us, the loyalists of Judaism, to heed the call of the Beloved more acutely, and to respond to it immediately with extraordinary effort."

Rav Soloveitchik held American Jews responsible for the slow pace of Israeli settlement of the land. He felt American Jewry should've answered God's knock and moved to Israel. The Rav wrote this admonition in 1956, as we look back 65+ years later does the Rav's question and criticism still hold true? Even without a mass Aliyah from America, Israel is largely settled. Jews from Arab lands, Russia and Ethiopia have largely settled the land. Setting aside the need to settle the land, has American Jewry missed the Divine knock of Israel's creation?

Only American Jews can answer this question, and each American Jew must ask the question themselves. After years of Israel's existence one thing is clear, the gates to Eretz Yisrael have remained wide open. Jews have been able to move to Israel throughout its existence. Even those that maintain American Jewry ignored God's knocking would have trouble arguing "the lover has left." Rav Soloveitchik wrote, "I fear that we Orthodox Jews are still enveloped in sweet slumber." It would seem God is still knocking and His people are still sleeping, but they can arise and answer the knock.

CHAPTER

SEVENTY-EIGHT

Is there Religious Zionism without Messianism?

The army radio crackled, "The Temple Mount is in our hands! I repeat, the Temple Mount is in our hands! All forces, stop firing! This is the David Operations Room. All forces, stop firing! I repeat, all forces, stop firing! Over." The voice belonged to the head of the Israeli paratroopers, Colonel Motta Gur, and he was announcing the Israeli army's victorious reuniting of Jerusalem in the 1967 Six Day War. Blessings were recited by soldiers, Rabbi Shlomo Goren, the IDF Chief Rabbi, recited a blessing, the memorial prayer for fallen Jewish soldiers and then sounded the shofar. All over the world Jews were thrilled with the Israeli victory. The thought began to creep into the forefronts of people's minds, with all of Jerusalem and the Temple Mount in our hands, could Moshiach be far off?

It's been more than fifty years since that glorious day, and Moshiach still hasn't arrived. The Six Day War wasn't the first time the State of Israel and messianic hopes were connected. Rabbi Eliyahu Guttmacher wrote, "It is clear to me that if 130 families of Israel begin to till the land in our holy land, this will be the beginning of the redemption even if the people are not yet worthy." Commenting on Rabbi Guttmacher's prediction, Rav Tzvi Yehudah Kook taught, "Certainly, this great saint desired the increase of Torah and its glorification, but the order of redemption is: agricultural settlement, the establishment of the state, and as a consequence the uplifting of that which is sacred, the dissemination of the teaching of Torah, its increase and glorification."

Arguing for the messianic significance of the State of Israel, Rabbi Yehudah Amital wrote, "When the State was established, some of the great

Torah sages in the world declared although we are not living in the time of "the revealed end" of the "footsteps of the Moshiach," there is still great importance to the political freedom of the State of Israel. For these reasons, the Chief Rabbis, including Rav Herzog zt"l, ruled that the establishment of the State of Israel is the beginning of the flowering of our redemption."

Belief in the State of Israel as a start of the redemption has become a litmus test of religious Zionism. It is not enough for a religious Jew to celebrate the State of Israel, serve in its army, and see God's hand in the State's formation; to be considered a religious Zionist, a religious Jew must believe the state is the harbinger of the messianic era. Jews who don't believe that the state of Israel is the beginning of the redemption have their Zionism and belief in God called into question by other religious Zionists.

Rabbi Yitzchak Yaakov Reines was one of the founders of Mizrahi, the religious Zionist movement. He wrote, "[Zionism] is an idea whose fundamental principle is to improve our physical situation and to obtain for our brothers of the house of Israel who are oppressed and pursued without respite a place of secure refuge in our Holy Land. This has nothing to do with spiritual or religious matters." Another stalwart of the religious Zionist Mizrahi movement was Rabbi Yosef Dov Soloveitchik. Rabbi Soloveitchik wrote, "Our historic obligation, today, is to raise ourselves from a people to a holy nation, from the covenant of Egypt to the covenant of Sinai, from an existence of necessity to an authentic way of life suffused with eternal ethical and religious values, from a camp to a Congregation." Neither Rabbi Reines not Rabbi Soloveitchik saw Zionism and the founding of the State of Israel as the start of the Redemption. Rabbi Herschel Schachter said, "Rav Soloveitchik did not specifically call [Israel] the "*atchalta degeulah*."

There are many arguments to make in favor of Zionism and the State of Israel being the start of the messianic era, three signs Messiah is coming are the nation of Israel's return to its land; the abolition of our subjugation to foreigners, and the blossoming of the Land of Israel. We see these three things happening today. There are also as many counter arguments to make against the claim. Many Torah scholars maintained the redemption cannot come about through a heretical movement that opposes Torah observance. Others felt we can't know God's plans without God telling us through prophecy. Rambam also warned against predicting when Moshiach would arrive, a warning that history has unfortunately proven correct with false messiahs causing untold damage and dashed dreams.

Rambam wrote we celebrate Purim to, "Inform the future generations of the truth of the Torah's promise 'For what great nation is there that has God so near to it, as the Lord our God is at all times that we call upon Him?'" Whether the founding of the State of Israel is the beginning of the redemption will remain a source of debate among religious Zionists, but God's answering the Jewish people's prayers to return to Eretz Yisrael, settle the land, govern, is undeniable. The countless times Israel and its people have survived wars has further demonstrated Zionism and the State of Israel's providential significance.

Zionism as a movement is designed to encourage and inspire the growth of the Jewish people. There shouldn't be a litmus test of any Zionist, and especially religious Zionists. The State of Israel is a wonderful blessing for the Jewish people and the world. The State of Israel should be appreciated and celebrated, and it should be used as a vehicle to unite the entire Jewish people.

CHAPTER
SEVENTY-NINE

Is Zionism consistent with the Torah?

To most Torah observant Jews, the question, "Is Zionism consistent with the Torah?" has an obvious answer. Certain Torah observant Jews would answer the question with a resounding yes, and others with an equally definite, no! The question of Zionism's consistency with Torah values is a source of great debate among Torah observant Jews. Zionism is one of the most fundamental issues of modern Jewish time; it is one of the most influential phenomena of contemporary Jewish life. How can Torah observant Jews especially Torah scholars, who share so many values, disagree on such a fundamental Jewish question?

Towards the end of the book of Bamidbar, God wrote, "You shall possess the Land and you shall settle in it, for to you have I given the land to possess it." In line with the command to settle in the land of Israel, the following lesson was taught in the Talmud, "The Sages taught: A person should always reside in Eretz Yisrael, even in a city that is mostly populated by gentiles. He should not reside outside of Eretz Yisrael, even in a city that is mostly populated by Jews. The reason is that anyone who resides in Eretz Yisrael is considered as one who has a God, and anyone who resides outside of Eretz Yisrael is considered as one who does not have a God."

In his commentary on the verse quoted above, the Ramban wrote, "In my opinion, this verse expresses a positive command. We are commanded to settle and dwell in the land for it was given to them, and we cannot reject the portion of God. If it would ever occur to us to go and capture the land of Shinar or the land of Ashur, or anything like it, and to settle there, one would be violating this positive command." Rabbi Moshe Feinstein maintained living in Israel isn't an obligatory mitzvah, but a mitzvah that one should strive to fulfill. Living in Israel is a Jewish value, if not an obligatory mitzvah.

The modern political movement of Zionism got its start in the late 1800's, and it was a source of great controversy throughout the world. Zionism was a source of division among the broader Jewish community, with most Jews rejecting it. Among the Jews that accepted Zionism, different forms of Zionism developed. There were Communist Zionists, practical Zionists, religious Zionists and secular Zionists among others. The different groups united on the cause of returning the Jewish people to the land of Israel.

With the abundance of Biblical, Rabbinic and contemporary Torah literature that encourages, if not outright commands, the Jewish people to live in the land of Israel, and the goal of Zionism to return the Jewish people to live in the land of Israel, all Torah observant Jews should align themselves with Zionism and consider themselves Zionists. Why have so many Torah observant Jews rejected and continue to reject Zionism?

There are several objections some Torah observant Jews have towards Zionism. There have been many books written that examine the objections of the Torah observant community to Zionism, and there is too much to quote here, but there are two primary objections. As Gregory Baum wrote in "Jewish Opposition to Zionism, "The principal theological argument [against Zionism] is that the Zionists have transformed the religious messianism implicit in Judaism into a political nationalism and tried to replace the religious definition of Jewish identity by one that is secular and political. The exile of the Jews from the Promised Land has been imposed on them by God as a punishment for their infidelity to the Torah. The return of the Jews to the Holy Land is a messianic promise: it will therefore take place as God's doing, not be the result of a political movement or, even less, of military action." In his book, "The Transformation," Neturei Karta's I. Domb wrote, "Zionism is basically the reverse of our emuna and religious ideology. To become a Zionist means to conceive Jewry as something temporal and earthly, utterly divorced from all the divine connections, upon which the whole of emuna is based."

The counterarguments that Zionist Torah observant Jews offer to the arguments of anti-Zionist Jews is that nowhere does Jewish tradition state that Jews must wait for a Messiah to come before returning and governing the land of Israel. Furthermore, there is a mitzvah for the Jewish people to return and settle the land of Israel, as the Ramban was quoted as saying earlier in this essay. Not only is Zionism consistent with Torah values, but it has also proven to enhance Torah study and observance. There are more people studying Torah daily in Israel today, many with Israeli government financial support, than at any previous point in Jewish history.

The debate over Zionism being or not being consistent with the Torah is not going to reach a conclusion any time soon. Both sides have been entrenched in their opinions for over a hundred years and short of a prophetic message from God, there isn't anything that can happen that would change either side's approach to Zionism or the Torah. It's important to note that those objecting to Zionism don't reject the land of Israel, or the right of the Jewish people to the land of Israel. Their objection rests in the values of the Zionist movement and their perception of their inconsistency with Torah values. Most importantly, it is crucial that this debate be waged for the sake of Heaven, and never violate the laws of civility, respect, and love for one's fellow Jew.

CHAPTER
EIGHTY

The lessons of the Jewish Past

This week we sat at our Passover Seder(s) and told the seminal story of the Jewish nation. The Exodus from Egypt is more than just a moment in Jewish history. This event is so important that Jewish custom mandates recounting the story of the Exodus from Egypt twice a day, mentioning it during Shabbat kiddush, during prayers, and of course, Jews dedicate an entire night to the story on Passover. The Jewish people learn lessons from their history and apply them to their present and future circumstances. As political Zionists began their internal and external campaign for a right to return the Jewish people to their land they used lessons from their past, especially the Passover story, to instruct them on how to successfully achieve their goals of creating a Jewish state on their homeland.

When Moses came back to the Jewish people from his forty-year escape to the desert of Midian, he told the Jewish people he was on his way to Pharaoh to demand their freedom. The Jewish people, accustomed to over 200 years of servitude, were nervous. Their fear proved to be foretelling as Pharaoh responded to Moses's boldness with harsher decrees on the Jewish people. Although resented by his people for their extra work, Moses persevered and continued taking a stand for his people's rights, demanding his people's freedom. Moses's determination taught generations of Jews to demand their rights.

Like Moses, Early Zionists weren't disheartened by initial setbacks and rejections. They persisted and used diplomacy, resistance and military attacks to create a Jewish state. When Chaim Weizmann and the Emir Feisal signed an agreement for close collaboration between their respective national movements and the agreement was later repudiated by Arab nationalists, Weizmann and the Zionists kept advocating for a Jewish state. In 1921 when Arab anti-Jewish riots and outbreaks of violence in Jaffa, Rehovot, Petah Tikva, Hadera and other places left 47 Jews dead and many wounded, the Zionists kept fighting for their freedom. In 1939 the British White Paper was published, restricting immigration and the sale of land to Jews. The paper could've been the death knell to the hopes of a Jewish state – but it wasn't; the Zionists continued with illegal immigration to populate Eretz Yisrael. Today's Zionists must stand up to Iranian nuclear aspirations, Hamas and Hezbollah rocket fire, Palestinian terror attacks and international delegitimization and demand Jewish rights, freedom and security like any other sovereign nation in the global community.

The trip to Eretz Yisrael from Egypt should not have taken more than a week. The Jewish people had a scheduled three-day layover at Mount Sinai to receive the Torah and then they were supposed to have a quick trip to their new home. In a tragic development, the people doubted God and believed the spies' report that the Jewish people could never defeat the Canaanites and settle their land. Their punishment was to stay in the desert for forty years and anyone over twenty wouldn't be allowed to enter Eretz Yisrael. If the Jewish people had given up at that point and refused to continue, history would've understood their despondence. Yet, the Jewish people focused on getting to the border, even though they knew they wouldn't be the ones to cross into Eretz Yisrael. They kept going in order to ensure that future generations would enjoy their own land.

Just as the Jewish people of the desert fought hard to ensure future generations were privileged with a free nation on land they themselves wouldn't be able to enjoy, the early Zionists worked hard knowing there was little chance they themselves would see the fruits of their labor. Theodore Herzl himself said, "At Basel I founded the Jewish State. If I said this out loud today, l would be greeted by universal laughter. In five years perhaps, and certainly in fifty years, everyone will perceive it." Herzl would die less than a decade after saying it, and fifty one years before he was proven correct. Zionists enjoying their ancestors' efforts to create the State of Israel must keep the focus on strengthening Israel and always move towards a stronger Israel - even in face of setbacks.

As the Jewish people traveled towards Israel and Egypt long in their rearview mirror, a nation from far away, with no previous interactions with the Jewish people, met the Jews in the desert and attacked them. The nation of Amalek, forever to be a Jewish enemy, didn't attack the strong leaders at the head of the people, but rather waited for the tired and weak Jews trailing behind. Their cowardly attack would forever teach Jews that antisemites would always attack the Jews without cause, and when they attacked, would do so spinelessly by attacking the weakest members of the nation. Moses did not take this attack silently, he appointed Joshua to lead the first Jewish army to counterattack and defeat Amalek. The Jewish people quickly learned they would always have enemies and they would have to fight to defeat their enemies.

Early Zionists took the lesson of the first Jewish army to heart. The Yishuv, the first Jewish settlements in Palestine, came under attack quickly from local Arabs. The Zionists quickly formed paramilitary groups to defend themselves against Arab attackers. Bar Giora turned into Hashomer, which turned into Haganah, and Irgun and the Stern Gang worked alongside them against Arab attackers. The Arab forces didn't attack the strong Jews, like Amalek they attacked convoys of nurses, farmers, women and children. Nothing was out of bounds for the cowards. The early Zionists were ready in 1948 when the Israel Defense Forces were formed and fought their first war – the Israel Independence War. The Jewish State has successfully remembered its lesson of fighting its enemies, winning war after war against enemies looking to annihilate it.

Jewish collective national memory is a powerful tool. The early Zionists called upon Jewish memory time and time again to find the courage to stand up for themselves. Moses, Joshua and the Jewish people weren't mere historical figures to early Zionists and they can't be to today's Zionists. Zionists must call upon their ancestors' actions to instruct them to keep standing up for their rights. The most important lesson for the Jewish people is to remember the Divine favor their ancestors enjoyed through their various trials. When the people followed God's commands they succeeded, when they forgot God's directives they failed. The Jewish people must never forget their success doesn't solely come at their own efforts, but with Divine providence.

As Zionists look forward to the 100th anniversary of the State of Israel it is the lessons of the Jewish past that will be key to their continued success. The Jewish people must stand up for themselves and demand their rights, they must always be on the way to a successful Israel, and they must be prepared to go to war. Most importantly, they must follow the word of God to ensure they merit Divine providence. The dream of thousands of years of Jewish lovers of Zion are coming true today, and it is today's Jewish people who are responsible to ensure those dreams continue to succeed.

CHAPTER

EIGHTY-ONE

The Three Oaths and the Opposition to Zionism

Religious Zionists are often confused by fellow Torah observant Jews who oppose Zionism and the State of Israel. The Religious Zionist community sees the State of Israel as one of the greatest gifts to the Jewish people; how, they wonder, could anyone oppose it?

The objection that many Torah observant Jews have towards Zionism is they see it as a violation of God's decree about the Jewish people's time to return to the land of Israel. According to their viewpoint, God punished the Jews with exile and only God will decide when the Jewish people merit to return to their land. The notion that Jews should take their future into their own hands, go to war, and return to the land of Israel without a direct prophecy and charge from God contradicts their belief in how the redemption of the Jewish people is designed to unfold.

This particular objection is based on a teaching in the Talmud and the Medrash commonly referred to as the "Three Oaths."The teaching is found in Mesechet Ketuvot page 110b and is grounded in a debate between two early Jewish scholars, Rabbi Zeira and Rabbi Yehuda. The two debated whether Rabbi Zeira should move from Babylonia to Israel. Rabbi Yehuda was Rabbi Zeira's teacher, and maintained, "Anyone who moves from Babylonia to the land of Israel transgresses a mitzvah. Rabbi Yehuda supported his position from a prophecy of Jeremiah, "They shall be taken to Babylonia and there they shall remain until the day that I recall them, said the Lord." Rabbi Yehuda maintained Jews shouldn't return to Israel without God bringing them back. When challenged about Jeremiah's prophecy and why he still felt he should move to Israel, Rabbi Zeira explained Jeremiah's prophecy was about the vessels from the Beit Hamikdash, not people.

As the discussion continued in the Talmud, another verse, this one from King Solomon, is mentioned, "I command you to take an oath, daughters of Jerusalem, by the gazelles and by the hinds of the field, that you not awaken or stir up love, until it please." Rabbi Yehuda used this verse to prove the Jewish people shouldn't perform an act of redemption, like returning to Israel, without a directive from God. Rabbi Zeira maintained that the oath mentioned by King Solomon meant that the Jews should not ascend to Eretz Yisrael as a people together whereas individuals may immigrate as they wish.

The Talmud's discussion moved on to highlight that there are three oaths mentioned by King Solomon, One, so that the Jews should not ascend to Eretz Yisrael as a force together, but little by little. The second, that God adjured the Jews that they should not rebel against the rule of the nations of the world, and the last one is that God adjured the nations of the world that they should not subjugate the Jews excessively. Opponents of Zionism point to the first two oaths as prohibitions against the Jewish people returning by force and founding a state.

The anti-Zionist case made from the three oaths is compelling. Verses from Tanach and teachings of the Talmud aren't always meant to be taken literally; many are metaphoric in nature. Torah observant Zionists understand the three oaths in a way that is consistent with their support of Zionism. Maimonides, in a letter to the Yemenite community wrote, "The prophets predicted that pretenders will appear in great numbers at the time when the Messiah will come, but they will not be able to make good on their claim and they will perish with many of their supporters. King Solomon foresaw that the prolonged duration of the exile would incite some of our people to seek to prematurely end the exile before the appointed time, and as a consequence they would perish. King Solomon adjured the Jewish people in metaphorical language to desist from trying." Zionists understood Maimonides to have interpreted the oaths as non-binding and meant to teach a lesson about Messiah's arrival. King Solomon wasn't teaching about the Jewish people returning to the land of Israel.

A proper attitude towards the Messiah was important to Maimonides. Elsewhere in his writings he explained Messianic times and how Jews should relate to Messiah's arrival. He wrote that the order of the occurrence of these events, or their precise detail are not among the fundamental principles of faith. A person should not occupy himself with the tales and homiletics concerning these and similar matters, nor should a person consider them as essentials, for study of them will neither bring fear or love of God. The events that occur before and during the coming of the Messiah cannot be definitely known by man until they occur for these matters are undefined in the prophets' words and even the early scholars have no established tradition regarding these matters except their own interpretation of the verses. Therefore, there is a controversy among them regarding these matters. Similarly, one should not try to determine the appointed time for Mashiach's coming. Jewish tradition stated there will be no difference between the current age and the Messianic era except freeing the Jewish people from the persecution of the gentile kingdoms. The Messiah will establish peace within the world.

Maimonides wrote that the Sages and the prophets did not yearn for the Messianic era in order to have dominion over the entire world, to rule over the gentiles, to be exalted by the nations, or to eat, drink, and celebrate. Rather, they desired to be free to involve themselves in Torah and wisdom without any pressures or disturbances, so that they would merit the world to come. It's counterproductive to make the Messiah and his arrival a fundamental of Judaism. The entire point of a Messianic era is to understand God better. If one makes their Torah study and mitzvah observance secondary to acts aimed at bringing the Messiah, they are confusing priorities. This is the lesson Maimonides taught from the "Three Oaths."

While the anti-Zionists' interpretation of the "Three Oaths" is well known it is far from a consensus understanding of the verses and the teaching of the Talmud. Only a small minority of scholars over the past fifteen hundred years have agreed with the anti-Zionists interpretation. The overwhelming majority of scholars understand the "Three Oaths" to be metaphoric just as Maimonides understood them to be metaphoric.

Not only do Torah observant Zionists maintain that there is no prohibition for individuals and the nation to return and govern the land of Israel, but they subscribe to the opinion of Nachmanides who wrote, "In my opinion, settling in the land of Israel is a command. We are commanded to settle and dwell in the land for it was given to them, and we cannot reject the portion of God. If it would ever occur to us to go and capture the land of

Shinar or the land of Ashur, or anything like it, and to settle there, one would be violating this positive command."

CHAPTER
EIGHTY-TWO

The Uniqueness of Eretz Yisrael

Since the day I moved to Israel almost 8 years ago I've counted every day I've been blessed to live in Israel and on many days I post that day's number with the hashtag #Livingthedream on social media. Living in Eretz Yisrael isn't only my dream, but it was my ancestor's dream as well. I've tried to understand Eretz Yisrael and what makes living in Israel so special.

At the very start of the Torah, God commanded Abraham to leave his home and to go. Abraham didn't know where he was going, but he obeyed God's command. Abraham landed in what was then called Canaan and would eventually be called Eretz Yisrael. Many of the Jewish people's most meaningful moments took place in the land of Israel. From Joshua bringing the people into the land of Israel to King Solomon building the Temple, the Jewish people have a historic connection to the land of Israel.

The Jewish people's historic connection to the land of Israel is the foundation of what many Zionists use to build a legal case for the Jewish right to Israel. The Jewish historic and legal connection to Israel is well established, but while the history connects the Jewish people to the land, what made the land of Israel unique that it was chosen for the Jewish people?

Explaining the land of Israel's uniqueness requires a philosophical approach to an area usually reserved for fact-based analysis. The Mishna in Mesechet Keilim offered a reason for Eretz Yisrael's uniqueness, "There are ten grades of sanctity: the land of Israel is more sanctified than all other lands. What is the nature of its sanctity? That from the land of Israel, the omer, the first fruits and the two loaves are brought, which cannot be brought from any of the other lands." According to the Mishna, it is the mitzvot that are dependent on the land that makes Eretz Yisrael so unique.

The Mishna's explanation is consistent with a discussion quoted in the Talmud where Rabbi Samlai asked why Moses desired to enter the land of Israel. Rabbi Samlai rejected the idea that Moses desired the luscious fruits of Israel, and instead taught that of the many mitzvot commanded to the Jewish people, some of them can only be fulfilled in the land of Israel. Moses wanted to enter the land of Israel to fulfill the mitzvot that can only be fulfilled in Israel. One quality that makes Israel unique is the mitzvot that can only be fulfilled in Israel.

Rabbi Yoel Sirkis, an 18th Century scholar known as the "Bach," disagreed with the lesson of Rav Samlia and argued that Moses did want to enter the land of Israel for its luscious fruits. Rabbi Sirkis taught that the fruits of Israel are nourished from the heavenly Israel and its sanctity. That sanctity comes directly from the Divine Presence and is found in the land of Israel. In Rabbi Sirkis's approach to the land of Israel, the land is unique because of a metaphysical quality found in the produce of the land of Israel. The Divine nourishment that feeds the fruits is the metaphysical quality that makes Israel unique.

The "Rashba," Rabbi Shlomo Ibn Aderet, a 12th Century scholar, offered an additional quality that made Eretz Yisrael unique. The Sages taught, "Eretz Yisrael is watered by God, Himself, and the rest of the entire world is watered through an intermediary." In his commentary to this teaching, Rashba wrote, "Since the Jewish people are the chosen people and Eretz Yisrael is the chosen land of God, He is not going to leave the people or the land to an angel as God did for the other nations of the world. Rather God's "eyes" are on the land and all that occurs in the land occurs under God's providence." According to the Rashba, Eretz Yisrael is made unique by God's specific providence on the land.

In a moment of brutal honesty Israel's first Prime Minister, David Ben Gurion said, "Since I invoke Torah so often, let me state that I don't personally believe in the God it postulates ... I am not religious, nor were the majority of the early builders of Israel believers. Yet their passion for this land stemmed from the Book of Books ... The Bible is the single most important book in my life." Whether Prime Minister Ben Gurion understood the land of Israel to be unique because of the mitzvot that could only be fulfilled in the land, the Divinely luscious fruit of the land, or the specific Divine providence on the land - or all three, it's clear that the land of Israel is unique because of qualities is possess that separate from other lands.

The Jewish people have a historic, legal and national connection to the land of Israel. They have a right to self-determination in their homeland, Eretz Yisrael. They also have an appreciation of the metaphysical and philosophical qualities that make the land of Israel unique and understand that even more than just the historic connection to the land, the land is exceptional. The Jewish people are blessed to have been given this particular land as their homeland.

CHAPTER
EIGHTY-THREE

The Past is the Present and the Future

Alan King was a famous Jewish comedian who entertained both on the Borscht Belt and the Tonight Show. I have an affinity for King and his humor because we share a birthday and a love of Cigars. King's most famous joke was about Jewish festivals, "A summary of every Jewish holiday: They tried to kill us, we won, let's eat!" The joke needs no commentary, and hits home for many Jewish families.

Jewish festivals and fast days are more meaningful than just commemorations of past events. Maimonides discussed commemorations of past triumphs and tragedies much the same way - as current events, not ancient history. When he wrote about past tragedies, (In the laws of fast days) he wrote, "There are days when the Jewish people fast because of the catastrophes that occurred to them, to arouse their hearts and inspire them to repent. The fast days remind the Jews of our ancestors' sinful conduct which resembles our present conduct. It is this sinful behavior that caused these catastrophes on them in their days and us in our days. By reminding ourselves of these matters through fasting, we will repent and improve our conduct."

In a similar fashion, when Maimonides discussed the Passover Seder, he wrote, "In each and every generation, a person must present himself as if he, himself, has now left the slavery of Egypt." When he discussed Purim and reading the Megillah, he wrote, "The prophets and the courts commanded that the Megillah be read in order to praise God, the salvation God brought us, and God's response to our cries, so that we will bless God, extol God, and inform the future generations of the truth of the Torah's promise, 'For what great nation is there that has God so near to it? The Lord our God is always [available] when we call Him.'" Maimonides understood the commemoration of past events to speak much more to the present than the past. Historic tragedies were caused by sins that are still repeated today and God's salvation is still seen in our times.

Mixing Zionism and theology has been a point of contention since the founding of the modern Zionist movement. Not all Zionists believe in God, and they understand the Zionist movement and its success to be a purely human development. Some Zionists who believe in God aren't convinced Zionism is providential. The range of opinions on God's involvement in Zionist success scale from a refusal to see God's "hand" in modern Israeli events, to Rav Soloveitchik's Divine knocking, to Rav Kook's belief that Zionism and Israel are the beginnings of the ultimate redemption

Israel and the Jewish people have been put in dangers' way on countless occasions over the past 75 years. The Jewish people have not only survived those dangers, but as a people, they have thrived. In 1948 the Jews beat the odds and defeated their enemies to win their independence. Israel's enemies battled the Jewish people again in 1956, 1967 and 1973. Each time the Jewish people were in peril but overcame the threat and were victorious. Through wars, terror attacks, intifadas and rockets, the Jewish people have called out to God and have been answered.

Maimonides's idea of Purim being a celebration of God's continuous salvation of the Jewish people helps put Israel's victories over the past 75 years into context. At modern Purim celebrations we don't only recall the miracles in Shushan, but the miraculous victories in Jerusalem, the Golan Heights and the Mitla Pass, among others. The message of Purim is that God answers the Jewish people at their time of need, and it is a parent's responsibility to teach this lesson to their children. This generation is privileged to have many modern-day examples to demonstrate the point.

Zionists didn't desire war with their neighbors. Ancient and modern Zionists debated how to settle their ancient homeland and live productively with its Arab neighbors. Israel's Declaration of Independence stated Israel "will ensure complete equality of social and political rights to all its inhabitants irrespective of religion, race or sex; it will guarantee freedom of religion, conscience, language, education and culture; it will safeguard the Holy Places of all religions. We extend our hand to all neighboring states and their peoples in an offer of peace and good neighborliness, and appeal to them to establish bonds of cooperation and mutual help with the sovereign Jewish people settled in its own land. The State of Israel is prepared to do its share in a common effort for the advancement of the entire Middle East." Our neighbors rejected our peaceful overtures. Forced to go to war, we experienced great victories.

Having modern day examples of God's salvation can make teaching their lessons to today's children easy and challenging at the same time. It's easy to point to an Israeli soldier and tank and explain the miraculous victories our people have experienced in contemporary times. Children can see the people, touch the tanks and visit the places of our greatest successes. At the same time children are accustomed to miracles occurring to ancient people and they might have trouble understanding that miracles can happen in their days as well. Every day between Purim and Pesach provides an opportunity to teach our children that miraculous Jewish victories aren't relegated to the past, they occur in our times.

During the 2,000 years of exile from the land of Israel, the Jewish people simultaneously celebrated Purim and Pesach and commemorated the destruction of the Temples and other tragedies. The 2,000 years of exile can be characterized more by the fast days of tragedy than the celebration of victories. The past 75 years of Jewish return to Eretz Yisrael have been characterized more by the celebration of victories than the commemoration of tragedy. In Maimonides's framework, the past has been more fast day than Purim, while Israel's resurgence has been a state of Purim. The recognition that God is available to answer the Jewish people's call for help is an everyday responsibility - the celebration of Purim isn't limited to two days. Living in a time of miraculous victories in the land of Israel is a dream come true for the Jewish people.

CHAPTER
EIGHTY-FOUR

We don't pray towards Jerusalem

I found an interesting description of Jerusalem and the Western Wall on a tourist website, "The Western Wall is the most religious site in the world for the Jewish people. Located in the Old City of Jerusalem, it is the western support wall of the Temple Mount. It is one of the major highlights in any tour of the Old City." This seems to be an apt description of the Kotel, except that it's wrong. The most "religious site" for the Jewish people isn't the Western Wall, it's the Temple Mount that sits behind the wall.

In June of 1967, the Jewish people reunited the city of Jerusalem. In an interview with Providence Magazine, former Ambassador Michael Oren talked about the Six Day War that reunited Jerusalem, "Even throughout the war, the Israeli government kept sending messages to the Jordanians saying that if they stopped fighting the Israelis would stop fighting. On the morning of June 7th, Prime Minister Eshkol sent a message to Hussein saying, "Stop fighting and enter peace talks and we won't even take the Old City. Think about that. On Jerusalem Day, we walk through the Old City with flags, celebrating the reunification. In 1967, the Israeli government was willing to forgo, willing to forfeit, that historic reunification of the Jewish people with its holiest sites in order to have peace with one Arab country. King Hussein never responds. Israeli paratroopers enter the Old City at about 9 a.m. Two hours later they report, "The Temple Mount is in our Hands," and the war is essentially over on the Jordanian front."

The religious Zionist community celebrates the 28th of Iyar as "Yom Yerushalayim." They consider the day no less miraculous than Chanukah. They recite special prayers and have a parade through the streets of Jerusalem. With a few exceptions the day hasn't really caught on with communities outside of Israel's religious Zionist community. Yom Yerushalayim isn't a day off for students or companies like Yom Ha'atzmaut (Israeli Independence Day.)

It's clear that Jerusalem plays a central role in every Israeli's life. Israel's first Prime Minister David Ben Gurion often spoke about Jerusalem. There are three memorable statements he made about Jerusalem that demonstrate the importance of Jerusalem to Israel. "No city in the world, not even Athens or Rome, ever played as great a role in the life of a nation for so long a time, as Jerusalem has done in the life of the Jewish people." He also said, "If the Land of Israel is the heart of the Jewish nation, then Jerusalem is its heart of hearts." Jerusalem is indivisible from Israel, "We regard it as our duty to declare that Jewish Jerusalem is an organic and inseparable part of the State of Israel, as it is an inseparable part of the history of Israel, of the faith of Israel."

Over two thousand years ago King Solomon said, "[The Jewish people] turn back to You with all their heart and soul, in the land of the enemies who have carried them off, and they pray to You in the direction of their land which You gave to their fathers, of the city which You have chosen, and of the House which I have built to Your name." The Talmud noted the direction the Jews prayed in and taught, "One who was standing in prayer in the Diaspora, should focus his heart toward Eretz Yisrael." Many knowledgeable people assume Jews around the world pray towards Israel, and some assume more, that Jews pray towards Jerusalem. Like the quote from the website quoted above, that isn't the entire picture.

Jews don't pray towards Israel or Jerusalem. The complete teaching in the Talmud, which Maimonides wrote goes back to the times of Moses, stated, "One standing in Eretz Yisrael, should focus his heart towards Jerusalem, one standing in Jerusalem, should focus his heart towards the Temple, and one standing in the Temple, should focus his heart toward the Holy of Holies. Consequently, one standing in prayer in the East turns to face west, and one standing in the West, turns to face east. One standing in the South, turns to face north, and one standing in the North, turns to face south; all of the people of Israel find themselves focusing their hearts toward one place, the Holy of Holies in the Temple." Jews don't pray towards Israel or Jerusalem; they pray towards the Temple. At a time when the Temple isn't standing, they pray towards the place it once stood, the Temple Mount.

The most sacred place for the Jewish people isn't Jerusalem or the Western Wall, it's the Temple Mount. There is a significant distinction between the two locations. Outsiders often claim the Jewish people can walk away from the Temple Mount as long as they keep the Western Wall and its Plaza. The claim that Jews are just provoking anger by praying on the Temple Mount is made with a pure heart but is based in a lack of awareness of how important the Temple Mount is to the Jewish people. As the Jewish people commemorate the reunification of Jerusalem it's important to note the most sacred part of the city.

CHAPTER
EIGHTY-FIVE

Zionists Didn't Wait for the Messiah

It surprises many to learn that Theodore Herzl, largely considered the father of modern Zionism, wasn't the first activist to encourage the Jewish people to return to the land of Israel. There were even Jews who preceded Dr. Herzl that had started spreading the message that it was time to create a Jewish state in the land of Israel. Before Herzl there was Rabbi Yehudah Alkalai who worked alongside Rabbi Zvi Hirsch Kalisher to promote Zionism, even publishing about the need for the Jews to return to Zion. Herzl, whose grandfather was friends with Rabbi Alkalai, was influenced by Rabbi Alkalai's writings. Even before Rabbis Alkalai and Kalisher, there was the Baal Shem Tov and the Vilna Gaon; two Rabbis who sent their students to settle in the land of Israel. Even before them, there was a famous religious community in Tzefat. While most of the leaders of the modern political Zionist movement weren't religious, the Zionists that kept the Zionist ideology alive over the two-thousand-year Jewish exile were almost exclusively religious Jews.

Zionism was a revolutionary national liberation movement. Like many liberation movements, Zionism drew its inspiration from religious ideals. Unfortunately, many of these movements slowly gave up their religious idealism and turned purely secular. As purely secular movements they lost much of the meaning that drew the early adherents to the movement. Zionism was inspired by the Jewish liberation movements of the exodus from Egypt and the Jews' return to Israel from Babylonia. As Zionism evolved from a movement to a State government, it was unique in that it never gave up its religious inspiration.

There is a movement that tries to sever the religious roots in both idealism and people from Zionism's start and success.

The link between the Jewish people and the land of Israel throughout the two-thousand-year exile was sustained by Jews praying three times a day to return to Zion. These same Jews, whether they were in in Tunisia, Shanghai, or America, faced Jerusalem when they prayed. At the end of these Jews' Yom Kippur services and Passover Seder, they declared, "Next year in Jerusalem!" When secular Zionists entertained the notion of founding a Jewish state in Africa, it was religious minded Russian Jews who insisted on the Zionist State being founded in Israel. Zionism, as secular as it might have turned at times, was always anchored in religious values.

Those who posit that Zionism was purely secular are being intellectually dishonest. They are trying to erase one of the most meaningful aspects of Zionism. Not only was the Zionist movement built on religious values, but many early activists in the Zionist movement were also religious. Just because Zionism didn't advocate a theocracy, didn't mean it was completely secular. There is a well-known strawman argument that secular Jews were the ones to bring the Jews back to Israel, while religious Jews opposed Zionism and insisted on waiting until God sent the Messiah before returning to Israel. While there were religious Jews who opposed Zionism and the Jewish return to Israel without a Divine mandate, there were also many religious Jews who partnered with secular Zionists to found the State of Israel. The notion that Zionism was a purely secular movement is factually incorrect.

The majority of early Zionists were secular Jews. These Jews found meaning in establishing a state of their people. They risked their lives and everything they knew for a dream. They changed the course of Jewish history forever, actualizing the Jewish right to self-determination in their homeland. The connection between Zionism and secularism is one of the parents of Zionism, but it is very far from being its only parent. Zionism and religious Judaism both share the same values; in fact, Zionism took its values from traditional religious Jewish values. Zionism was successful not in spite of its partnership with religious Jews and religious ideology, but because of it.

In their actions and positions, Zionists rebelled against two thousand years of Jewish passivity. Religious and secular Jews together said to the Jewish people that they no longer have to live in exile, they can return home. They no longer have to face the persecution of the Gentiles. To those who believed in waiting for the Messiah, they said we can return to Israel without a Messiah. Religious Jews called on their brethren to fulfill the mitzvah to settle the land of Israel and to live on it. The unfortunate irony is that as Zionism succeeded, religious and secular Zionists didn't graciously share the credit, they each claimed the credit for themselves. They should have celebrated their diverse partnership.

There is a significant difference between seeing Zionism as a secular movement and a secular takeover of the Zionist movement with a complete lack of understanding of religion and religious people's contributions to Zionism and the founding of the State of Israel. There are multiple causes to Israel's success, human innovation, investment, and energy. Those aren't the only factors to Zionism's success. God's providence can't be overlooked. It is close to impossible to credit Israel's military, economic, and social success to just human ingenuity and luck. God's providence is perceived in Israel's success. Prime Minister David Ben Gurion said, "In Israel, in order to be a realist, you must believe in miracles...Life is more than blind forces. There is something more than we can see or perceive, something behind, beyond, and inside man. Nobody can define God, He is beyond definition. He is boundless, infinity, and without end. If we understand religion as not just ritual, then this is religion, the fact that fate alone does not govern history or man, that there is a will that can be exercised, that life is more thana game played by blind forces."

The Jewish people have always struggled with themselves. Internal strife and struggle is an unfortunate feature of the Jewish people. In fact, many people explain the name Israel to mean to struggle with God. From the Biblical stories of the division between Jewish people to the shocking divisions that plagued the warriors of the Warsaw Ghetto uprising, the Jewish people are plagued by infighting. The tragedy of Zionism and Israel today is that with all of its success, the Jewish people are still divided and not ready to unite. We've even repeated the Biblical mistake of our ancestors and invited foreigners to interfere with our internal affairs.

The partnership between religious and secular Jews that created Israel and built the State of Israel is the model that the Jewish state should follow going forward. The answer to creating an even more successful Israel will not be found in erasing Israel's history or trying to ignore the secular or religious aspects of the State. Israel's success to date has been the partnerships and compromises made between religious and secular Zionists. Israel's future depends on ensuring the rightful place of all Jews, irrespective of their political and religious positions.

CHAPTER
EIGHTY-SIX

Does Zionism and the State of Israel have intrinsic value?

Zionism is a diverse movement, made up of various different streams that extend from communist Zionists to cultural Zionists. Due to the early Zionists having never defined Zionism, the movement has accepted many different variations of Zionism and hasn't banned any particular stream from joining as fellow Zionists. Religious Zionism is one of the larger streams within Zionism. This stream is made up of Zionists who combine their observance of Torah and Halacha with Zionist thought and action.

Within the religious Zionist "camp," there are even more extensive streams of Religious Zionists. The different streams of religious Zionism might seem too similar for differentiation to someone who isn't a religious Zionist, but analysis of the different streams demonstrates the different approaches each stream of religious Zionism takes to the overall Zionist movement. Even religious Zionists who are part of one stream might not be aware that other religious Zionists take a completely different approach to Zionism. These different approaches can best be seen in how various religious Zionist scholars and leaders taught Zionism's role in the Jewish people's philosophy and daily life.

One of the major differences found between the different streams of religious Zionism is whether Zionism has intrinsic value or is valuable in so far as it serves a greater value. In Halacha and Jewish philosophy there is a division between actions that are ends in of themselves and actions that are means to an end. A well-known example of the division between ends in of themselves and means to an end is the building of a sukkah. Although fulfillment of the mitzvah to live in a sukkah is dependent on building a Sukkah, in Halacha and Jewish philosophy, the action of building a sukkah is considered a "hechsher mitzvah," a means to the ends of the mitzvah of living in the sukkah and has no intrinsic value in of itself. A division among religious Zionists is whether Zionism, and today's State of Israel, has value in of itself, or is its value merely one of "hechsher mitzvah," and a means to another end.

The stream of religious Zionism that maintains Zionism and the State of Israel have intrinsic value perceive Zionism and the State of Israel as part of the redemption process, claiming it is the first step towards the ultimate redemption and the Messianic era. As Rav Boruch Weider, Rosh Yeshiva at Yeshivat Hakotel in Jerusalem's Old City and student of Rabbi Tzvi Yehuda Kook explained, with the founding of the State of Israel and the beginning of the ultimate redemption, Halacha and Judaism has changed forever. In Rav Weider's and those in his camp's view, the founding of the State of Israel was such a momentous event in Jewish history it changed Jewish destiny in the most fundamental of ways – it changed halacha itself.

Rabbi Efrem Goldberg and Rabbi Josh Broide hosted Rabbi Moshe Meiselman, Rosh Yeshiva of Yeshivas Toras Moshe in Jerusalem, on their weekly show, "Behind the Bima." At one point in the show Rabbi Meiselman, whose uncle was Rav Joseph B. Soloveitchik, was asked about Rabbi Soloveitchik's views on Zionism. Rabbi Soloveitchik is considered one of the foremost leading Rabbis of the religious Zionist movement. Rabbi Meiselman qualified his remarks by telling of the many extensive discussions he shared with his uncle about Zionism. The Rabbi Soloveitchik's position on Zionism, as Rabbi Meiselman explained it, is different than the path many Religious Zionist Torah scholars teach Zionism's role, and how Rabbi Weider explained it. Rabbi Soloveitchik saw Zionism and the State of Israel as a vehicle to understand Torah and observe more mitzvot. Rabbi Soloveitchik maintained the Zionist movement and the State didn't have intrinsic value, but was a "Hechsher Mitzvah," that allowed other mitzvot to be achieved.

The overwhelming approach of religious Zionists today, especially of its leaders and Rabbis, is consistent with Rabbi Weider's approach that Zionism and the State of Israel have intrinsic value. Israel's Chief Rabbinate included the description of the founding of the State of Israel as "The Beginning of the Redemption" in the prayer for the State of Israel recited by many religious Zionist communities every Shabbat and festival. I discussed Rabbi Soloveitchik's view with a leading religious Zionist Torah scholar, and he lamented that expressing the view of Rav Soloveitchik and Rav Meiselman can get one pegged as anti-Zionist by many in the religious Zionist community. Instead of celebrating the diversity of views within the religious Zionist camp, it is unfortunate that some prefer to cancel those with differing views than their own.

The religious stream of Zionism is one rich with scholarship, activism, and loyalty to the Jewish State. Its schools, seminaries, and Yeshivot have produced leading Torah scholars and IDF officers. A sizable percentage of Knesset members boast of being members of the religious Zionist camp, and its popularity has spread outside the borders of Israel. Countless Orthodox Synagogues around the world consider themselves part of the religious Zionist camp and fly an Israeli flag in the front of their Synagogues, right next to the Ark. Religious Zionists and its philosophy will grow richer with the celebration of diversity of thought and opinions within its camp.

CHAPTER
EIGHTY-SEVEN

The Antisemitism Equation

One of the most hotly debated topics in the Israel space is whether anti-Zionism is a form or cover for antisemitism. Jonathan Greenblatt, the Director of the Anti-Defamation League gave a groundbreaking speech where he stated, "To those who still cling to the idea that anti-Zionism is not anti-Semitism, let me clarify this for you as clearly as I can—anti-Zionism is anti-Semitism. I will repeat: Anti-Zionism is anti-Semitism." This was the first time a recognized authority on antisemitism had stated unequivocally that Anti-Zionism is antisemitism.

The colloquial definition of Zionism - the right of the Jewish people to determine their own future in their historic homeland- should be accepted by all; after all, why should Jews be singled out as not having the right to self-determination or living on their ancient homeland? There is debate over whether criticism of Israel qualifies as antisemitism. These debates are often visceral and lacking the metrics necessary to judge which position is more accurate.

There are many books, articles and position papers written about when criticism of Israel crosses into antisemitism. The most well-known is the International Holocaust Remembrance Alliance definition of antisemitism which states, "Antisemitism is a certain perception of Jews, which may be expressed as hatred toward Jews. Rhetorical and physical manifestations of antisemitism are directed toward Jewish or non-Jewish individuals and/or their property, toward Jewish community institutions and religious facilities." The IHRA provided a few examples, "Manifestations might include the targeting of the state of Israel, conceived as a Jewish collectivity." If accusations against Israel include lies or if they are applied in a double standard, where only Israel is singled out, the IHRA defines that criticism as having crossed a line into antisemitism.

The IHRA's definition of antisemitism and the examples given help us understand antisemitism and when it should be applied, but how did the IHRA reach its conclusions about what criticism of Israel qualifies as antisemitism? To explain I'll posit an equation that can help us understand and then offer a few examples to show how the equation is applied.

Using a simple formula of A+X=C, we can formulate an effective manner of identifying antisemitic criticism of Israel. When A is the criticism (for example, criticizing checkpoints) and added or included in the accusation or criticism is discrimination (the 'X' in our equation) the criticism or accusation becomes antisemitic. If the criticism or accusation lacks discrimination it is legitimate and not antisemitic. The factor that determines whether criticism is antisemitic is if it includes discrimination or hate.

If someone criticizes Israel's checkpoints separating the West Bank from Israel, and their criticism is based on facts without exaggeration of falsification and doesn't single Israel out for crimes anyone else is doing, their critique is without discrimination and isn't antisemitic. If an accusation is levied against the Israeli policy of sterilizing Arab children, it is easy to determine the accusation includes falsification and is therefore antisemitic according to IHRA definition of antisemitism.

One more factor needs to be mentioned when discussing the line of when criticism of Israel qualifies as antisemitism. There are certain accusations and criticism levied against Israel that are inherently antisemitic. These include accusations that are made of classic antisemitic tropes, like controlling political systems, uses a double standard, calls for the death or harm of Jews, or makes dehumanizing, demonizing or stereotypical allegations against Jews. These inherently antisemitic accusations are different from accidentally antisemitic accusations that require the addition of hate or discrimination to be considered antisemitic.

The Antisemitic Equation is a technical method of determining whether criticism of Israel is antisemitic. Most Zionists shy away from methodical determinations of antisemitism, preferring the gut or intuitive calling out of antisemitism instead. Their argument makes sense; after thousands of years of antisemitism, Jews know it when they see it. Although the technical look at antisemitism isn't the favored choice, it is a crucial instrument in the Zionists' arsenal of tools to be used when calling out unacceptable hate directed at them. If Zionist responses to hate was based solely on intuition and feelings, their haters could easily deny the claim against them. With a highly technical way of defining the line of when anti-Israel criticism becomes offensive antisemitism there is an undeniable metric to call out antisemitism.

CHAPTER
EIGHTY-EIGHT

Why do people hate Zionism?

One of the most shameful episodes in United Nations history was when Yasser Arafat threatened the United Nations: (after removing the gun from his holster) "Today I have come bearing an olive branch and a freedom fighter's gun. Do not let the olive branch fall from my hand." That threat bullied the United Nations into granting the Palestinians observer status at the United Nations. One year later the United Nations passed resolution 3379, stating "Zionism is racism." 75 countries agreed with this sentiment about Zionism. Ultimately the resolution was revoked, but the stigma against Zionism remained.

While not all anti-Zionism is based in antisemitism, it's difficult to divorce the two from each other. The IHRA principles of antisemitism include, "Denying the Jewish people their right to self-determination, e.g., by claiming that the existence of a State of Israel is a racist endeavor." Zionism is a political movement that aims to achieve and protect the Jewish right to self-determination. When one objects to Zionism, they object to the right of self-determination for the Jewish people – which is antisemitic. It's no coincidence that a report on antisemitism from ADL's Center on Extremism found anti-Israel groups on US college and university campuses frequently demean and ostracizes pro-Israel Jewish students, and occasionally descend into antisemitism.

The most prevalent motivator of anti-Zionism is antisemitism. Thousands of years of research has offered a myriad of theories to the causes of antisemitism, but no definitive cause has been demonstrated. In an ironic twist, some of the theories are themselves antisemitic! People who hate Jews – for whatever reason – obviously don't want the Jewish people to have their own state on their own land. Antisemitism often presents itself as anti-Zionism.

The Jewish people aren't just a religion, they are a nation. A Jew who doesn't maintain Judaism as part of their life, having rejected the Torah's values and axioms, is still a member of the Jewish nation. All nations deserve the right of self-determination. The nation of the Jews, historically known as Israelites, deserve to determine their own future. Anti-Zionists view Jews as belonging to one religion, not one nation. Their denial of Jewish nationhood is a more heinous immorality than their hatred of Zionism, but one undoubtedly leads to the other.

Zionism wasn't just a movement to actualize Jewish self-determination – it focused on a place as well. The Jewish people are the indigenous people of the land of Israel. Zionism aimed to bring the Jewish people back to their ancestral homeland, the land of Israel. When anti-Zionists deny the nationhood of the Jewish people, they're also denying the Jewish people the rights to their land. The same claim made against the Jewish people – they're not a nation so they don't deserve to determine their own future as a people – is applied to the Jewish people with land. They're not a nation, so they don't deserve their own land. More insidious of an accusation is the denial of the historical connection of the Jewish people to their own land. Anti-Zionists frequently peddle the false claim that Jews are colonialist foreigners who came from Europe to occupy a native people's land.

Whether it's antisemitism, the denial of the Jewish people as a nation, the refusal to recognize the right of Jewish self-determination, or the validity of the Jewish nation to their own homeland, or the historical connection between the Jewish people and the land of Israel, anti-Zionism is unjustifiable. Anti-Zionists aim to cancel the Jewish people and their rights, and the only legitimate response to that hate is to shine a light on it and call it out for what it is – ignorant slander.

Inherent to the values of Zionism is proclaiming the movement and its values' legitimacy. For two thousand years the people of the world, whether they were Pagan, Christian or Muslim, denied the Jewish people their rights as a nation. Zionism dreamed that Jews should be equal to the other nations of the world and reclaim their rights. Allowing others to decry Zionism as racist, illegitimate or without validity is to abandon the battle Zionists have successfully fought for over 150 years.

Many argue that Zionism is a movement that has lived past its expiration date. They claim that Zionism aimed to establish a Jewish homeland in Israel, and it achieved its goal in 1948. Now that there's a state of Israel, Zionism is no longer a necessary movement. Zionism is the philosophical backbone of the continuous existence of a Jewish state and as long as the world lends credence to anti-Zionists, it remains a necessary cause. Zionists must stand up for themselves and their rights.

CHAPTER
EIGHTY-NINE

Meeting people where they are but not on Israel

Rabbis in Europe in the *alter heim* were solely responsible to answer the Jews of their town's questions on Jewish law. If one of their followers had a chicken whose kashrut was questionable, they'd bring the chicken to the town's Rabbi, and he'd examine the chicken and decide whether it was kosher or not. The Rabbi would usually only deliver a speech twice a year, on the Shabbat between Rosh Hashanah and Yom Kippur and the Shabbat preceding Passover.

Most of today's Rabbis understand their role as more multifaceted. Rabbis still answer their congregants' questions on Jewish law, but they also teach more, encourage greater mitzvah observance, and some even discuss politics. Zionist Rabbis discuss Israel and the events occurring in the land of Israel. "kiruv," which is encouraging or teaching non-observant or unaffiliated Jews the beauty of Torah and Mitzvot, has become a large part of every Rabbi's role and responsibilities.

There is an important technique in teaching people about mitzvah observance - meet the people where they are, not where they should be in their Torah observance. When teaching someone who isn't observant about the Mitzvot, piling on about all they're doing wrong and all they must change in their life isn't effective and will likely turn them away from Torah more than it will turn them towards Torah. A slow and patient introduction to enjoyable Mitzvot, like Shabbat meals, Chanukah candle lighting, and Simchat Torah celebrations, are effective and attractive introductions to the world of Mitzvot and Halacha.

Many Rabbis understand this and practice it every day of their lives. Unfortunately, for Rabbis who talk about Israel, some think that because a slow introduction to Torah works for Mitzvot and Halacha, it also works for all other areas of their Rabbinate as well. This is incorrect when it comes to Israel.

Many – but thankfully not all – of the younger generation of Jews today are highly critical of Israel. Many Rabbis make the mistake that to connect to the younger generation they must meet the younger generation where they are - with heavy criticism of Israel. They'll defend Israel's raids to stop terror but introduce their defense of Israel with an acquiescence to Anti-Zionists' claims of Israeli occupation and oppression. "Sure, Israel denies Palestinians their rightful freedoms," they'll give in, "but you have to understand Israel's security needs." This is a dangerous approach because in admitting to the slander Anti-Zionists throw at Israel, they're undermining their support of Israel.

When a Rabbi tells their congregation or students that Israel has robbed Palestinians of their land, mistreats Palestinians, or has apartheid policies, they're not meeting their audience where they are and opening their minds to a different perspective. Instead of supporting Israel, they've reinforced the slanderous accusations Anti-Zionists and Israel's enemies have been lying about for decades. That reinforcement undermines the support for Israel they think they're giving to the Jewish state and the Jewish people.

There is a significant difference between meeting someone where they are when it comes to Torah observance and when it comes to Israel. Rabbis will not permit violations of Halacha by saying explicitly that it's acceptable to not fulfill or violate Halacha since the Jew they're teaching is working towards better observance. There are no general allowances for allowing Torah violations. Rabbis should apply the same principle of not allowing slander against Israel when discussing Israeli events or policies to a more critical audience.

If a Rabbi wants to support Israel, they must do two things. One, don't defend Israel. Israel is older than half the nations in the world, is one of the world's top ten economies and militaries, and its people the fourth happiest in the world. It is widely praised for its moral treatment of minorities under its control. Supporters of Israel only weaken Israel by trying to answer the slander its accused of on a daily basis. Second, no matter the calculations and strategy, don't undermine support of Israel by admitting to the slanderous accusations made by Israel's enemies.

Israel and her people appreciate all the support it gets from around the world. Rabbis play an important role in supporting Israel. As community leaders, teachers, and role models, many look to Rabbis for guidance and moral direction. When a Rabbi supports Israel, the Rabbi's congregants, students, and followers are taught that Israel is a nation worthy of the Jewish people's support. In a world that follows "influencers," a Rabbi can play the role of Jewish influencer and bring a great deal of support to Israel.

The phone call came at dinner time in Israel; a distraught former student was calling from his college campus in Texas. "Rabbi! There are 20 students from my school holding a rally against Israel. They have Palestinian flags and large posters accusing Israel of war crimes, apartheid, and racism against Palestinians. I want to shut them down, what do I do? What should I say?" I could hear the pain and frustration in his voice. I calmly reminded him that he shouldn't try to debate or prove them wrong. I advised him to purchase a large piece of oak tag and in big letters make a list of his five favorite parts of Israel and stand near the rally. When they go negative, I told him, we go positive and talk about our values and achievements. People walking by will be more attracted to positive messaging about Israel than negative attacks against Israel. He got his oak tag, made his list and proudly reported back to me that many of the students walking by the rally approached him to talk to him about Israel and Zionism.

The Pro-Israel community in Israel and the Diaspora has taken a largely defensive approach to talking about Israel. Activists' talking points largely center around the antisemitic and ineffectual nature of the BDS movement and other boycotts of Israel. Online activity is spent disproving Palestinian accusations against Israeli control of land and answering the Squad's charges against Israeli policies. While there's nothing wrong with self-defense, and effectively disproving Palestinian charges against Israel is important, it's become almost the entirety of Pro-Israel messaging.

If we rewind 150 years, we see much different Zionist messaging than today. The Zionist Congresses were about planning a Jewish state in Eretz

Yisrael. They were full of hope and optimism and the sky was the limit to their dreams. From 1900 until the establishment of the State of Israel in 1948, Zionists were getting down to brass tactics. They were bringing people from Europe to Israel and creating institutions like the Jewish Agency and Keren Kayemet L'Yisrael. After the establishment of the State Zionists focused on transitioning from a movement to building a Jewish State. After Israel's stunning victory in the 1967 Six Day War, euphoria turned to complacency as Palestinians began organizing as a people and took an offensive against Israel.

A surprising dichotomy between Israelis and their opponents' talking points is that it's only Israelis that are on the defensive. When our enemies are accused of using terrorism, being intransigent, and violating human rights, they don't try to defend themselves – they ignore the charge and go on to their next point. They don't seem to mind the accusations. Jewish values don't allow us to be immoral, cruel or insensitive to suffering. Jews value morality, generosity and helping the downtrodden. Jews become defensive when accused of actions that take away from the values we hold dear. We also can't discount the defensiveness that the exile in foreign lands, under constant attack, ingrained into our national DNA.

Zionism is one of the foundational points of Judaism. That statement might sound shocking considering how much of the Jewish world rejected Zionism in its early years. The idea that Jews should live freely, determining their own future and in their own land, is a consensus point Jews from across different communities all maintain to be authentic Jewish values. As a foundational point of Judaism, Zionism should be taught, boasted about and promoted across the world. Most Jewish anti-Zionists don't disagree with these fundamental points. Their opposition stemmed from timing, tactics and consequences.

Zionism has been largely replaced by supporting Israel in various different ways. Instead of expressing Zionist values, the message is to lobby for Israel, support Israel on social media, and recruit people to be supportive of Israel. This support of Israel is commendable and necessary, but it doesn't focus on Zionist, Israeli, and Jewish values. Outside of vigorously defending our rights, we've stopped talking about being a free nation, determining our future in our own homeland and how that transforms our nation.

We can't allow being Pro-Israel to cannibalize our Zionism. If we don't focus enough on Zionism and its values we're going to become a people who can easily forget the values that make us unique. The student mentioned at the start of this essay thought the best way to support Israel would be to confront and shut down Israel's opponents. He quickly learned the best thing to do is discuss Israel's values. Zionists have a great deal to be proud of; it's time we focused on our values and achievements.

CHAPTER
NINETY

Warning! Being Pro-Israel could be taking away from your Zionism

The phone call came at dinner time in Israel; a distraught former student was calling from his college campus in Texas. "Rabbi! There are 20 students from my school holding a rally against Israel. They have Palestinian flags and large posters accusing Israel of war crimes, apartheid, and racism against Palestinians. I want to shut them down, what do I do? What should I say?" I could hear the pain and frustration in his voice. I calmly reminded him that he shouldn't try to debate or prove them wrong. I advised him to purchase a large piece of oak tag and in big letters make a list of his five favorite parts of Israel and stand near the rally. When they go negative, I told him, we go positive and talk about our values and achievements. People walking by will be more attracted to positive messaging about Israel than negative attacks against Israel. He got his oak tag, made his list and proudly reported back to me that many of the students walking by the rally approached him to talk to him about Israel and Zionism.

The Pro-Israel community in Israel and the Diaspora has taken a largely defensive approach to talking about Israel. Activists' talking points largely center around the antisemitic and ineffectual nature of the BDS movement and other boycotts of Israel. Online activity is spent disproving Palestinian accusations against Israeli control of land and answering the Squad's charges against Israeli policies. While there's nothing wrong with self-defense, and effectively disproving Palestinian charges against Israel is important, it's become almost the entirety of Pro-Israel messaging.

If we rewind 150 years we see much different Zionist messaging than today. The Zionist Congresses were about planning a Jewish state in Eretz Yisrael. They were full of hope and optimism and the sky was the limit to their dreams. From 1900 until the establishment of the State of Israel in 1948, Zionists were getting down to brass tactics. They were bringing people from Europe to Israel and creating institutions like the Jewish Agency and Keren Kayemet L'Yisrael. After the establishment of the State Zionists focused on transitioning from a movement to building a Jewish State. After Israel's stunning victory in the 1967 Six Day War, euphoria turned to complacency as Palestinians began organizing as a people, and took an offensive against Israel.

A surprising dichotomy between Israelis and their opponents' talking points is that it's only Israelis that are on the defensive. When our enemies are accused of using terrorism, being intransigent, and violating human rights, they don't try to defend themselves – they ignore the charge and go on to their next point. They don't seem to mind the accusations. Jewish values don't allow us to be immoral, cruel or insensitive to suffering. Jews value morality, generosity and helping the downtrodden. Jews become defensive when accused of actions that take away from the values we hold dear. We also can't discount the defensiveness that the exile in foreign lands, under constant attack, ingrained into our national DNA.

Zionism is one of the foundational points of Judaism. That statement might sound shocking considering how much of the Jewish world rejected Zionism in its early years. The idea that Jews should live freely, determining their own future and in their own land, is a consensus point Jews from across different communities all maintain to be authentic Jewish values. As a foundational point of Judaism, Zionism should be taught, boasted about and promoted across the world. Most Jewish anti-Zionists don't disagree with these fundamental points. Their opposition stemmed from timing, tactics and consequences.

Zionism has been largely replaced by supporting Israel in various different ways. Instead of expressing Zionist values, the message is to lobby for Israel, support Israel on social media, and recruit people to be supportive of Israel. This support of Israel is commendable and necessary, but it doesn't focus on Zionist, Israeli, and Jewish values. Outside of vigorously defending our rights, we've stopped talking about being a free nation, determining our future in our own homeland and how that transforms our nation.

We can't allow being Pro-Israel to cannibalize our Zionism. If we don't focus enough on Zionism and its values we're going to become a people who can easily forget the values that make us unique. The student mentioned at the start of this essay thought the best way to support Israel would be to confront and shut down Israel's opponents. He quickly learned the best thing to do is discuss Israel's values. Zionists have a great deal to be proud of; it's time we focused on our values and achievements.

CHAPTER
NINETY-ONE

Not all inequalities are equal

Israel is not to blame for the Palestinians' poor choices.

Western nations share the belief that all people are created equal. Yet treating all people equally is not something that comes automatically. So, creating equality is an important objective for all nations and communities. There is no justifiable reason why one human being should be held back due to institutional policies. State-imposed disadvantages for one group of people—like slavery—are clearly immoral.

A just society ensures inequalities do not develop. A progressive society actively seeks out inequalities and seeks to correct them. In fact, the Torah commands Jews to do precisely this. While the Torah cannot be pigeonholed into a single modern political movement, on this issue, the Torah is progressive.

However, not all inequalities are equal. While inequalities imposed on others require correction, inequalities that result from a person's choices are not society's responsibility to correct. For example, if a person chooses to spend years in medical school and earns a high salary, while their friend decides to skip school for a lower-paying job, the inequality that results cannot be blamed on society at large.

Such self-imposed inequalities can result from forgoing education, financial recklessness and criminal activity. A person in prison is unequal, but has no one to blame but himself.

Moreover, at times, leaders make choices that create inequalities that affect their entire society. The individual citizen is not at fault for their leaders' choices, but they nonetheless suffer the consequences. Thus, if leaders are unjust, the people must rise up, rebel and overthrow those leaders, even at the risk of life and limb. Free nations usually become free only by toppling despotic rulers.

People, especially progressives, often see all inequalities as societal faults that require correction, including inequalities that are the result of poor personal or political choices. For example, we often find apologists for the Palestinians and many Jews characterize the inequalities brought about by poor Palestinian choices as unjust inequalities.

In 1948, the Arabs who lived in then-Palestine made the choice to oppose and fight the Jews who declared a Jewish state. They could have accepted the U.N. partition plan, but chose not to. This poor choice led to their defeat. For the next two decades, the State of Israel extended its hand in peace to the Arab nation. The Israelis' offer was repeatedly rejected, and the Arabs chose to attack the Jewish state instead of making peace. Over the next five decades, Israel continued to offer peace. Countries like Egypt, Jordan, the UAE and Bahrain accepted and enjoy the resulting benefits. They made the right choice.

The Palestinians, however, consistently chose to reject every offer of peace. They made poor choices and have suffered the consequences. This is their own doing and their own fault.

There are great inequalities between Israelis and Palestinians. These inequalities are not unjust inequalities that are Israel's obligation to correct. They are inequalities caused by the Palestinians' poor personal and political choices. Israel cannot force the Palestinians to make the right choice and choose to end the Israeli-Palestinian conflict via a peace deal.

There are Palestinians who want peace with Israel and an end to the Israeli-Palestinian conflict. They blame the Palestinian leadership for refusing to make peace. It is possible that the Palestinian people can only achieve peace with Israel by overthrowing their leadership and taking life and death risks to improve their situation. While the world would prefer a smooth and bloodless transition to freedom and prosperity, it is not likely.

Blaming Israel for the inequalities Palestinians face due to their poor choices is intellectually dishonest. Characterizing the Palestinians' predicament as "oppression," "occupation" or "apartheid" blames Israel for the Palestinians' poor choices, which is deceitful.

Progressives interested in improving the Palestinians' situation should not act as Palestinian apologists and blame Israel. They should push the Palestinian leadership to reform or for Palestinians to overthrow it.

CHAPTER
NINETY-TWO

The progressive argument for Zionism

Judaism has a long and rich history of caring for other people and making kindness towards others a top priority. The Jewish tradition of caring for others is expressed strongly with a statement by Maimonides, " We have never seen nor heard of a Jewish community that does not have a charity fund." The Jewish people raise their children to care about other people, teaching them at a young age to think past themselves and see the needs of those around them. Over two-thirds of Israelis give charity regularly, and when world Jewry's donations to Israel are counted, that number rises significantly. Jews are a caring people who prioritize looking out for the poor and unfortunate.

Progressivism is a movement that hopes to direct political power to improving people's lives. Progressives believe humanity has the potential to move on a constant course of development, but it requires political action to hasten its advancement. Unfortunately, and for no good reason, many progressives maintain an anti-Zionist and anti-Israel position. In the American Congress, a small group of progressive representatives, self-coined "The Squad," offer constant anti-Israel vitriol. The trend among progressives is to oppose Israel and accuse it of being an oppressive nation towards the Palestinians who live within the areas Israel controls. Even progressives who aren't familiar with the Israeli and Palestinian conflict are pressured by identity politics to oppose Israel.

It's almost in Jewish DNA to care about events in the world. Many Jews who advocate, donate, and support Israel are critical of Jews who are concerned about a myriad of causes except Israel. These Jews, many of whom identify as progressive, answer this criticism by questioning the foundation of the challenge. Why should they care more about Israel and Jews than other countries and human beings? Why should Jerusalem's Jews matter to them more than China's Uyghurs? In his essay, "The Jewish Question" Bruno Bauer addressed the way Jews can gain freedom, "No one in Germany is politically emancipated. We ourselves are not free. How are we to free you? You Jews are egoists if you demand a special emancipation for yourselves as Jews. As Germans, you ought to work for the political emancipation of Germany, and as human beings, for the emancipation of mankind, and you should feel the particular kind of your oppression and your shame not as an exception to the rule, but on the contrary as a confirmation of the rule." Progressives champion universalism over a particularism that focuses on helping Jews first.

If progressives would take a fresh and honest look at today's Israel, they'd see a nation that lives up to almost all progressive ideals. The policies and values Israel holds dear are consistent with progressive priorities. Israel offers universal health care for all its citizens, and it offers some of the top medical care in the world. Israel puts an emphasis on equality among all its citizens, irrespective of race, identity, or religion. Israel's placing primacy on equality is the envy of its region. The availability of higher education for low affordability is another progressive gem of Israel. There may be areas progressives can see need improvement in Israel, but in comparison to other nations of the world, and especially in the Middle East, progressives should champion Israel.

Israel's Declaration of Independence includes progressive values, "The State of Israel will be open for Jewish immigration and for the Ingathering of the Exiles; it will foster the development of the country for the benefit of all its inhabitants; it will be based on freedom, justice and peace as envisaged by the prophets of Israel; it will ensure complete equality of social and political rights to all its inhabitants irrespective of religion, race or sex; it will guarantee freedom of religion, conscience, language, education and culture; it will safeguard the Holy Places of all religions; and it will be faithful to the principles of the Charter of the United Nations." It's nothing short of a tragedy that progressive Jews express their identity by standing in opposition to a nation committed to protecting the values progressives hold most dear.

It is common sense for Jews to care about their people and nation first and make them a priority. Advocating a Jewish approach that puts Jews and

Israel at the bottom of the Jewish caring tree solely because those that need are also Jews lacks in common sense that people will care about themselves and their people first. Zionism is designed to not only help the Jewish people but to create a Jewish state that will help the rest of the world. Israel's record of being the first medical and search and rescue teams on the ground at so many tragedies around the world demonstrates its priority of helping the entire global community.

The progressive argument for Zionism is strong. American Congressman Ritchie Torres put it best, "Progressivism is about the struggle for liberation, and Zionism is the struggle for Jewish liberation." A similar perspective came from Arizona State Representative Alma Hernandez mirroring Torres's sentiments, "I am a progressive because I am a Zionist." Progressives that consider their values as inconsistent with Zionism are making a grave error and robbing themselves and their movement of a strong partner in their activism. Progressives who want to see their values advance around the Middle East should join the Zionist movement and support a progressive Israel.

CHAPTER

NINETY-THREE

Can antisemitism be stopped?

As a target of hate for decades there is hardly a better person to explain hate and how to get past it than former South African President Nelson Mandela. He wrote, "No one is born hating another person because of the color of his skin or his background or his religion. People must learn to hate, and if they can learn to hate, they can be taught to love. For love comes more naturally to the human heart than its opposite." Mandela's words are powerful and seem to make sense, but there's one problem with them. Mandela's idea is predicated on teaching people to love instead of hate. If society is racist and hateful and they're taught to love, they can overcome their hate. The problem with this theory is that if society is hateful, who is going to teach the next generation to love?

Criticism of Israel isn't antisemitic, there are 120 members of Israel's Knesset who consistently criticize Israel. Calling for Israel's annihilation, delegitimizing Israel, slandering Israel, or holding Israel to a double standard reserved only for Israel and not other nations, is antisemitic. So much of today's anti-Zionism is fueled by antisemitism and so many anti-Zionist organizations are full of antisemites. Jews have always worried about antisemitism; anti-Zionism is another layer of hate that causes Jews even more concern.

Understanding when antisemitism began is a challenging undertaking. Is the first person to hate a Jew considered an antisemite? The Talmudic Sages taught that antisemitism is a constant of Jewish existence, and they used the phrase "Esau hates Jacob" to express the sentiment. Their teaching hearkens back to the biblical twins, seemingly suggesting that antisemitism goes back to our patriarchs and matriarchs in biblical times. Jewish tradition understands antisemitism to be a rule of Jewish existence just as much as any other aspect of Jewish life. The Passover Haggadah expressed this acutely, when more than a thousand years ago it wrote, "In every generation the [Jewish enemies] stand up to wipe us out, and God saves us from their hand." Not only is antisemitism ancient, it seems to be eternal and infinite.

Antisemitism reached a crescendo in the late 19th Century in Eastern Europe. Pogroms were a consistent feature of life for Jews of Poland and Russia. The future for Jews looked bleak and no one had a solution to the plague that was killing Jews and making life impossible for the survivors. A journalist at the time, Theodore Herzl, was becoming increasingly despondent over the situation. Later in life he wrote of that time, "In Paris... I achieved a freer attitude toward anti-Semitism, which I now began to understand historically and to pardon. Above all, I recognized the emptiness and futility of trying to "combat" anti-Semitism."

As Herzl's thoughts on antisemitism began to develop, his positions did as well. Dr. Gil Troy, a Zionist scholar, wrote of journalist Herzl covering the Dreyfus trial, "How could this happen, Herzl wonders, reeling, even before it becomes obvious that conniving Jew-haters framed Dreyfus. We Jews have worked so hard to be accepted. Yet, we are always suspect. Even if one of us is guilty, why does that crime condemn us all? Only when Jews have a proper sense of nationalism, a proper state of our own, a Jewish state, will we be respected - and truly free."

As an answer to antisemitism Herzl thought of returning the Jewish people to their homeland, the land of Israel. In the introduction to his book, "The Jewish State" Herzl wrote, "The idea which I develop in this pamphlet is an age-old one," Herzl wrote, "the establishment of a Jewish State.... What matters is the driving force. What is that force? The distress of the Jews... Everywhere we have sincerely endeavored to merge with the national communities surrounding us and to preserve only the faith of our fathers. We are not permitted to do so. In vain are we loyal patriots, in some places even extravagantly so; in vain do we make the same sacrifices of life and property as our fellow citizens; in vain do we strive to enhance the fame of our native countries in the arts and sciences, or their wealth through trade and commerce. In our native lands where, after all, we too have lived for centuries, we are decried as aliens..." Herzl also wrote, "I think the Jews will always have sufficient enemies, such as every nation has. But once fixed in their own land, it will no longer be possible for them to scatter all over the world."

Although Israel was designed to address antisemitism, it wasn't thought to end it, and it hasn't. In their paper "An End to Antisemitism!" Armin Lange, Kerstin Mayerhofer, Dina Porat, and Lawrence H. Schiffman wrote, "The long-term eradication of antisemitism will take generations and will only be possible through concerted efforts of cultural and religious institutions worldwide. The short-term combating and restraining of antisemitism are possible in this generation. To achieve both key aims of the fight against antisemitism, we recommend a five-step process that combines both short-term and long-term strategies." Their five steps are, "Assessment, comprehending the problem, awareness-raising, application of policies for combating antisemitism, and adjusting the general policies to combat antisemitism." The paper's goals are commendable, but not convincing.

It's difficult to see an end to antisemitism. As a four-thousand-year-old plague with no tested solution that has worked, there is little cause for optimism to think antisemitism will end. While Israel has done an admirable role in providing a place of refuge for Jews fleeing antisemitic persecution, it hasn't ended antisemitism. In many ways it has centralized antisemitism and provided a new avenue for antisemites to attack Jews. Zionism allowed the Jewish people to manage antisemitism for the first time in Jewish history, maybe one day it will be the method Jews use to end it. If Zionism isn't successful on its own to stop antisemitism, Jewish Sages have promised that the nations of the world will no longer hate, and instead will support the Jewish people, when the Messiah arrives – may that day come soon.

CHAPTER
NINETY-FOUR

Other People's Perceptions of Israel

One of a parent's biggest challenges is ingraining the value of not worrying about what other people think of them in their children and encouraging them to do the right thing. Children feel peer pressure more than adults and when children face the judgment of other people it isn't easy for them to act correctly. A child must be courageous to stand up to their friends' pressure to do the wrong thing. Standing up to this pressure as an adult is much easier, but it still presents a challenge.

Nations also face pressure from other nations and their leaders must withstand that pressure and judgment to do the right thing. Like children facing social consequences for standing up to the bullies in their classroom, nations face economic and military consequences for standing against international pressure. Nations with moral fortitude stand up to pressure from the global community and make the right policy decisions.

Israel isn't immune to international pressures, and it seems to be overly sensitive to those pressures. Israelis and their advocates constantly worry about the opinions of American college students. Jonathan Greenblatt, the head of the Anti-Defamation League said, "What we're seeing on campuses across the country is a kind of virulent anti-Zionism that purports to be about Palestinian rights, but in reality, results in the marginalization and the demonization of all Jewish students." These same people are worried about a perceived drop in support for Israel among American adults and are constantly worried about American support for Israel in the United States Congress.

Israeli concern for American's opinions about Israel is a curious phenomenon. One never reads about Americans concerned over Israelis' opinions about America and its policies. President Obama's approval ratings in Israel where dismal, yet his low ratings didn't seem to factor into his decisions about American policy in general and especially not towards Israel. Not only does America rarely consider Israeli opinion, but it also rarely takes world opinion into consideration when making policy decisions. What can explain Israeli and Israel advocates' obsession with American opinion of Israel?

The obvious explanation for why Israel and its advocates put so much emphasis on American opinion is because of the significant amount of American diplomatic and military aid Israel receives from the United States. The fear is that if American support dips below some imaginary line Israel will lose American aid. The fear over college students' opinions is that today's American college students are tomorrow's American leaders and if they don't appreciate the U.S.-Israel relationship as college students, they won't support it as America's elected leaders when they "grow-up."

The United States gives military and diplomatic aid to Israel not because they like Israel (or because of Jewish money as Congresswoman Ilhan Omar tweeted) but because it's in America's best interest for America to have a strong alliance with Israel. Many people become cynical when discussing the U.S.-Israel relationship and assume Congresspeople don't really put America's interests first, but especially when it comes to American foreign policy Congress prioritizes America's interests when deciding on supporting allies.

A strong U.S.-Israel relationship has and will always be in America's best interests. Israel has become a dominant world player on many global stages. Its military innovation is world famous, with innovations that can bring down hundreds of enemy rockets and hunt terrorist masterminds hidden in labyrinths of tunnels. Israel is also a technological hive, the "Start-Up" nation second only to America's Silicon Valley. Israel is a strategic ally that many consider America's best friend and America's guiding light in a dark neighborhood of tyranny, dictatorships and oppression.

Israel also shares values of life, liberty and the pursuit of happiness with America. It is a moral country known as having the "most moral army in the world." Americans are well known for coming to Israel and leaving thinking that Israelis are just like them. They appreciate Israel's role as the only true

Democracy in the Middle East. American support of Israel is guaranteed because of Israel's role as an American strategic partner and the values the two nations share.

While Israel has little to fear from a drop-in American support, the obsession over American support detracts and weakens Israel's sovereignty. Strong nations do what is in their best interests and don't fear other nations' concerns. American aid is important to Israel, but Israel is no longer the weak and small country dependent on American aid. It would take Israel years to recover from a loss of American aid – which isn't a concern – Israel is a developed and strong country that doesn't need to hold back from adopting policies in its best interests out of fear of American public opinion.

No sensible advocate of Israeli strength would argue for ignoring America's leaders, but a healthy balance between caring and obsession must be found when it comes to Israeli concern over American support. Israel must take actions and policies it thinks is right and not be concerned with American or other people's perceptions. Israel has reached a point in its history and destiny when it can take policy steps it feared in its past. Israelis and their advocates should no longer fret over what opinion polls seem to rate Israeli support on American college campuses and instead focus on progress on the ground in Israel.

CHAPTER

NINETY-FIVE

Zionists don't need to plead their case

"Here's your opportunity, you'll have five minutes to explain your position, and then we'll open for questions.". The moderator of this discussion explained that her organization wanted me to explain why I live in Israel and why I think Israel's positions on various issues are justified. I found the moderator's directions odd. Why would I need to justify where I live or the policies of my government? I've never seen a similar talk given by people who live in other countries unless they were an official spokesperson of their government. I'm an educator, not a spokesperson for the government of Israel.

For two thousand years, Europeans and Arabs persecuted Jews and accused them of being imposters in foreign lands. Jews were told to "Go back to Palestine!" Jews were forced to justify their presence in lands not their own. With the advent of modern political Zionism in the late 1800's a movement began that aimed to not only give Jews the freedom to determine their own future in their own land, but to never have to make excuses or justify their presence again.

In 1948 Zionists achieved their goals, founded the State of Israel, and declared to world Jewry they could return home to their historic homeland. Furthermore, Zionists called to their fellow Jews they had a right to return to Eretz Yisrael. 74 years later, Israel is an established State with a leading military and economy.

In today's Israel, Jews live in their ancestral homeland where they govern it as free people and determine their own destiny. It is a dream come true, and some believe it to be miraculous. Yet, some see Israel as an immoral nation and Jews have no excuse to live in their own homeland.

Israelis aren't the only people who celebrate a successful State of Israel. Zionists around the world celebrate a successful and thriving State of Israel. Zionists around the world support Israel through financial donations, activism and lobbying their governments to support a strong relationship with the State of Israel. As my friend Jonah wrote to me, "As a Jew in the diaspora who has friends, family, and a connection to the Land, I feel I have a say to a certain extent on where the country is headed for the sake of its safety and survival because that has an effect on Jews in the diaspora as well. Israel is in a volatile region and therefore requires a lot of critical thinking to propose ideas for the sake of the safety and well-being of Israelis (and Palestinians) and the ideas I propose are based on my honest assessment on what I believe is best for both Israelis and Palestinians."

For the most part Israelis are greatly appreciative of the support global Zionists lend Israel and completely understand their desire to influence events in Israel. Many suggestions from Zionists around the world are helpful and are creative ideas. Some Zionists from around the world are left wondering why Israelis don't respond to their ideas.

Whether ideas come from friendly Zionists or opposing anti-Zionists, many Israelis no longer feel the need to respond to every critique or suggestion offered to them. After 74 years of success and having created a thriving state in the face of enemy armies and economic boycotts, Israelis should be forgiven when they don't respond to suggestions that seem impractical or unfairly critical to them.

Zionists don't need help, nor do they need a case made for Zionism. If people want to oppose Israelis' choice to live on their ancestral homeland, that's their prerogative. Either way Israelis are still going to live on their land, as they have for thousands of years and govern as they have for over half a century. As a Jew living in Israel, I find it somewhat amusing those foreigners living thousands of miles away from me, come up with ways I should lead my life, while I would never presume to do the same to them.

I explained to the moderator who wanted me to justify where I live and the policies of my Israeli government that Zionists never need to plead their case again. Zionists have succeeded, are well established and no longer have to justify their existence. If activists in London, Paris, New York or San

Francisco accuse Israel of stealing other people's land or mistreating others, Israelis have no reason to answer their accusations. Israel is a reality and people can accept it or pointlessly oppose it, but Jews no longer have to justify their existence to opponents.

CHAPTER

NINETY-SIX

What is Aliyah?

The Talmudic case is a strange one; it takes place in a divorce court with a couple who have reached the breaking point in their marriage. One of the partners has made a decision to move to Israel and the other one doesn't want to move. Facing an irreconcilable difference of where to live, the couple decides to divorce. The court must decide which partner was responsible for the end of the marriage and will receive less favorable terms in the divorce. The Talmud rules that the partner that doesn't want to move to Israel is to receive less favorable terms in the divorce settlement.

When reading this section of the Talmud, the student is drawn to a linguist oddity. Instead of writing that one of the spouses is interested in moving to Israel, it uses the words "To go up to Israel." Throughout Jewish history, moving to Israel has been called an "Aliyah," an ascent. The corresponding move out of Israel is called a "Yeridah," a descent. These terms were chosen to demonstrate the uniqueness of the land of Israel. "Aliyah" has been reserved for moving to Israel. On that same page of Talmud, Rabbi Yehudah is quoted as maintaining it was forbidden to leave Babylonia, the center of Torah scholarship at the time, to move to Israel. Even though he maintained it was forbidden to move to Israel, he still called moving to Israel an "Aliyah."

For a time in Jewish history all Jews lived in the land of Israel. Starting at the destruction of the first Temple in 586 BCE and the subsequent forced Jewish exile, Jews began moving around the world. The dream of returning to Israel began immediately and Jews, no matter where they lived, prayed everyday to return to Israel. Throughout the subsequent exiles Jews always looked back to Israel. There was always a small Jewish community in the land of Israel, but few Jews moved to join them. The dream of "Making Aliyah" was always alive and well for over two thousand years.

Jews dreamed of and made Aliyah for different reasons over the past two thousand years. Many Jews didn't make an Aliyah of choice. These Jews lived in countries that began persecuting their Jewish citizens and had nowhere to go but back to the land of Israel. Historically, many Jews made Aliyah for religious reasons. While the Chassidim and Misnagdim, two groups of religious Jews in the 1700's, didn't agree on much, the leaders of these two groups, the Baal Shem Tov and the Vilna Gaon, both sent their students to move to the land of Israel and create communities.

In the late 1800's antisemitism in Eastern Europe rose to frightening levels. Jews began thinking of escape routes out of the pogroms plaguing Russia and Poland. Many European Jews moved to America, but a new movement, Zionism, rekindled the dream of Aliyah in the eyes of Jews from America to Russia. Theodore Herzl began preaching to Jews around Europe that it was time to make Aliyah to the land of Israel. In 1880 there were between 20,000 and 25,000 Jews living in what was then called Palestine. In the first of five waves of Aliyah between 1180 and 1900, approximately 35,000 Jews moved to Israel. Over the next fifty years hundreds of thousands of Jews moved to Israel.

The British restricted Jewish immigration into British Mandate Palestine at the behest of political pressure from the Arabs living in Palestine at the time. Just at the time when Aliyah no longer became a choice but a necessity for Jews fleeing the German, the Arabs of Palestine pressured the British, who made the decision to limit Jewish immigration. Had the Arabs and British not opposed Jewish Aliyah at the time, millions of Jews who ended up in German gas chambers could have made Aliyah and started new lives in Palestine. When placed in the context of saving millions of lives it becomes understood how Aliyah became such a significant movement in modern Jewish life.

Today, Zionism has kept Aliyah a strong and vibrant movement. Every year Jews from around the world make Aliyah and make Israel their home. Over the past 75 years the State of Israel has made Aliyah a priority, taking Jews from the four corners of the world into its warm embrace. Israel has welcomed Jews fleeing persecution from Arab lands, European countries, Russia and Ethiopia. Israel has also welcomed Jews who made Aliyah to realize the 2,000-year-old Zionist dream of gathering the exiles back to Israel from North and South America and many peaceful countries scattered around the world.

Jews hope that future Aliyah will be made by choice and in mass numbers. The Zionist dream wasn't to just create a vibrant state, but to have the Jews from around the world settle and live in that State. Immigrants who made Aliyah like David Ben Gurion, Golda Meir, and Menachem Begin all became Israel's Prime Ministers. Today's Knesset, regional councils and city municipalities, are full of elected leaders who proudly boast of their Aliyah to Israel. There are millions of people around the world eligible to make Aliyah. The State of Israel and her people are eager to welcome them.

CHAPTER
NINETY-SEVEN

Aliyah isn't a sacrifice

Before the advent of the internet there was no way to see videos of Israel or helpful pictures that could have given first time visitors a sense of what Israel felt and smelled like. The first time trip was one to remember. It was wonderful to experience Israel for the very first time. Years ago everyone would pack very little of their own stuff to make sure they had room for two suitcases worth of supplies and clothing for their Israeli cousins. These goods weren't available in Israel, and Israeli cousins loved getting American goods.

Bringing supplies like Zip Lock bags to Israel has always sent me the message that Israel didn't have it all and people who lived there were lacking some of the most basic goods found easily in any American supermarket. Jokes like, "How do you make a million dollars in Israel? Bring two million dollars!" just reinforced the message. Americans that lived in Israel earned respect from their American friends and family, but many were discouraged from living in Israel themselves. Why would anyone want to live in a place that was missing so much?

When Israel was founded in 1948 the country was in economic despair. The new nation had no resources, no industry, and no prospects. For hundreds of years the Jewish "Yishuv" in Palestine sustained itself on the generosity of Diaspora Jewry. The Jewish community in Israel couldn't see its way out of poverty and hopelessness. Just as the country was finding its feet in the early 1950's, Israel's Arab neighbors evicted 850,000 of its Jewish citizens. The Jews of Arab lands were successful people of industry, but almost overnight they were left penniless.

The nascent State of Israel was forced to make a horrible choice, accept almost a million destitute Jewish refugees and risk the economic collapse of the country or turn down needy Jews seeking a place of refuge – the very cause of the State of Israel. Israel's leaders made the right choice and accepted the refugees. Without housing for them, hundreds of thousands lived in tents for years, and many never recovered from their economic collapses. Ben Gurion famously explained to Israelis that they'd support this wave of immigrants, but in the future, the immigrants' children would support the State.

Israel grew and developed, existing cities were expanded and new cities were built. The country was still socialist and this hampered its growth, but private industry wasn't ready to play a managing role in Israel's economy yet. While certain innovations in Israel made it seem like a fully developed country, even as late as the 1980's, the dearth of certain basic necessities still made Israel seem backwards and underdeveloped. Things like getting a phone line installed in a new home could take between six months and a year. Only the most dedicated American Zionists made Aliyah to Israel. Aliyah was seen as a great sacrifice, and those who made the move to Israel were looked upon as something between an Abraham following God's order and a Ben Gurion pioneer. Those who made Aliyah had the admiration of friends and family but were also looked upon as strange for making such a great sacrifice.

Today, things are much different. Zip locks and all necessities, even most luxury items, are available in Israel. There's nothing Israel lacks that makes it seem like an underdeveloped country. Yet, many still consider making Aliyah a great burden and sacrifice. They talk about the challenges and difficulties that come with moving to Israel. They bring up the barriers of language and culture that all immigrants face – let alone the Israeli bureaucracy. They talk about being separated from friends and famly. They argue that in any discussion with immigrant families, they'll each have many trials and tribulations to relate. Without hesitation they say that making Aliyah, even in the 2020's is a great sacrifice.

I disagree and don't think of Aliyah as a sacrifice. Moving to Israel, like moving to any country, has its challenges and can be very difficult. Getting used to a new language and culture, children making new friends and learning a new educational system, and dealing with the Israeli bureaucracy is very tough. Yet, life isn't easy. There's a tendency to think that life is always easy in one's native country. It's true that certain things are easier in a country one is accustomed to living in, but that doesn't mean that life is a breeze anywhere.

Aliyah presents its own set of challenges, but that doesn't mean life in Israel is uniquely overburdensome and challenging.

Most importantly, living in Israel has its own advantages. Besides simple things like inexpensive cell phone plans and delicious shawarma, living in the historic homeland of one's own people is a privilege. For thousands of years Jews only dreamed of returning to the land of Israel, and today's Israelis and olim (immigrants) are given the opportunity to live in Israel every single day.

Living through difficulties doesn't define sacrifice. Living in a place that presents challenges and is tough doesn't mean someone has sacrificed. There is a significant difference between difficulty and sacrifice. When a person gives up more than they've gained, they've sacrificed. Moving to Israel, especially from America, requires people to give up comforts and luxuries. At the same time, the benefits of living in Israel, especially since it's no longer a country lacking any resources and necessities, far outweighs its challenges.

Living in Israel is better described as a privilege than a sacrifice. Living in Israel is the fulfillment of our grandparent's dreams. The Jewish people prayed, dreamed, and waited thousands of years to return to the land of Israel and govern it. The opportunity to live in Israel in relative comfort and ease compared to just twenty or thirty years ago can not realistically be considered a sacrifice. The Sages of the Talmud taught there are three gifts that God gave to the Jewish people and each comes with pain. One of those gifts was the land of Israel. Nothing valuable comes without pain – no pain, no gain – especially immigrating to Israel. With all the difficulty, it's still a privilege to live in Israel.

CHAPTER
NINETY-EIGHT

Aliyah; No pain, no gain, but, oh, the gain!

The most significant development in Jewish history over the past one hundred and fifty years is the establishment of State of Israel. After two thousand years of forced exile, the Jewish people can determine their own destiny on the Jewish people's historic homeland, Eretz Yisrael. The Zionist dream is more a reality than a dream. The second most significant development is the mass Aliyah of the Jewish people from all four corners of the Earth. I imagine when the Jewish people were exiled out of their land they looked and sounded the same, but upon their return, 2,000 years had transformed them to different shapes, colors and languages. Over the last one hundred- and twenty-years millions of Jews have left their adopted lands and returned to Eretz Yisrael.

As the humorous Jewish saying states, "Two Jews, three opinions," if a poll were taken asking why millions of Jews moved from their birthplaces to Israel there would certainly be as many reasons as people polled. There is no *one* reason to move to Israel. Some moved to escape an antisemitic land, others to achieve the Zionist dream of developing a Jewish state, and others because God commanded the Jewish people to live in Israel, as God said, "You shall possess the Land and you shall settle in it, for to you have I given the land to possess it."

In his comment on this verse, the Ramban wrote "In my opinion, this verse commands a mitzvah. Jews are commanded to settle and dwell in the land for it was given to them, and they cannot reject God's portion (*nachalas HaShem.*) If it would ever occur to the Jewish people to capture the land of Shinar or the land of Ashur, or anywhere like it, and to settle there, they would be violating this mitzvah." In this comment the Ramban states his well-known opinion that one of the 613 mitzvot is to live in Eretz Yisrael. In truth there are two laws in this verse according to the Ramban, the law to settle the land and the law for the individual to live in the land.

Many Jews look to Avraham for inspiration to move to Israel. Avraham was the first Jew charged to move to Eretz Yisrael when God told him, "Go forth from your land, your birthplace and from your father's house." The Ramban's comments on this verse point out the seeming repetition of the words, "your land, your birthplace and from your father's house." He wrote, "The reason for mentioning all three descriptions of what Avraham would be leaving to move to Israel is that it is difficult for a person to leave the country where they live, where they have their friends and companions. This is all the more true if this be his native land, and all the more if his whole family is there. It was necessary to say to Avraham that he leave all for the sake of his love of God." It seems leaving one's birthplace is so difficult it isn't worth it without a greater objective - in Avraham's case, his love of God.

The Talmud included a teaching of Rabbi Shimon the son of Yochai who taught, "God gave the Jewish people three precious gifts, all of which were given only by means of suffering. The three gifts are Torah, Eretz Yisrael, and the World-to-Come." The Talmud doesn't record why Eretz Yisrael (and the other gifts) were given only by means of suffering. It's easy to apply the modern axiom, "No pain, no gain," to settling in Israel, and expand our understanding to posit the Jewish people wouldn't properly appreciate the gift of their own land without suffering to settle it, but there's more to it than just appreciation.

It is rare to find a Jew who has moved to Israel as a random choice. It's hard to even imagine a Jew having trouble deciding where to move and just ending up in Israel. Jews move to Israel for a greater objective, and as mentioned above, each Jew has their own reason. There is also a collective dream being actualized by each Jew who moved to Israel, irrespective of their personal reasons.

Together, the Jewish people have returned to their land and gathered together to build their own nation-State. Even Jews who don't ascribe to a nation state still participate, each in their own way, in the building of this state. When the people join to create something great, there are going to be growing pains. The Jews haven't joined together to build something in over two thousand years. It's impossible for the success of something as significant as the Jewish people reestablishing their homeland to be painless.

One of my good friends likes to say, "Every oleh has their story," and they're right. Whether they've walked thousands of miles (!!!) over the burning hot sands of the African desert, escaped a collapsing Communist Soviet Union, or gingerly walked on to a charter flight from New York, every Jew who followed Avraham's path has a story. That story inevitably includes some pain – but ask that new immigrant and you're almost guaranteed to hear the pain was well worth it. The two-thousand-year-old dream of living in Israel made all the struggle worth the pain.

CHAPTER
NINETY-NINE

The future is here!

When I was preparing to move to Israel (the second time) I often wondered if I would become used to Israel and not feel how special it was to walk the streets of Israel like I felt when I visited Israel. After moving to Israel I can attest that I have never been happier in my life. My prayers to live in Eretz Yisrael were literally answered. For a decade that I lived in America I dreamed that I'd be able to live in Eretz Yisrael. I prayed for it, I wished for it and I imagined it. Today I live it. I am living mine and countless others' dreams. I live with the excitement of destiny fulfilled, and dreams realized. It is absolutely amazing.

Since the day my family and I moved to Israel I count each day that I've been here. We live in an amazing community, Mitzpe Yericho, with people who respect each other, help each other and share our values. I have neighbors who seem to help us in a new way everyday. My family and I live in a beautiful large home that we could never have afforded in America. It has a view that overlooks the Judean Desert, Jericho, the Jordanian Mountains and on the walk to my Synagogue, the Dead Sea. My children attended a public school that rivals any observant day school in America (forget about the tuition difference!). My kids are learning Hebrew better than Jewish high school seniors and transitioned seamlessly into a new school, with new friends.

I work in a fantastic job; Everyday I commute to and from work through Jerusalem and pass the Old City. My view is of the Temple Mount! This is remarkably different from my commute from Exit 44 to Exit 16 of the I-95 in Florida over the past few years.

Not everyone shares my experiences. Aliyah is tougher for some than others. I moved to Israel once before and after eight years moved back to America, where I lived for ten years. I know of the financial, emotional, and physical struggles families suffer when coming to Israel. Yet, with all the challenges moving to Israel can incur, I know one thing that makes it worth it.

While in America, we aimed to strengthen our Jewish identity. We created programming, curricula and events to ensure the continuity of Jewish life, culture and tradition. We extolled our connection to Israel, taught Zionism and Israel Advocacy. Yet we were on the sidelines of the Jewish future.

It is naive to think that the future of the Jewish people is anywhere but in Israel. Whether you're religious, secular, or somewhere in between, leading Jewish thought, tradition and culture is all taking place in Israel. In Israel we aren't strengthening our identity, we are creating it. The excitement in the streets of Israel, the constant building, growth and development is palpable. We've all felt it on visits, missions and vacations here. There is a sense of pride, of shared enthusiasm, of a partnership in something much larger than ourselves that is happening all around us.

When I drive to work and look out my car windows and see the Temple Mount, I know that our future has arrived. When I look out over my porch at the Western Bank of the Jordan River, in my small town, something my grandfather could only have dreamed of while lying in barracks in Auschwitz, I know our future has arrived. When F-35s fly by my porch and dip their wings, so close that I can see the star of David on their tail, I know our future has arrived. But most of all, when I see hundreds of Jewish children skipping through the streets of Jerusalem's Old City on their way to study their first words of Torah, I know that our people's future is here in Israel. New immigrants to Israel don't want to be on the sidelines for our people's future, we want to play a part in it.

Maimonides wrote that one who truly loves something - he was talking about the love of God - can't stop talking about it. He wrote that love of God was the driving force that pushed Avraham to tell everyone and anyone, even at the risk of his life, about God. I think fresh olim, new immigrants to Israel, are so excited about creating our future, of being a part of something so much larger than themselves, and of setting Jewish destiny, that they can't stop talking about it.

People ask me if I ever see my excitement of living in Israel dying down. I know in my first month here I couldn't sleep through the night I was so overjoyed to be here. I sleep fine now, exhausted by a day's work. Yet, as I watch the sunrise each morning over the Jordanian mountains, and its shadow set over the Western Wall each night, it's hard for me to believe I'll ever get used to living in Israel.

CHAPTER
ONE HUNDRED

Stop Aliyah shaming American Jews

I made a fool of myself at my wedding. It's tough to admit, but I was an arrogant 21 year old, coming off of three years of post-high school study in Israel and had returned to America for my wedding. As is customary, I spoke at my "Chosson's Tish," and with a return to Israel scheduled for two weeks after my wedding, I lectured people much smarter than me about their need to move to Israel. Thankfully, the speech was recorded on VHS tape and will never be watched again. Six years later I ate crow when I moved back to America for ten years.

Thankfully, I am now "living the dream" in Israel and my family and I were able to remake Aliyah and live a wonderful life in Mitzpe Yericho. The Talmud instructs, "A person should always live in Eretz Yisrael." Even the Rambam, the sole medieval scholar who maintains living in Israel isn't a mitzvah, quotes that same passage from the Talmud. It is undeniable that it is better for a Jew to live in Eretz Yisrael than outside of Israel.

Many American Jews who made Aliyah love talking about living in Israel. Olim - Jewish immigrants to Israel - are very proud of themselves for the sacrifices they've made. They gave up the comfortable life they were accustomed to and moved to a land with a very different culture, a foreign language (sic) and no Amazon Prime. Olim know the Jewish future rests in Israel, and they're excited to play a part in it. Unlike those we left behind in America, we made the tough, but correct choice, and we feel everyone should follow our footsteps.

There is a way we should be encouraging Aliyah. We should talk about the benefits of living in Israel. We should talk about the wondrous chagim, when everyone celebrates Sukkot, Chanukah, Purim and Pesach, and not Halloween, Christmas, and Easter. We should talk about the solemn Yom Hazikaron and the festive Yom Haatzmaut. We should tell American Jews about living in the place of our ancestors. We can start the morning at the Kotel, take a walk through the shuk, spend the afternoon skiing at the Hermon, and end the day at the beach in Tel Aviv. There is so much to boast about in Israel, and we should exude that excitement.

We should never shame and guilt American Jews about living in Chutz la'aretz. There is no prohibition to live outside of Israel, in fact the Rambam wrote, "A person can live wherever they choose except Egypt." It is wholly unjustified to rebuke someone when they're doing nothing wrong. It is also counterproductive to guilt people to move to Israel. I don't know anyone who speaks of making Aliyah out of guilt and shame. Why would anyone want to move to a place where the people are judgmental and obnoxious?

America in the 21st Century is not Germany in 1938, it is not a few years away from a second Holocaust. While antisemitism is on the rise, most Jews are safe and haven't personally experienced antisemitism. Judging America as a dangerous place based on news reports is the same error that frustrates so many Israelis when Americans judge Israel to be a dangerous place based on news reports of terror attacks. Israelis are out of touch when they tell Americans they need to move to Israel before it's too late for them. Americans rightfully ignore Israelis and their warnings.

Aliyah is important, but it isn't one of the most fundamental mitzvot of the Torah. Listening to some Israelis you get the sense they consider Aliyah the 14th fundamental of Jewish faith. Unfortunately, there are many mitzvot not observed properly today, and many of those mitzvot are more important to correct than Aliyah. I'm fascinated by the psychological phenomenon that leads Americans who made Aliyah to reprimand American Jews for not making Aliyah. If their rebuke was based on Torah values, they'd be talking about other mitzvot before encouraging Aliyah.

The 500,000 American citizens living in Israel should encourage the five million Jews in America to think about making Aliyah. Living in Israel is a wonderful experience, and every Jew should get to enjoy it. To successfully inspire American Jews to move to Israel our messaging must be positive. We should never shame an American Jew for living in America. By publicizing the beauty of Eretz Yisrael we'll encourage more Americans to join us – and if we're successful enough, maybe Jeff Bezos will open Amazon Prime here too.

CHAPTER
ONE HUNDRED AND ONE

Do Zionists need to live in Israel?

I was a naïve teenager and like most teenagers I thought I was wiser and more knowledgeable than my parents. My father had just been named president of the local branch of an American Zionist organization and was excited to begin his new role. Always the smart aleck, I joked that in just a week or two he should expect to be promoted to the national president of the organization. After all, I reasoned, the national president of the Zionist organization is the top Zionist in America and should make Aliyah immediately. The person who filled their position would also need to move to Israel almost immediately, and so on, until my father would shortly become the national president of this Zionist organization. My father didn't find my joke as humorous as I did.

Behind my wise guy joke was the idea that you have to live in Israel to be a Zionist. This idea that Zionists must live in Israel isn't without merit. Zionism was a modern political movement that started in the late 1800's and among the movement's many facets was encouraging the Jewish people to move to Israel. Theodore Herzl traveled Europe trying to inspire Jews from London to Russia to leave their homes and move to their homeland. Jews that ignored Herzl's message did so for various reasons but there's no question they didn't fully buy into the Zionist movement of the time. There's an argument to say the full buy-in to Zionism is still lacking today for those who don't move to Israel.

The twelfth century scholar Nachmanides wrote that one of the Torah commandments God charged the Jewish people to fulfill is to live in and settle the land of Israel. He wrote that "Jews cannot reject (me'us) the portion of God (nachalat Hashem). If it would ever occur to capture the land of Shinar or the land of Ashur, or anything like it, and to settle there, one would be violating this positive command." Some Zionists make the argument that by choosing to live outside of the land of Israel, either by moving from Israel to a different land or by neglecting to move to Israel from one's birthplace, they are violating the Ramban's dictum and rejecting the portion of God. There are even some religious Zionists who maintain that the Messiah will not arrive until all the Jews live in Israel. A Jew who chooses to live outside of Israel not only denies themselves the benefits of living in Israel but denies the Jewish people the messianic era. A Zionist, the argument flows, would never consider such anti-Zionist actions.

Early Zionists debated whether there was an ongoing need for the Diaspora after the Zionist movement had gotten started. Their debate kicked into high gear when the State of Israel was founded in 1948. Now is the time for all Jews to move to Israel, one side of the debate argued. They negated any need for the Diaspora and saw the mindset of the Diaspora Jew as harmful to the spirit of the new Jew being molded by Zionism. Other Zionists countered these arguments by looking at the rich history of the Diaspora and the dedicated Jews who still lived in the Diaspora today. These Jews had a great deal to contribute to Zionism, the Jewish people, and the State of Israel. It would be foolish to nullify their existence or put them down as lesser Zionists. The debate is still going on between Zionists today.

As much merit as there is in the argument that Zionists must live in Israel, it isn't necessarily correct. There are strong counter arguments to make that while Herzl tried to inspire all Jews to move to the land of Israel to create a Jewish state, the Zionist movement didn't aim to move all of the Jewish people to Israel. The idea of fifteen million Jews moving within the space of a few decades to a barren land without the infrastructure to support a million people let along fifteen million, is absurd. Zionism aimed to create a Jewish State in the land of Israel were all Jews would have the right to live in if they chose. Zionism succeeded in meeting that challenge by creating the State of Israel with a law of return that has acted as a shelter for Jews who made Aliyah out of choice and due to persecution.

Scholars that have studied Nachmanides' writings understand his warning not to reject the portion of God by settling an area outside the land of Israel as a warning to the nation, not to the individual Jew. The Jewish people would be rejecting the portion of God if they would move to Uganda and establish a Jewish State within its borders. An individual Jew who moves out of Israel or decides not to move to Israel isn't rejecting the portion of God. That same Jew is making a choice for themselves that doesn't affect the nation as a whole. There is no tradition among our Talmudic or early scholars' writings that says the Messiah will only come once all the Jewish people move to Israel, rather it is the Messiah that will inspire the Jewish people to gather back themselves back to Israel.

A Zionist is someone, Jew or Gentile, who is dedicated to the right of the Jewish people to determine their own future in their historic homeland, the land of Israel. A Zionist isn't required to take any action to be a Zionist. The belief that there are litmus tests to qualify as a Zionist is foreign to early Zionist writings and positions. From Moses to Herzl, the Zionist movement is full of great people dedicated to the Jews living in their homeland who never lived in Israel themselves. To call their commitment to Zionism and its principles into question is baseless. The State of Israel and its people is open for all Jews to return to its borders, and they look forward to the day when all Jews live in the land of Israel. Until that day, Zionists will live in and outside of the land of Israel.

Conclusion

My journey as a Zionist wasn't the usual one. I was raised in a Zionist home and in a Zionist town. In high school I was required to learn about Zionism. I visited Israel a number of times between the ages of 10 and 18 and then after graduating high school I left America for a gap year in a Zionist Yeshiva in Israel. Instead of returning to America after my gap year I stayed in Israel for the next eight years. I married, started a family, continued my studies in a Zionist kollel, and began teaching. I was drafted into the army (although ultimately never served) and didn't utilize the exemption I was entitled to from being a kollel member.

After eight years in Israel I moved back to America and felt that I should contribute to Israel from America. I was introduced to AIPAC and helping Israel through political lobbying. I quickly brought students into the AIPAC camp and offered them a concrete way of helping Israel from America. I had my heart set on returning to Israel and after ten years of being away from the land I loved, I was privileged to return with an extended family.

My story sounds like the usual Zionist story, but there's a twist. Ironically, the more I felt closer to Israel and did to help it, the less connected to Zionism I felt. As a Torah observant Jew who spent a great deal of time studying the Torah, I was put off by modern Zionism's move away from the Torah and to more universal values. I also read the Zionist essays of the leading religious Zionist Rabbis and felt their focus on Messianism and heavy emphasis on living in Israel more than other mitzvot was inconsistent with the classic Torah works of Chazal and the Rishonim. I began thinking of myself as a post-Zionist. I supported the State of Israel and put hours of my day in helping it and training students in helping it, but its core philosophy, Zionism, didn't appeal to me.

One of my students, Elie Codron, bought me a gift that changed my life. A book is a powerful tool, it activates our imagination and opens our mind to new options we've previously never considered. Different from a lecture, a podcast, or a short form essay, the length and depth of a book invites the reader to think about a topic in more depth. Elie bought me Dr.

Gil Troy's "Zionist Ideas," a large collection of articles on Zionism by over 170 Zionist writers. Among the 170 articles I found a combined religious-practical Zionism absent of messianism. I had found my place in Zionism.

Zionism is an ever-evolving movement. Its principles and values don't change, but its applications are constantly changing. To be a Zionist today requires one to be both a dreamer and practical, spiritual and rational, hopeful that the Messiah will come today but cognizant that the past instructs us to be prepared for a longer exile. We must think like those not yet redeemed, while preparing for an imminent redemption. A Zionist today is a walking contradiction; someone who believes the impossible is possible and takes the steps to make the impossible possible.

To be Zionist today is a brave position. A Zionist today requires a person to stand up against enemies and opponents who slander you and don't allow you the space to defend yourself. A Zionist today must dream about Israel's future and how to ensure the Jewish people not only survive but thrive.

I am a proud Zionist. I don't agree with everything Zionism stood for or has achieved. I certainly don't agree with everything Zionist thinkers and activists have said. I am not a proponent of every policy of the Zionist State. Zionism isn't about loyalty to a movement, ideology, or a State. Zionism is about improving the Jewish people's circumstances. Zionism today is working towards a better Israel and a better Jewish people. I'm proud to take part in Zionism today.

About the Author

Rabbi Uri Pilichowski grew up in Fair Lawn, New Jersey. He studied in Mevaseret Zion for eight years, earning a Bachelor of Talmudic Law and Rabbinic Ordination. After receiving his ordination, Rabbi Pilichowski moved to Beverly Hills, CA to become the Assistant Rabbi of the famed Beth Jacob Congregation. After his time in California, Rabbi Pilichowski spent three years in Boca Raton, Florida where he was the Rosh Beit Midrash at Scheck Hillel Community School and one of the Rabbis at The Boca Raton Synagogue.

Rabbi Pilichowski is proud of his involvement with the Pro-Israel community in America. He created the first teen pro-Israel group in the country that taught students to advocate in Congress for a stronger US-Israel relationship. His students gained a national reputation that has even reached the White House. Rabbi Pilichowski continues to teach his students from Israel via Zoom as the director of Israel Advocacy for Southern NCSY.

In July 2014, in the midst of Operation Protective Edge, Rabbi Pilichowski and his family moved back to Israel. He is a columnist at the Jerusalem Post and Jewish National Syndicate. He is a senior educator at numerous educational institutions.

Rabbi Pilichowski also enjoys writing and speaking; he is the author of three other books, a book on time management, on the weekly Torah portion and on the Jewish festivals. He has been a scholar in residence in synagogues across America, from Richmond, VA to Santa Barbara, CA. Rabbi Pilichowski is happily married to Aliza and has six wonderful children and lives in Mitzpe Yericho.To contact Rabbi Pilichowski or have him speak in your community or school, please email him at **uri@uripilichowski.com.**